D0847186

DREAD TRIDENT

Liverpool Science Fiction Texts and Studies, 60

Liverpool Science Fiction Texts and Studies

Recent titles in the series

DREAD TRIDENT

Tabletop Role-Playing Games and the Modern Fantastic

CURTIS D. CARBONELL

LIVERPOOL UNIVERSITY PRESS

First published 2019 by
Liverpool University Press
4 Cambridge Street
Liverpool
L69 7ZU

British Library Cataloguing-in-Publication data
A British Library CIP record is available

ISBN 978-1-78962-057-3 cased

Typeset by Carnegie Book Production, Lancaster
Printed and bound in Poland by BooksFactory.co.uk

Contents

Note on References

Throughout *Dread Trident*, all game titles are unitalicized. This non-standard use differentiates games (unitalicized) in a general sense from core gametexts (italicized), which often use the name of the game as the title of its primary rulebook.

Chapter 1

Introduction

Theorizing the Modern Fantastic

Dread Trident investigates the rise of imaginary worlds, the continued expansion of an ironic impulse this book frames as the modern fantastic. Etched in clear relief, this dynamic emerges in the most detailed of such worlds, those found in tabletop role-playing game (TRPG) texts. While one might look to the literature of fantasy and the fantastic to best find such an understanding, the most expansive of TRPGs provide textured canvases ripe for scholarly comment. They are populated with both engineered and discursive gametexts and tools, literal analogues of their digital counterparts that most thinkers associate with the rise of fantasy popular culture. We encounter them as analog rulebooks, settings books, adventures, etc., many of them also digital gametools from virtual tabletops, online forums, digitized cards, virtual dice. Extensive imaginary worlds, be they analog or digital, must first be built, and in the process of persons engaging them, they become realized fantasy worlds, a curious configuration this book explores in theorizing the modern fantastic.

The technologized world is changing in curious ways that demand explanation. One such change is the dramatic rise of the modern fantastic as a cultural referent and gaming as a dominant cultural mode. During the initial writing of this chapter, *Pokémon Go* (2016) was released, ushering in augmented-reality gaming to mass culture. Before that, any number of cultural milestones saw the fantastic carve new inroads. The popular HBO series *Game of Thrones* (2011–19) has dominated torrent downloads during each of its seasons, as well as many people's social network feeds. A host of other fantasy series have filled recent TV programming, reaching back to the entry of game changers, the *X-Files* (1993–2005; 2016) and *Buffy the Vampire Slayer* (1997–2003).

Fiction, as well, with the rise of Amazon's Kindle-Direct Publishing (K.D.P.), has widened its reach by allowing anyone to publish and find an audience. Within traditional publishing, the realized world of Harry

Potter's Hogwarts demonstrated that kids read, especially fantasy. Even serious literary publishing has hosted debates over fantasy's inclusion, or, rather, its acceptance by major literary figures such as Haruki Murakami and Kazuo Ishiguro. The debate, some claim, is over.[1] Fantasy has arrived. Film has been no exception, the amount of sophisticated fantastic films increasing in the last two decades, obscuring the fact that even earlier mavericks such as *Rosemary's Baby* (1968), the *Exorcist* (1973), *Star Wars* (1979), *Close Encounters* (1979) were such anomalies when released.

The acceptance of fantasy within popular culture continues to grow. Digital gaming, of course, is its most dominant offspring, with role-playing games (RPGs) forming one of the most played types. However, the digital supports redoubtable embodied experiences that reaffirm material, analog life. Before the rise of the digital, TRPGs made popular-culture history with the success of Tactical Studies Games' (TSR) Dungeons and Dragons (D&D) in the 1980s. Since then, the broad category of RPGs has been subjected to a considerable amount of critical commentary. Monographs by Sarah Lynne Bowman and Jennifer Cover examine TRPGs beyond Gary Alan Fine's seminal sociological study *Shared Fantasy* (1983) and Lawrence Schick's early history of the industry, *Heroic Worlds* (1991). Jon Peterson's *Playing at the World* (2012) and Shannon Appelcline's *Designers and Dragons* (2015) both offer expansive histories of TRPGs. What ties these works together is fantasy's seminal role in opening horizons of possibility for new technological-driven world creation and subject formation. Gametexts that outline analog TRPG procedures, be they paper or available on PDF through *DriveThruRPG. com*, *DMsGuild.com*, and/or *Kickstarter.com*, continue to deliver foundations for the creation of realized worlds.[2]

While digital game studies and analog game studies have carved important niches in the face of disciplinary challenges so that games are examined as seriously as other forms of cultural production, within the border-shifting fields between new media, literary studies, and cultural studies, the written texts of TRPGs still remain undertheorized

---

[1] See Ursula K. Le Guin and Ishiguro's conversation over the nature of fantasy, as summarized in Miller 2015.

[2] For representative academic monographs, see Mackay 2001; Fine 2002; Bowman 2010; Tresca 2010; Cover 2010; King and Borland 2014; and for books written in the popular sphere, see Barrowcliffe 2009; Gilsdorf 2010; Ewalt 2014. For anthologies, see Williams, Hendricks, and Winkler 2006; Torner and White 2012, as well as detailed scholarly work by Harrigan and Wardrip-Fruin 2010 that broadly explores how role-playing works across varying media.

as important archives in the history of popular culture, especially by literary historians and theorists.[3] Within the past decade, game-studies theorists have gained headway in the professional realm of discipline creation, detailing how game systems and mechanics function, often outside the purviews of narrative-driven theorists. "Games are not a kind of cinema, or literature, but colonizing attempts from both these fields have already happened, and no doubt will happen again" (Aarseth 2001, online). While digital game studies works to outline its own disciplinary space, *Dread Trident* seeks acceptance in the literariness of TRPGs by analyzing its archive of written gametexts.

This introduction presents a variety of threads that weave their way through this study. In starts by offering literary studies as a foundational discipline, one whose discursive methods, while suffering many blows to its credibility, has survived. TRPGs are primarily comprised of literary gametexts. They are open to traditional hermeneutics, even as they are used as manuals for engineered play. Another major thread is how this play emerges within the modern fantastic. Thus, the 'modern' is a concept that drives much of the analysis in this study. It is the development toward our technologized present that infuses the modern with its renewed vigor as posture of continual critique. Combined with this is a particular use of the 'fantastic' as a dominant impulse seen in two prevalent tropes, the draconic and the posthuman. This modern fantastic tenor within modernity can be seen in a type of space *Dread Trident* theorizes as 'realized' worlds, imaginary worlds constructed through a curious combination of analog and digital tools. This process is one of posthumanization, a reworking of the discourses of trans-and-posthumanism away from focusing on how bodies are written to the spaces in which subjects emerge. This focus works within the broader context of the critique of modernity through its continued shaping of the human, a drive within humanism itself or, better, a drive within more recent (neo) or (post) humanisms. The result? This introduction foregrounds a few key effects of how TRPGs allow us to understand this process. In particular, a focus on embodiment and materiality at the table means the dominance of the digital must take a backseat. The concept of gameplay here is one that requires the analog, physical objects, alone with digital and discursive ones. The end result is a type of "magification," a touch of ironic enchantment that infuses the modern with a requisite positive fantasy.

---

[3] For an attempt at inclusion with media studies, see Dovey 2006, and for an argument that game studies should be included within cultural studies, see Nieborg and Hermes 2008.

Literary Studies

Mid-twentieth-century literary studies thinkers once asked if popular literature can be useful or instructive, rather than simply about escape.[4] This instrumental demand belies a prejudice that the escapist, imaginative tenor is a problem and that such mechanisms are suspect. Such a pejorative insistence that escape is juvenile is being reassessed in the context of a dominant new mode of cultural production: games. The creation of realized worlds and their engagement is an activity synonymous with the creation of subjects and their desire for play. Escaping is a fruitful process of contemporary life that provides healthy mechanisms against the many-headed beast of a complex technologized world. These mechanisms are often palliative, a way to release the tensions of work and adult life.

Escapist experiences of the fantastic, though, are still often viewed as simplistic. Granted, those of TRPG leader D&D are notorious for their dualistic notions of good vs. evil.[5] D&D also has rudimentary literary qualities similar to earlier adventure romances of the American pulps and British penny dreadfuls, while foregrounding complex non-literary game mechanics, all of it scaffolded by a combination of system-focused play peppered with degrees of performance-based experience. And while even more introspective games like that of its Gothic-inspired rival the World(s) of Darkness[6] provide complexities in character development and motivation, compared to the most sophisticated written forms, they are often less complex.

While a shift in importance is occurring within popular culture from the literary to the gaming mode, the modern fantastic relies on a literary past rife with a contested historiography in justifying its own worth. The recognition of literature as a stable cultural mode of understanding has suffered much since the poststructural challenge to formalism,

---

[4] See Wellek and Warren 1949.
[5] Yet, a comprehensive look at how 'alignment' works in D&D allows for plenty of middle ground. For example, a player may play a character with neutral qualities between lawful vs. chaotic (unlawful) or between good and evil. Neutrality in any configuration means such a player opts for a pragmatism that demonstrates how complex the categories are in specific contexts. You can also have lawful devils (evil), as well as chaotic characters who do good (a good-hearted barbarian, for example).
[6] In this book I use the plural term 'Worlds of Darkness,' rather than the singular 'World of Darkness.' This is to note that the different, but compatible settings can be recognized as maintaining some uniformity, while also maintaining its differences.

one among many assaults from the canon wars to the dominance of theory, to theory's own supposed dissolution.[7] One of the most valiant attempts to define literature as a reliable, stable discipline occurred when eminent mid-century literary critic Northrop Frye argued in the *Anatomy of Criticism* (1957) that major forms of literature in Western history move through five modes, beginning with the mythic, then romantic, into high and low mimetic, and ending with the ironic. He saw the ironic (our diminishing transitional moment) returning to the mythic (a possible nascent moment). Frye's cyclic modal impulses operate on a critical level dismissive of the rhetoric of modern publishers and their constructed genres. Granted, many fantasy genres must be viewed, in practical strokes, emerging because of market pressures but also, with more cryptic strokes, because of a perceived disappearance of traditional mythos and the failure of literary realism in the face of modernity's various 'isms': mechanism, materialism, instrumentalism, positivism, rationalism, scientism, secularism, skepticism, consumerism, etc.

But Frye's insight that the mythic returns should alert us to its possibility as an ironic mythos. Such irony cushions its mythic tenor, shielding the literary mode from perceived ineffectiveness by those who would condemn literature as antiquated because of its insistence on narrative, story, character, all the elements of Aristotle's use of mythos for how a work of art provides humanistic understanding. We are, following Frye's reading, able to mine such works for viable direction in today's modern world. The ironic mythos within the modern fantastic requires no such heavy metaphysics. Instead, it offers an experience. This is the shift from Frye's literary use to *Dread Trident*'s offering of the modern fantastic's focus on gameist play. Even if Frye is no longer a critical reference for literary scholars, he still helps as we view our current return to mythos through ironic lenses.

This process, though, should be no surprise. The traditional conception of the literary humanities as a 'first culture' containing an elitist and narrow view of the human in opposition to a technocratic 'second culture' presents a narrative problematized by the rise of fantastic-gameist space. The privileging of the serious and real over the fanciful and unreal (i.e., imaginary) has surfaced many times in Western history in an anti-aesthetic, utilitarian insistence on the common good instead of personal transcendence; with Protestant doctrine about the virtue of work over play; or with Realists' focus on the struggling working or middle classes. Debates between T.H. Huxley and Mathew Arnold,

---

[7] To take only one example from this discussion that reaffirms the continued need for critique; see Eagleton 2003.

DREAD TRIDENT

later to be labeled by C.P. Snow as tensions between the Two Cultures, act as precursors for the recent challenges to canons over high and low literature, as well as to the role of the liberal arts in the university. Today, we even see this divisive legacy in the row over the digital humanities, another debate far beyond the scope of my study.[8]

Instead of deconstructing what is viewed as an upstart dominant mode (the technocratic) in opposition to a waning, traditional mode (the literary), the modern fantastic collapses the two. The cultures of science and engineering are emerging with the same valorized status that critics like Matthew Arnold and F.R. Leavis once attributed to classical literary culture: that they are examples of quintessential human creativity and spirit. An engineering ethos invigorates the mechanics of realized worlds, enough so that tools of material culture inspire the imaginative aspects once associated with literary culture. The discourses of the humanities, especially traditional literary culture, find new fields of study by accepting this adjustment.

The realized worlds of the modern fantastic offer a positive affirmation of human activity rather than a pessimistic view of subjectivity as loss or as a flattening of human potential under the maligned behemoth known as technocratic capitalism. Pessimistic critical tendencies have previously led to destructive science wars and culture wars, with proponents of the sciences reacting defensively in the face of a perceived postmodernist assault on knowledge legitimation and, with even more vehemence, science as a cultural practice.[9] While popular culture has accepted the artifacts of engineering, humanist and posthumanist discourses confront complex representations of materiality, yet now with an openness to the relevance of engineered fantasy space.[10]

Dread Trident's analog-games' approach differs from most found in established literary studies, which should intrigue thinkers interested in gametexts as worthy of critical study. Momentum is in favor of its approach. We have seen this type of development before. Science fiction (SF) now has acceptance in the professional academic sphere; its journals are respected, its monographs increasing in numbers. Fantasy

[8] For Huxley, Arnold, Snow, see Cartwright and Baker 2005. Also, for tensions over the role of the liberal arts, a place to start is with Readings 1996; Newfield 2004; 2011; and for debates over the digital humanities, see Hayles 2012; Gold 2012.
[9] See Segerstråle 2001.
[10] Focusing on engineered space with the context of the modern fantastic refracts these issues so that the fantastic gameplay experience becomes the problem that needs solutions. These occur through the methods detailed in this book as part of the analog/digital dynamic.

studies is following the same trajectory, but more slowly, although I believe this will change in the future. While traditional North American scholarship has largely overlooked gametexts, role-playing games have attracted increased commentary in Northern European and Nordic academic spheres.[11] In the last decade, digital game studies has seen rapid momentum and acceptance. Its aim is to provide a theoretical understanding of video game culture and mechanics. Analog game studies has emerged to fill an important gap, one rooted in the artifacts of materiality and embodiment that resists the dehumanizing aspects of screen culture.[12]

Dread Trident ultimately examines fantasy and SF gametexts from a literary and cultural studies approach by focusing on TRPGs' rich written gametext archives of the fantastic. While more people engage in fiction reading, film viewing, or video game playing than in playing analog games, this difference in popularity does not diminish the importance of the written archives used by the much smaller, niche groups in analog fantasy gaming. The massive amount of TRPG gametexts as written fantasy-and-SF archives is impressive. These must be addressed with scholarly rigor, along with attention paid to cinema, literature, video games, and other popular-culture artifacts. Even more so, when we look to them as vital elements in a gameist mode that requires active participation, we recognize a broader shift in focus within the modern fantastic from novels and film to gametexts. The number of players may be smaller, but the largest of the archives examined in this book rival if not exceed many of the most popular media franchises of imaginary worlds.[13]

Most TRPGs begin as written words on a page, reminding us that a *literary* understanding is as important as an engineering understanding. These TRPG gametexts require players to engage in the traditional techniques of reading, annotating, and composing. This literary process reminds us, though, of how such an activity requires flexible theoretical models to engage with engineered play as a different mode of consumption. For example, while many of the traditional elements of hermeneutics in literary studies apply, they alert us that the complexities involved in textual analysis must be expanded to involve play. Plato's

---

[11] For an in-depth look into the popularity of Nordic LARPing, see Stenros and Montola 2010.

[12] See the online journals *Game Studies* at http://gamestudies.org and *Analog Game Studies* at http://analoggamestudies.org.

[13] In particular, the imaginary worlds of D&D are vast, with forty years of development, while those of 40K, although newer, demonstrate impressive narrative complexity across a variety of media.

censure of poets in the *Republic* would also censure imitative play because poetry (i.e., literature) is a type of play itself. Aristotle's demand for catharsis in proper tragedy also relegates the ironic play now seen in imaginary realized worlds as less than serious, or effective as tragic poetry. Classical literary studies' admonition that poetry delight and instruct provides further constraints. Conversations over the sublime, or allegory, or mimesis remind us that, in play, language is secondary to experience. Yet, even the Derridean insistence on the inherent tendency for linguistic play to emerge reveals itself as a fundamental aspect of texts.

Thus, *Dread Trident* is predicated on a theoretical frame within the modern fantastic that values a literary-inspired *gameist* cultural mode of consumption. The written gametexts and tools analyzed in this book are mechanisms of the imagination, and they are part of the cultural dynamic that gave us SF and fantasy and that is now changing the technologized world around us into ever more fantastic modes. We see this as fantasy percolates through popular culture. Imagining oneself as a dragonborn or a cyborg, whether in a game or at a convention, with only pen and paper to describe your character or a painstakingly built costume, leads to notions of the (post)human as a plastic subject imbricated in analog/digital technology. Not only is subjectivity important, but these gametexts and tools demonstrate that spaces have been erected in which such conceptions can occur. And these spaces are becoming increasingly complex, ubiquitous, and realized. They are the ultimate result of the modern fantastic.

Modernity

Modernity itself has encouraged this proliferation of realized game worlds and is a key element in theorizing the modern fantastic. Historian Stephen Toulmin suggests that the received view of the Modern Age was never stable, a view that insisted on the dominance of modern philosophical 'Reason' as a defining factor. Modernity's appearance and disappearance was and is a discursive phenomenon, and it now exists in a less-than-dominant fashion as a phenomenon with myriad definitions contextualized in specific cultural moments, many of which are still superstitious and traditional (the two bugbears of optimistic European rationalism).[14] Our words become engineering blueprints. The modern fantastic, a discursive (written) and engineering (systemic design) phenomenon based on empirical principles of constructing worlds with

---

[14] See Toulmin 1992.

fantasy qualities, now drives an inflection of modernity in which lived spaces oscillate between the real and the imaginary.

Many thinkers have considered what follows modernity or, at least, what is different about the mid- to late twentieth century and, today, about the particulars of our current century. For some, modernity as a theoretical concept has run its course, yet a beleaguered rationality still exists that drives a variety of modernities in a globalized world. While many thinkers have focused on a historical approach predicated on beginnings and endings, such as the emergence of the printing press or the beginning of Cartesian philosophy and Galilean astronomy or the rise of the nation state, a way to escape such constraining frames is to examine the major impulses of what drove the modern (e.g., representations of the human, the change wrought by technology, or the changing landscape, etc.) and how those are still at work today in refined and variegated fashion.

Realized-modern-fantasy space as a controlling theoretical concept should offer no surprise in a book rooted in modern studies in which our technological tools expanded our vision far into the galaxy, as well as deep into the smallest parts of physical matter. To theorize the beginnings of the *modern* fantastic, we can look back to as early as 1609 when Galileo combined the refined science of optics and technological advances in machining to spot the moons of Jupiter, thereby extending the reach of our vision.[15] Our imaginations followed with tales of space travel. By the nineteenth century, with H.G. Wells and Jules Verne, and Lovecraft in the early twentieth, space becomes part of our imaginative territory, what we now consider 'geographies of the imagination.' No wonder that the following pulp articulation of SF exploded with the space opera, a literary form that required technological tools in the forms of space ships to extend our reach into these new fantastic frontiers. Advanced technology found its fantastic face, the history of SF a testament to this imaginative landscape.

The artifacts of the modern fantastic began in earnest at the end of the nineteenth century, when print manufacturing exponentially distributed more material to a wider reading public. Yet, our current imaginary tenor reimagines a longer past in its very (post)modern construction of the fantastic and its marvelous/fantastic fiction. The fantastic here is broad, rather than narrow. This nostalgic rethinking germinated with the early revival of European chivalric romances during the sixteenth and seventeenth centuries, famously satirized by Cervantes.[16] Today,

---

[15] See Galileo's *Sidereal Messenger*, or *Starry Messenger*, published in 1610.
[16] For example, fantasy writer Michael Moorcock sees the chivalric romance

such genre elements as knights on quests have become common to the point of cliché; locating them within a continuum before the emergence of twentieth-century fantasy foregrounds these precursor elements that emerged at the same time as the birth of the modern novel. These elements of the fantastic resulted in the solidification of perennial fantasy tropes that we still see. But they also encouraged a blurring of boundaries to the point the fantastic as, Kathryn Hume has argued, must be considered a persistent impulse in Western thought that reaches back to the Ancient Greeks.[17]

This impulse responded to the dominance of the Enlightenment project's focus on reason and order, encouraging a contrarian tone in literature, the arts, and even philosophy that challenged the beating

---

Palmerín de Inglaterra (1547–48) as an analogue to the twentieth century's popular epic fantasy. It and other adventure romance poems like it are "packed with wizards, magic weapons, cloaks of invisibility, beautiful sorceresses, flying machines and diving bells of various unlikely kinds, magic cups, rings, crowns, shoes, horses, and castles; ogres, dwarves, monsters, malevolent spirits, helpful spits, black curses, doom, tragedy—and a hero of incredible youth, good looks and prowess who is out to rescue a heroine of incredible youth, beauty, and virtue" (Moorcock 1987, 22). These are now stable elements within the sort of high fantasy exemplified by D&D and a host of other gametexts, novels, films, video games, etc.

[17] Critical for my approach is Kathryn Hume's *Fantasy and Mimesis: Responses to Reality in Western Literature* (1985). Fantasy as a foundational type of fiction is a recognizable descendant of what Hume calls a "blindspot [...] a long shadow" (1985, 6) that began in the West with Plato and Socrates' critique of the fantastic. For Hume, her correction is in seeing the schema of mimesis and fantasy as two impulses that work together in fiction, one sometimes weighted more heavily than the other. She charts the earlier failure of mythos as critical in allowing a triumphant realism, a failure due to the skepticism of Socrates toward traditional mythology and later due to the Enlightenment's critique of Christianity. This was a short-lived victory because literature is about human experience, both the rational and the mystical. Fantasy, according to Hume, emerges through the tensions with an upstart realism that refuses to admit its weakness. She states more than once her intention to avoid an exclusive approach that would "isolate fantasy from the rest of literature" (1985, xii). She follows the accepted idea that fantasy is "the deliberate departure from the limits of what is usually accepted as real and normal" (1985, xii), her approach most helpful because it moves beyond genre and publishing demands to view fantasy as an impulse that emerges in a variety of literatures. In particular, SF has become such a borderless phenomenon, Hume's recognition of the fantastic and the mimetic working together to reorient the reader to SF. In this sense, I read Hume as less detailing fantasy and more detailing the fantastic in SF, or crime fiction, or romance, etc.

drum of technologically driven progress. Such an intellectual–literary history reveals this response as the cataloging of German fairy tales and the resurgence of Gothic romances in the eighteenth and nineteenth centuries. Grouped together, the earlier chivalric and later Gothic romances formed idyllic landscapes with adventurous narratives that blossomed into a return to the exotic and fabulous. As the mid-eighteenth century came and went, Romantic impulses such as these lingered as critiques against a new domineering ethos of machine industry.

The cultural logic of the modern fantastic, then, emerged with vigor in the late eighteenth century, the 'Age of Technology.' The 1880s and onward are, thus, important in understanding the fantastic and its ties to technology with the emergence of scientific romances/fantasies later labeled SF. During this pivotal time, the secular ethos of technology and science, the new dynamos later described by Henry Adams in 1907, offered novel ways of looking at ourselves and the universe that fueled the promise of progress and its technical tools.[18] But along with the rise of these new forms of progress and power during the Age of Technology's mechanical wonders, a discourse of disenchanted pessimism emerged alongside new hopeful forms of romance and fantasy fiction (see below). This complex time of the early twentieth century led to a battle between the championing of progress and skepticism in which, for many thinkers, sacralized transcendence looked suspect, while for others progress would solve our social problems. Alternatives were needed. The modern fantastic provided this relief in the form of imaginary and now realized worlds.

According to the standard account, Max Weber's 'iron cage' and Oswald Spengler's 'decline of the West' dominated such outlooks; however, combating the effects of these skepticisms, a populist form of enchanting discourse emerged that fueled the perennial return of fantastic tales.[19] This exploded into a variety of genre forms, from romance and the detective story, the western, eventually SF and epic fantasy.[20] This mechanistic saturation foregrounded the rise of the first

[18] See Adams 1918.
[19] See Weber 2001, 123, where he mentions his metaphor of the "iron cage." Also, Spengler's first volume of *The Decline of the West* (1926) for a representative pessimism.
[20] Historian Roger Luckhurst locates the rise of a machine aesthetic during this Age of Technology as critical for the nascent formation of what would become modern SF. "SF is a literature of technologically saturated societies" (Luckhurst 2005, 3), and it concerns itself with what Luckhurst calls 'mechanism' and how this impacts culture, as well as, he notes, human subjectivity. Thinkers such as Luckhurst recognize that this process of

virtual and realized worlds,[21] and while early modern SF was situated to present fictions of society's encounter with mechanism, the stories did more than just this; they created rudimentary realized spaces via material objects (analog magazines, books, films, and later computer screens driven by digital representation, etc.). We see this most clearly with the modern fantastic's critical conceptual move from representation to realization, a similar move made by game studies thinkers who argue that to understand the experience of story-telling-games one must think of configurations over representations.[22]

A confluence of modern pressures drove the rise of this imaginary (and later gameist-realized) mode, both its broadly fantastic and more science-focused versions. Hugo Gernsback's didactic scientifiction and the 1926 creation of *Amazing Stories* attempted to systematize this new ethos. Soon after, John W. Campbell's strong version of modern SF—seen in its most refined articulation as a move from Gernsbackian naiveté and simplicity to narrative sophistication whose stories posed problems answerable by science and engineering—failed in its attempt at creating a twentieth-century, modern, rationalist mythos. The threat of the 'bomb' and continued ecological devastation resisted such myth-making, as well as resisted the perception that science's domain could guide us in how to be human. The imaginary, though, was ripe for its explosion within popular culture, far beyond SF's reach.

The *modern* as a foundational concept within the modern fantastic remains intractable, especially if attempting to find meaning based on its terminology. If so, we are faced with parsing the concept from its broadest scale relative to its predecessor, the *medieval*, and its supposed successor, the *postmodern*. From such a centuries-spanning view, the latter, though, becomes an inflection of the modern, rather than a true break. Deciding if one should locate modernity's beginnings with the rise of industrial technology, or with the Enlightenment, the Renaissance, or even the shift from the Late Medieval Period, still deserves investigation. Such determinations, though, have a long and convoluted historiography, with the modern still contested across disciplines. The historical or philosophical concept of modernity comprises the largest scale, while the literary, critical, and artistic modernisms help because they have

---

mechanism, this primary drive within the modern fantastic toward realized space, did more than reduce everything to machine-culture. Resistance emerged that reworked the effects of industrialization on culture.

[21] See Michael Saler's use of 'virtual' worlds in *As If: Modern Enchantment and the Literary PreHistory of Virtual Reality* (2012).

[22] For a helpful overview of the topic, see the Ludology section of Harrigan and Wardrip-Fruin 2004, 60.

captured the minds of many important producers of culture, such as Marx's materialist view of political economy, Nietzsche's critiques of rationalism, Freud's destabilizing of the self, Heidegger's erasure of the humanist subject, etc.

Key categories such as progress, nature, the self, reason, etc., have served as definitive frames for the modern consciousness, especially in the critique of these concepts that has led to the modern crisis. In theorizing the modern fantastic, we could consider the gripes of the Romantics, plus Freud's discontents, or even Weber's disenchantments. Searching for clues closer to our present, we see Andreas Huyssen's 'great divide' often referenced with tensions between high art and mass culture providing much material for a burgeoning modernism, especially as a point of origin for the postmodern collapse of such categories.[23] We might seek clarity with Baudelaire's transitional newness in understanding the period, but the new becomes obsolete, like the fashions of Benjamin's Parisian *flâneur*, and must be rethought.[24] Out of these tensions, we might broaden our perspective toward political economy and the construction of the modern state and its empire-driven successors.[25]

Yet, the most consistent endeavor within modern studies, which continues to be a determining factor in the modern fantastic, has been the examination of the modern subject, especially how it is formed, pressured, seduced by the above influences. In this comprehensive sense, the modern subject has been a locus of inquiry in many working definitions, especially within critical theory; we might even focus on the thought of the Frankfurt School and its critique of mass culture. This leads us to Theodor Adorno and Max Horkheimer's famous argument that the Enlightenment moves through a dialectic with myth or Jürgen Habermas's incomplete project of modernity and the attempt to recover a communicative reason.[26]

However, the most useful, elegant, and simple conceptual tool for *Dread Trident*'s use can be found in the prescient thinking of Michel Foucault's call for an enlightened modernity defined by continued critique. This book seriously considers the Foucauldian idea that the "attitude of modernity" (Foucault 1980, 38) (i.e., a perennial 'Enlightenment') works

---

[23] See Huyssen 1987.
[24] See Benjamin's reading of Baudelaire within a modern context (Benjamin 2006).
[25] See Hardt and Negri 2000.
[26] One of the most important comments here is Horkheimer and Adorno 1972, one of many texts that unravel the myth of the Enlightenment. Also, see Habermas's attempt to salvage value from the Enlightenment (Habermas 1985a; 1985b).

through continual self-critique and, thus, is not limited historically to a single moment in time or even to a series of events. His reading of Kant's *Was ist Aufklärung?*[27] demonstrates an attempt to save what is valuable from the Enlightenment, its insistence on *sapere aude*, or 'daring to know,' as a consistent impulse inherent in the modern.[28]

Within the context of the modern fantastic's construction of realized worlds, one analogue for Kantian 'tradition' equates with the idea that human beings occupy environments with clearly defined borders between the real and unreal. Common-sense tradition and current naive realist thinking demand that these must remain separate to avoid dangerous confusion. The imaginary, the fantastic, the marvelous, the sacred, etc., all suggest a mental, or non-material ontology. Yet, this binary is less than helpful in explaining the experience of the modern fantastic, which reworks another type of fantastic space we have imagined for centuries, but now have the capability to live within for extended periods. How we speak and think about this new spatial factuality of the *imagined* or *realized* fantastic is crucial in how we experience it, often in a ludic fashion, but always with a sense of irony. Games encourage this experience, one reason they are now a dominant mechanism within the cultural mode of the modern fantastic.

Foucault was also concerned with theorizing modern space, suggesting "that today's anxiety concerns space in a fundamental way" (1998, 177). For Foucault, knowledge, space, and power are always qualified by reciprocal relations and their effects.[29] His most famous example is panopticism in *Discipline and Punish: The Birth of the Prison* (1977), a system of surveillance that works via the perceived absence of authority to create, through self-regulation, docile bodies. For Foucault, "space is fundamental in any exercise of power" (Foucault and Rabinow 1984, 252). Embedded in his various biopolitical studies is this language of space.[30]

---

[27] The full title to the essay is *Beantwortung der Frage: Was ist Aufklärung?* (1784).

[28] I am aware of Foucault's thinking in the *Order of Things* (1970) concerning the limitations of the modern episteme and the dissolution of 'man' as a thinking subject limited by finitude. It is this sense of reaching that inspires the positive use of such insights that a renewed modernity will constantly seek answers to such lack.

[29] He provided a historical example of railroads creating new relationships, such as confusion for individuals who might want to marry "between Bordeaux and Nantes" (Foucault and Rabinow 1984, 243).

[30] He was challenged on his minimal published commentary elucidating the discipline of geography, even though his thought is filled with the language of territories, fields, domains regions, horizons, etc. (Foucault 1980, 68).

Echoing theorist of play Johan Huizinga, Foucault clarifies his use of space within a modern context, suggesting that a major difference between the medieval conception of space and our current epoch's is the notion of sacred space, or sanctified space. He sees that even with modernity's desanctification, many spaces retain a touch of the sacred:

> For example, between private space and public space, between the family space and social space, between cultural space and useful space, between the space of leisure activities and the space of work. All these are still controlled by an unspoken sacralization. (Foucault 1998, 177)

Foucault defines these 'heterotopias' as places situated between impossible utopias (pure intellectual fantasies) and environments set aside by society as alternate places, but very real. They are typically places of crisis, or often of deviation. The boarding school, the honeymoon bed, rest homes, psychiatric hospitals, prisons, cemeteries, but also spaces of the imagination like the theater, cinema, and even gardens, museums, and libraries. Among others, he suggests that brothels and colonies are also heterotopias, leaving the ship or sailing vessel as "the heterotopia par excellence" (1998, 185). Also, his use of the mirror is a telling element because it has aspects of the unreal utopia and the intermediate heterotopia that stand between the real and the unreal. These landscapes of internal space are "haunted by fantasy" (Hurley translation in Foucault 1998, 177), a nod toward a cultural inflection already on its upward ascendance that the fantastic often has an inseparable neo-Gothicism of haunting in its tone.

Dread Trident argues that fantasies of internal space can now be realized in sophisticated fashions with the tools of the modern fantastic, tools that can act as forms of resistance to the disciplinary exercise of power and knowledge but may, just as easily, reinforce categorical and social norms. In a way, these realized worlds function like heterotopias or magic circles.[31] All of these spaces speak to the notion that the binary

---

[31] While a sacralized magic circle hints at the importance of such spaces in pre-modern cultures—for example, those detailed in earlier sociological work by Émile Durkheim and later Mircea Eliade—such a space becomes realized within the frame of an ironic, modern fantastic. For a good introduction to Durkheim, see Alexander and Smith 2005, and for Eliade's representative work on the sacred and profane, see Eliade 1987. Only a misunderstanding of what fantasy role-playing is would suggest real spells are cast or devils summoned. The 'magic' circle is not magical, and its circle is not a truly circumscribed space. We must see that the metaphor is helpful

of real-and-unreal is unhelpful in understanding the complexities of modern spaces. Instead, it demands we examine how mediated spaces function. Realization of fictional/imaginary spaces, in their fantastic versions, is unavoidable as a modern phenomenon, and one that will continue to expand its reach. Yet, the separation of real and unreal, while thoroughly problematized in postmodern studies, still retains its hold on the minds of individuals in the everyday, popular spheres of thought. The shift to realized spaces clarifies how the unreal in the form of imaginary worlds foregrounds itself as a major impulse in modernity, and one that demonstrates how unreal, constructed, or, in my language, *fantastic* reality is.

SF and Fantasy

Imaginative elements of the modern fantastic inform the entire process of consuming TRPGs. Genre studies helps in understanding the case studies in this book, but primarily as a departure field that points to genre's inherent instability. SF, of course, is a genre many thinkers have dedicated much thought in separating from mythic fantasy. Yet, post-Campbellian, post-New Wave, post-cyberpunk SF is a multi-headed beast with tendencies, often, toward the improbable and fantastic. The amount of SF-fashioned films, TV programs, novels, etc. that demonstrate these fantastic qualities are great. To take one, in the Wachowskis's film *Jupiter Ascending* (2015) god-like, posthuman aristocrats vie for control of planets; werewolf and dragon soldiers battle; and Gothic spaceships that, in an aesthetic nod to Games Workshop's Warhammer 40,000 (40k) setting, soar through space like flying cathedrals. The final scene screens a stunning image in which Jupiter (Mila Kunis) and Caine (Channing Tatum) jump from a building, Jupiter with rocket boots and Caine with wings. The image reconciles the opposing tropes of traditional SF (mechanistic rocket power) and fantasy (mythological Daedalian wings).[32]

---

because it is suggestive, rather than descriptive. Such misunderstandings fueled the anti D&D craze of the 1980s. See Peterson 2012.

[32] One can pick and choose examples from the plethora of genre-bending films, TV shows, novels, video games, comic books that resist any tidy classification. To take one, the *Sherlock* (2010–present) TV show from the BBC is just as fantastic as realist because of how it represents Sherlock's cognitive powers as almost a magical form of ratiocination, an expansion on the original fictional stories with their quasi-fantastic representations of observation and intuitive logic.

Such miscibility within the popular genres of the fantasy-adventure-romance (often classified within the many sub-genres of SF and fantasy) point to the symbolic power of these stories to reflect a deep concern we still see in our dominant story-telling tropes, i.e., the *posthuman* becoming the quintessential SF-flavored technological trope of the near future on its way to superseding the rocket ship, the alien, the ray gun, etc. Only the *draconic* in the form of the dragon, the white knight, the black knight, the mad mage, the wizardess, etc., appears to have as much staying power. We see these twinned tropes as constant players in the rise of fantastic realized worlds that, themselves, function as drivers within the cultural logic for this wider process within the modern fantastic.[33]

We repeatedly see this *draconic–posthuman* motif–pattern in contemporary media, and often both draconic and posthuman define the experience of engaging realized worlds—both of which are fantastic. Whereas within the genre of epic/high fantasy, we find the draconic, and all of its ancillary motifs in the forms of dragons themselves, as

---

[33] Frederic Jameson's use of a 'cultural logic' helps ground *Dread Trident*'s use. His has also been one of the consistently strongest voices in American literary theory who maintained his authority as a Marxist literary critic most celebrated because of his earlier interest in, of all things, a way to re-read Freud by engaging with a Lacanian notion of the real in its material and historical contexts and, then, even more surprisingly, with postmodernism. See Adam Roberts's understanding of Jameson in 2000. His other interests from realism and modernism to utopia and SF all fall under the framework of how history, and its capitalist inflections, inform artistic expression. What informs them all, of course, is the socio-economic 'logic' relevant to their time periods. *Dread Trident* avoids engaging whether we are modern or postmodern, or whether modernism has ceded the high ground to postmodernism, or even at what stage in capitalism we find ourselves. What is helpful, though, in looking at how posthumanization emerges through the modern fantastic, is Jameson's explication of cultural logic within postmodernism. For Jameson, we have more than a postmodern style. Its logic acts as a type of container, or space, for modes of expression. This is not a grand meta-narrative that Lyotard so famously presented as the target of postmodern thought (see Lyotard 1984). Instead, Jameson's description of the shiny, glass encased, disorienting-and-depthless Westin Bonaventure hotel exemplifies a postmodern spatial sensibility that so many other thinkers have also explored. For *Dread Trident*, the most interesting tenor of our contemporary moment's logic is a resounding fantastic impulse realized through a variety of texts and tools. Most critically, they are creating many imaginary spaces within which modern subjectivities emerge, more and more of them pushing into actual space, rubbing up against our shoulders in shopping malls, grocery stores, schools, and the home. See Jameson 1991; 1998.

well as other magical creatures such as elves, dwarves, mages, warriors, vampires, werewolves, mythic monsters, etc., and whereas within SF, we find the roboticized, genetically enhanced, nano-altered, augmented, hyper-intelligent posthuman, these combined tropes do more than entertain in film, TV, comic books, video games, and written fiction or provide a way to theorize SF, fantasy, and the modern fantastic. They prove to be templates for subject formation in the realized worlds of TRPG spaces.

The draconic defines four decades of D&D and its numerous fantasy-game descendants, as well as the neo-Gothic Worlds of Darkness. The altered draconic/posthuman now emerges in a wealth of more recent fictive SF texts but can be seen in condensed form in gametexts from the 40k setting, as well as Eclipse Phase and Numenera. Gametexts are a perfect unmined archive that reveal these tropes through a process that now requires gameplay. Fantastic realized worlds must be engineered for such tropes to be experienced agentially. Posthumanization within this study explains how this occurs through the curious admixture of analog/digital forms within the context of perennially redrawing the modern human (see below).

As *Dread Trident* demonstrates with its case studies, the draconic-posthuman figure is central in framing discourse within the modern fantastic, and, in doing so, it carries an unavoidable mythic tenor recognizable as part of the technologized present. With certain TRPGs such as Eclipse Phase and Numenera this genre diffusion is a selling-point. Borders are unstable in such blatant science-fantasy contexts that hearken back to Poul Anderson, Jack Vance, L. Sprague De Camp, etc. Magic exists alongside super-tech. Amongst dragons, elves, dwarves, and wizards we encounter alien races with psychic powers, ships that speed through the galaxy at faster-than-light, and new modes of existence beyond the physical. Fantasy tropes are not restricted to wizards in pointy hats, to unicorns, orcs, or faeries. The most imaginative tropes are persons transformed into space habitats, 'uplifted' animals, disembodied egos, etc., all of these elements functioning within a modern-fantastic mythopoetic frame just as myth, legend, and folklore do within fantasy. Teasing apart the purely fantastic elements from the extrapolative, though, becomes a test of strained credulity. Ultimately, we must admit that such 'supra'-natural elements speak to Arthur C. Clarke's famous Third Law concerning advanced technology indistinguishable from magic.

However, modern fantasy's well-theorized cousin, SF, is often granted a seriousness in its content, while fantasy is not. This acceptance and dismissal is curious because SF suffered disciplinary scorn for much of its literary history, one that since at least the sixties has sought to separate itself from fantasy into "separate beasts" (Mendlesohn and James 2009, 66). Much work has been done by professional academics carving a place for SF at the High Table of disciplinary acceptance, with SF containing several competing definitions. Differentiating it from other forms of fantastic writing has been a defining factor of much criticism. However, genre classification only provides so much help. Brian Attebery's "fuzzy sets" (1992, 12) as well as Gary K. Wolfe's 'evaporating genres'[34] metaphors, among others, reveal that generic borders are not and have never been stable. Even more so, countless examples of such intermixing demonstrate that in today's world of creative production, such restrictions will never be stable.

Two of the most dominant conceptualizations of SF seek an understanding through its historiography or through its form. One popular approach, and assumed fact, is to define SF beginning with Mary Shelley's 1818 *Frankenstein* (Aldiss and Wingrove 1986, 18–19). Others sometimes view the science romances of Verne and then of Wells as inaugurating this new form of modern science-oriented fiction. Still, others find its historicity less convincing than its form. Darko Suvin's requirement that SF be defined by a *novum* that causes estrangement enshrined SF as a serious form of literature (1979). But the story of SF has never been so stable. Criticism grew, none more so than in the period that followed, the New Wave, whose admirers like J.G. Ballard, Samuel R. Delany, Joanna Russ, and others used language as a tool to wrest the genre from the hands of its stodgy grandfathers such as Robert A. Heinlein and Isaac Asimov or its narrower focus under Suvin. As the story goes, popular culture continued to produce new forms, cyberpunk reinfusing the genre with an awareness of the cultural logic of capitalism, issuing in a final hurrah for the power of SF. It would be superseded (or balkanized) by a variety of border-shifting genres and unforeseen market pressures like Amazon's K.D.P. self-publishing. The genre has returned to the hands of fans-turned-writers. Biopunk and the new weird are but two of the newest forms of SF, not to mention postcolonial SF and continued inflections of feminist SF.

A resistance to my argument that SF is inherently fantastic might be found in utopian studies and by SF's "commitment to visions of human transformation" (Parrinder 2000, 2), one of many critiques that elevates SF as a written or screened art form, in the tradition of Suvin.[35] Such a long view sees SF reaching back to Sir Thomas More's *Utopia* (1516).

---

[34] See G.K. Wolfe 2011.
[35] For a good example of the sort of lofty aim for SF hoped for by Suvin, see Freedman 2000.

It utilizes Suvin as a critical cartographer of SF because Suvin helped couple SF and utopia, as well as removed SF from (according to him) the taint of fantasy; his concept of a novum creating cognitive estrangement is a mechanism for seeing our world in a new, defamiliarized light, thus providing a way to affect it. We are to recognize that, as in science, in proper SF we wonder at the universe so that we can better it. Suvin's novum must do such heavy lifting in literary SF. The cognitive and intellectual side of estrangement, for him, must be bolstered by the textual and narrative elements. Modern myth-making requires stories to be told, and this occurs both in science and in SF. A gap often exists, though, between the estrangement of science exploration and that of SF. For critics such as Suvin and those who would follow his approach, narrative fills this space. SF, then, is a new world to discover, just like our solar system, and one to be regarded with care.

Dread Trident's approach makes no such demands. In fact, it recognizes a quite upsetting fantastic impulse that often runs counter to these lofty goals. Limiting the fantastic to fantasy as a genre or to an array of sub-genres, with narrow requirements predicated on the impossible or inexplicable, runs counter to the notion of the fantastic that precedes the many sub-genres both of fantasy and SF. My use allows the *modern* fantastic to be impossible, and explicable; however, it is best juxtaposed with the *mundane*. High fantasy with its dragons, elves, and magic is impossible, as is much in SF (such as time travel and Star Trek-like teleporting technology). But often in high fantasy these elements are explained rationally, especially, say, with the Vancian magic use in a game like D&D.[36] What makes them interesting for my study is their shattering of the mundane world.

These elements reach beyond our mundane reality to posit a tenor loaded with the imaginary. *Dread Trident* focuses on the fantastic rather than on the genre descriptors of fantasy (which would highlight the distinctions between SF vs. fantasy) not just to sidestep the insightful, professional debate that views SF about the possible (and improvable) and fantasy the impossible, but to foreground the commonality that both are imbued with the fantastic. The fantastic in this sense is a catalyst from the mundane world, pointing elsewhere, sometimes to the transcendent, sometimes to the immediate present, but in most cases away from the commonplace, from the mundane.

The term (*fantastic*) in this use means more than 'great,' or 'wonderful,' or 'terrific,' or the 'fabulous,' etc.; it means a surprising rupture within

---

[36] For example, 'impossible' spells work because of a rational arcane magic system based on somatic, verbal, and material rituals.

everyday reality. For example, if a safe fell from the sky and landed at your feet, breaking open to reveal a million dollars in diamonds, this would certainly galvanize a mundane world. In this sense, such a story represents a strong-mimetic version of the modern fantastic; in fact, such adrenaline-filled energizers are very much a part of the modern fantastic. These elements can be found in the genre of the modern thriller, with its super agents like James Bond or Jason Bourne saving the world from destruction and saving us from our mundane lives. The more mimetic of these are highly charged elements possible in the actual world, while the more outrageous border on the fantastic.[37] However, if thumb-sized plastic army soldiers marched out of the safe, we have entered the realm of the modern fantastic favored by TRPGs, with highly imaginary draconic (or posthuman, or a combination of both) inflections.[38]

I admit, though, that my non-standard approach requires some convincing. Along with the calling for a serious SF that separates it from other forms of fantastic literature, genre boundaries continue to exist for a variety of reasons, from marketing needs to sell packaged materials to the actual desire of consumers for specific types of content. I will not attempt another full argument for definition or classification of SF or fantasy beyond the claim that grounds *Dread Trident*: that SF, along with the modern horror genre, is just as much a part of the modern fantastic as are the varieties of fantasy genres. In fact, the modern fantastic is comprised of two poles, with hard SF and epic/high fantasy opposite each other at both ends. Horror floats between the two but rarely dominates.[39] We see both of the polarized versions flourishing in the types of fantastic realized spaces emerging, as well as in the most interesting of TRPGs, while horror, like many of its tropes, often hides in the shadows, yet in moments of confidence steps directly into view.

Rather than in Tolkien's lofty aims for fantasy, TRPGs found inspiration in the pulps. R.E. Howard and other sword-and-sorcery writers like Jack Vance and Fritz Leiber provided the inspiration. The reason for this is that fantasy's misunderstood favorite, D&D, is an artifact of popular culture, rather than high culture, a divide that is less and

---

[37] Note how these become fantastic when they stray from what is actually possible. In the Jason Bourne films, Bourne borders on a superhero with his fighting abilities, while a thriller such as *Collateral* (2004) posits an assassin with exceptional but very human abilities.

[38] See the short story "Battleground" by Stephen King, in *Night Shift* (1978). In the story, King posts a package to be opened rather than a falling safe.

[39] Other genres also float between the two, often appearing in both SF and high fantasy as elements from romance, to the detective story, to adventure, etc.

less stable today. With TRPGs of both the sword-and-sorcery/epic fantasy genres of Howard (low) and Tolkien (high), as well as the varied genres of SF, from space opera to cyberpunk and the old and new weird, we see game systems of realization that exemplify the modern fantastic's move toward technologically created realized worlds. The most popular of these, e.g., D&D, do follow Tolkien in presenting massive campaign settings and extended lore, yet also follow Howard and Leiber in creating dashing characters full of vim and verve, and follow Lovecraft in offering pantheons of mysterious, terrifying deities. The gametexts that provide the basis for such disparate play often feature stunning imagery, a nod to the role of the visual arts in providing representation of these unimaginable objects.

One of the pulps' most important writers is fundamental in understanding the reach of the modern fantastic. The influence of Lovecraft features extensively throughout *Dread Trident* as the originator of a stellar imaginary/realized world called the 'Cthulhu' Mythos. Unfortunately, Lovecraft's personal views on race mark him clearly within a cultural frame prior to a progressive social consciousness now being led by D&D and its continued championing of inclusiveness for all persons. The one positive outcome of how he responded to the pressures within modernity is the reach of this Mythos that others have extended far beyond his initial conception.[40] *Dread Trident* also uses him to foreground his type of cosmic horror as a sophisticated inflection within the modern fantastic, especially its constant shifting between the two poles of SF and fantasy. What is most interesting about Lovecraft as a component of the modern fantastic is his posthuman cosmicism, a belief in an indifferent universe and humanity's response of horror to this knowledge of itself and nature, and how his Mythos provides a fictive way to represent this cosmicism. What is significant is how his cosmicism prefigures a fantasy/SF-inspired posthumanism-as-post-anthropocene discourse that now forms a supplement within critical posthumanism (see below).

Theorists typically view posthumanism as a philosophical response to the limits of humanism, driven by technology's rise. Yet, *Dread Trident* argues that Lovecraftian cosmicism has little to do with this and much to do with grasping the temporal scale of geological deep time that minimizes, if not erases, humanity's importance. His posthumanism is postanthropocene-'ism.' His horror is one of erasure. Such intriguing

---

[40] Unfortunately, Lovecraft also responded to the pressures of progressive modernity with racial hatred and bigotry, a fact documented in his correspondences.

insights are surfacing across several disciplines interested in SF, fantasy, horror, Lovecraft, cosmicism, etc.[41]

Realized Space

When thinking of realized worlds, *space* must be considered within the context of the modern fantastic. Such gameist 'geographies of the imagination' (see Anderson 1991; Said 1979) function at the level of the gametext, and these require a discursive-and-material conception of space as an environment that allows for engineering solutions to solve particular problems. This is fair because space has never been a simple concept. In the modern period, the architectural dream of designing clear and clean perspectival space in a stable manner suffered blows by increased forms of social, artistic, and philosophical spatial dynamism. Modernism formed such a challenge in architecture with the radical work of Le Corbusier, Gropius, Frank Lloyd Wright, and others. Like Deleuze's attempt to understand the real, the space of the modern fantastic offers theorists a minefield of complexities and abstractions

One important way to conceptualize the fantastic aspect (i.e., the strangeness) of realized-modern-fantasy space can be seen when looking at Walter Benjamin's unfinished project, *Das Passagenwerk* (*The Arcades Project*). In it he uses the language of paradise, a concept of the marvelous, as a modern tool to critique earlier biblical usage.[42] This language was

---

[41] For example, philosopher Graham Harman's object-oriented ontology acknowledges the odd existences of things outside of human perception. For him, the literary 'weird' becomes relevant in a universe constantly rendered strange. Also, Eugene Thacker has examined how an indifferent universe is the most interesting evolution of the horror genre. See Harman 2018; 2012; Thacker 2015b; 2015a; 2011.

[42] Most serious commentary on the fantastic and its difference from the genre of fantasy starts with Tzvetan Todorov's structural thoughts in *The Fantastic: A Structural Approach to a Literary Genre* (1975). He argued that the fantastic is seen as a hesitation that both a character in a literary work and a reader experiences when encountering an uncanny event. Foregrounded here is a tension between "two orders, those of the natural world and those of the supernatural" (Todorov 1975, 27). When characters or readers encounter an event that makes them question the type of order, the fantastic enters as a hesitation. For Todorov, the primary tension exists between determining an event as either illusory/imaginary-and-real (the fantastic uncanny) vs. real-but-supernatural (the fantastic marvelous). This is a very narrow, specialized way to address the subject. Turning Todorov on his head suggests that the fantastic is the complete opposite; it becomes any event that one

applied by Benjamin to the city of Paris, a place for him in which commodities acted as religious icons. Benjamin wrote of arcades as temples designed to tempt passers-by. Objects for sale acted like the phantasmagoria seen in the lantern shows at the time, a technique that projected fantastic imagery in entertainment shows, as well as in seances. His foregrounding of objects as illusory but affective phantasms moves beyond a critique of modern capitalism's fetishes to a recognition that in projecting fantastic objects between the imaginary and the real, they become (what today we would call) *realized*.

The supreme examples of such phantasmagoria were arcades written large: the world expositions and, in particular, the Crystal Palace in London being the first, with Paris hosting several as well. These examples of the magical power of industry represented an apotheosis of modern capitalism; for Benjamin, they presented phantasmagoria as objects of modern myth-making. These illusions of progress, industry, nationalism, etc., all sold products within spaces whose existences as objects defined the new. The construction of such objects could be seen not only in arcades but in "urban phantasmagoria [...] railroad stations, museums, winter gardens, sport palaces, department stores, exhibition halls, boulevards" (Buck-Morss 1991, 92). These are actualized spaces that demonstrate their true unreality.

Dread Trident's use of realized worlds follows this trajectory that combines the imaginary with the real, switching the binary to the analog and the digital. In such theorizing, posthumanization drives such a fantastic-inflected modernity. The fashioning of the unreal world of Paris as a symbol for the modern leads, through the proliferation of fantastic things, to the construction of analog/digital realized worlds. Paris, through the eyes of its creative interpreters such as Benjamin, was a symbol of the modern imaginary. When people today play in the realized worlds of RPGs, they reflect how selves are fashioned in actualized worlds. We are not that far from a nineteenth-century Parisian *flâneur* strolling along the boulevard, even in our most virtual of realized worlds.

Insights of the realized such as these also find their roots in the broadest of existential concerns, also seen in the phenomenology of Maurice Merleau-Ponty and the reworking by neo-phenomenologists such as Don Ihde.[43] The very notion of 'place,' instead of space, as an

---

would consider to be a commonsense falsity in our own world. It requires no hesitation at all. And, most importantly in terms of the reading experience, or, in the context of realized worlds' broader experience of gameplay, no real belief must occur that such events are true.

[43] To begin with Ihde, start at Ihde 1990.

ontological category in which a human being exists, speaks to the heart of Heidegger's project in critiquing technology, as well as the turn toward a post-existentialist understanding of life.[44] It also speaks to Bachelard's insights into domestic space as integral to the creative imagination.[45] The modern crisis, itself, the very crucible in which Heidegger critiqued late nineteenth- and early twentieth-century humanism, was understood to be built through a modernity populated by increased industrialization.[46] We are reminded that the modern context is one, like Dostoevsky's Underground Man, concerned with the human and his or her place in the world. Space as containing a lived place, even if often distressed, returns as a focus for any understanding of the modern fantastic's imaginary worlds. In what space do these realized worlds exist? An urban one, a cybernetic one, an imaginary one, an embodied one? A realized one.[47]

[44] For a helpful introduction to Heidegger's thinking on the being of technology, see Harman 2002.

[45] We can't forget that most realized worlds emerge at home, in the bedroom, the living room, the garage, on a tabletop, in a book, on film. Bachelard wrote of a poetics of "felicitous space" (1994, xxxv), what he called a 'topophilia' of domestic spaces such as a house. This is a type of space, or place, wherein a person thrives through the power of the imagination. For him, his material focus on door knobs, cellars, nooks, etc., awakened another space, one embedded within the walls of comfortable containers, but walls that allow for the opening of imaginative space that he tied, very closely, to the poetic imagination. He even apologized for why a philosopher dedicated to the rational explication of the philosophy of science would turn his mind to a possible "philosophy of poetry" (1994, xv). In his study, he begins with the image of the house from a psychological perspective, but he quickly moves into containers themselves, objects within houses. Not stopping there, he presents shells and nests from the natural world, uninhabitable places, metaphors for the intimate nooks and crannies in which to daydream. Such a perspective is helpful because it demonstrates how the imagined emerges out of the actual and, in fact, is complicit in complicating any suggestion that they remain fully separate categories.

[46] For a comment from the popular sphere, World Economic Forum founder Klaus Schwab argues that the digital is driving a '4th' industrial revolution. See Schwab 2017.

[47] The modern fantastic works as a charged space, like that of sacred space or a magic circle, but one that is understood to be imaginary. The medieval fantastic, to take one example, viewed from a modern perspective, can be seen in Hildegard Von Bingen's believed-to-be-true, yet clearly imaginary, visions. The sincerity and earnestness of her belief in her mystical visions provides no bulwark from a modern view that admits her inherent misplaced fantasy. Within the modern fantastic's required irony we have proper footing. Even if someone misunderstands a realized world, maybe with the rise of more immersive virtual and mixed reality, such a space is no

Understanding the 'real' within the modern fantastic requires a brief comment on one major influence: Gilles Deleuze's[48] ontological philosophy of difference, multiplicities, flows, assemblages, forces, and intensities, especially how they relate to the abstract concept, the 'Real.' Deleuze, along with Derrida, Lacan, Foucault, and Lyotard, considered the transcendence of Western thought (i.e., relying on external grounds such as God, Truth, the Self, etc., for rational judgment) and how this transcendent philosophy affects the conceptualization of the modern subject, as well as the discursive practices used to define it. Deleuze informs *Dread Trident*'s approach to theorizing the modern fantastic because of his move not just to erase ingrained dualities like subject/object but the textual attempt to corral the movement of material forces, what he calls 'flows,' which emerge in a variety of forms and operate without our full cognitive understanding.

A difficult aspect of Deleuze's thought helpful in conceiving analog gametexts as the basis for realized worlds is his conception of the 'virtual' as a creative space for thought.[49] Deleuze's concept of the virtual, though, serves the modern fantastic more completely; he expands the term to describe the complex process of becoming. For Deleuze, the virtual emerges out of 'actual' material life as the 'real.' Before the virtual is the 'flow' of life. With perception, we see or experience the virtual. And the virtual is needed to make the actual *real*, slowing the flow of life to actualize it into the real. Deleuze has conceived of the virtual in a capacious fashion, robust enough to handle the complexities of realized worlds and their various game manifestations. Embracing this realism rejects the naive inflection surrounding most fantasy, i.e., that the fantastic only works in imaginary texts because the world is knowable in an uncomplicated and straightforward manner.

How can we expand the real beyond this naive conception? Like Deleuze, engineers are also interested in problems related to material reality. And while they do use discursive tools, they are not bound by them but, ultimately, rely on engagement with the material world for

less part of the fantastic as is something fully understood to be imaginary. The experience, though, for an individual thus deceived, requires its own analysis. A new type of fantastic might occur here, possibly the posthuman-fantastic or the hyper-real-fantastic.

[48] Often along with Félix Guattari. Henceforth, Deleuze.
[49] Historian Michael Saler also chooses to treat the virtual as non-digital. He frames the virtual, though, within a historical context prior to its use defining technological virtual reality. For him, virtual worlds are "acknowledged imaginary spaces that are communally inhabited for prolonged periods of time by rational individuals" (Saler 2012, 6).

reliable and verifiable results. If engineers failed to find some sense of an actual world, they would fail at their jobs too. But we have clear examples of successful results. Engineering provides the ultimate challenge to naive realism, rather than to Deleuzian thought. We should read Deleuze as pursuing the difficulties in generating human meaning and in understanding thought in a world with complex systems that often yield little meaning or transcendent answers of any kind.

Realized worlds multiply by the day as game designers work, and the raw material of TRPGs constitutes part of the real, rather than simply the imaginary. They are part of a massive assemblage of real and imaginary parts. Moreover, these realized worlds undermine the actual world's stability as simplistically real, a perennial theme in SF, especially from Philip K. Dick onward, and one to which the discourse of posthumanism is finely attuned.[50] Herein lies the beating heart of a Deleuzian philosophy of becoming in which the material world is empirically knowable and the virtual/realized world key. In such an understanding, science charts the process of the actual/virtual world becoming real, and philosophers of science, engineering, and technology push back in the opposite direction so that the philosophical creation of concepts do, in fact, affect the actual/virtual (real/realized) world in a material manner.

[50] In a key writer such as PKD, contemporary concerns emerge beyond those of the earlier pulp and Golden Age writers that, often, championed science as a tool of progress. PKD, though, found himself in the Digital Age, with all of the troubling ontologies inherent in its new media. Of central concern is the human being in contested realities where the virtual replaces the real in the form of, to take one example, androids hiding in plain sight as human beings. Also, the 'kipple' found in *Do Androids Dream of Electric Sheep?* (1968), so like the kitsch of postmodern culture, clogs society, as does imagined nuclear fallout, or mind-bending drugs, or hallucinatory reality. These issues of problematizing how reality and its objects are fabricated and made real/unreal lie at the heart of PKD's worldview and why he is read with such focus today. His narratives speak to the same impulse that drove Baudrillard to write of simulacra and Deleuze to interrogate the flows of life. PKD's interest in fakes, replicants, and falsities speaks to a concern that the world is fantastic-real, a fear of the imaginary not just as unreal, inauthentic, childish, etc., but as challenging an atavistic belief in a golden age of ontological stability and reality. PKD's recurrent return to the beleaguered human speaks to his core humanism and its existential quest for authenticity. And as a key figure in SF, many theorists choose to see him through those lenses rather than through the more problematic lenses of fantasy. This classification is historical, of course, and thinking of PKD as a SF writer, rather than as a fantasist, collapses horizons that need more expansion to better understand his role in the modern fantastic. See Kucukalic 2009 for PKD's inherent humanism.

Many other thinkers, as well, have alerted us to a variety of theories to understand modern space, materiality, and subjectivity from teasing apart the psyche along its symbolic, imaginary, and real dimensions (Lacan); to thinking about the different inflections of space and place and the activities that define them in our 'everyday' lives (De Certeau and Lefebvre); to space as a resurgent realist realm through which the multiplicities of life flow (Deleuze), etc.[51] Deleuze, again, is helpful because he recognizes that space is complex and material, and he draws theories from the sciences on how to understand these multiplicities, and, in particular, how morphogenesis occurs within virtual space. Any close examination into how we conceptualize modern spaces must look at the mechanisms of drastic material change—for example, not just those that altered the landscape with railroads and electric wires, with sprawling cities, with physical (and later digital) highways, all of which disrupted landscapes while creating new spaces within which to live, but those fantastic spaces emerging as real assemblages at the intersection of the analog and digital.

Dread Trident follows these and other theorists in using the idea of this Deleuzian force situated behind the world of differentiated matter, much like Manuel DeLanda does as a form of pre-thought, a pre-human categorical concept that allows for creativity to emerge in material ways.[52] The modern fantastic follows such a trajectory with the increasing proliferation of realized worlds. Gametexts and gametools, then, become part of this Deleuzian posthumanization process of creating realized worlds within a perennial modernity whose key attribute is a Foucauldian continued critique. These material objects must be considered within assemblages of complex networked analog/digital relationships that also help in understanding today's massively connected communication systems, as well as explain how human beings fit into such a matrix of human and non-human elements like individuals playing TRPGs. Ultimately, *Dread Trident*'s reading of Deleuze clarifies how something as complex as the creation of the realized worlds of, say, D&D functions today.

[51] For representative texts from each thinker, see Deleuze and Guattari 1987; Lefebvre 2000; 1992; DeCerteau 2011; Lacan 2006.
[52] For example, see DeLanda 2002.

Humanism, Posthumanism, and Posthumanization

At the intersection between modernity and fantastic realized worlds are the discourses that follow humanism and their focus on the problems Cartesian dualism poses for subjectivity. Just as the legitimation of science and modernity paradoxically interrogates the central doctrine of Cartesian dualism, critical (post)humanism attacks Cartesian abstraction and universalism. In response, it encourages the acceptance of qualities similar to the Renaissance humanists' love of particulars, skepticisms, varieties, i.e., lived individual affairs.

Pre-Cartesian humanism is rejected as a model for critical posthumanism because it retains stable ontological borders between the human and nature. If we can agree that human essentialism is problematic, that discussions of human nature are always predetermined by discourse, we see that realized worlds engender a variety of humans and humanisms, plenty to account for the differences that allow a plurality to thrive, without the need for a controlling definition.[53] Our attempts to engage in realized worlds foregrounds the flourishing of such details. TRPGs in their current aesthetic form should please both traditional humanists and posthumanists: they encapsulate humans as social beings telling oral, ephemeral stories as well as imagining what systems and complexities transcend them. What is most radical is not imagining the limits of constructing the human and transgressing them, but in imagining new fantasy spaces in which intelligent beings can live in a multitude of forms and places.

The realized worlds of the modern fantastic encourage creativity and agency for the broadest number of persons, as well as the expansion of these fantasy spaces across a variety of platforms. From this vantage point, the modern fantastic emerges as a very *human* process that has been occurring in detail since at least the late nineteenth century with the rise of the popular novel and its many fictional worlds. But if we take the long view—and this impulse is already present in Cervantes's *Don Quixote* (1615), the protagonist of which seeks disappearing myths in the face of disruptive change—such change is helping us tell our myths. Technological myth-making speaks to my insistence that the modern fantastic's key dynamic, *posthumanization* (see below), must retain aspects of the human worth saving. We enter realized worlds of our own making, wherein we leap into the enchanted present powered by stats, maps, etc., and our capacity for narrative. This is not only an

---

[53] One recent RPG example is Caitlynn Belle and Josh T. Jordan's transhuman-dating sim *Singularity* (2016).

intellectual process, but an experiential one. Without venturing into these simulated worlds, we cannot know them.

Critics of my focus on realized spaces might offer an expected objection: the modern, technologized subject is not exhausted, much less completely understood. For them, my focus on space erases the human and posthuman subject. The human, though, is more than a body or bodies. It is a discursive and material concept, and one constantly under pressure. *Humanism* has been described as the guiding ethos and watchword of modernity (Davies 1997, 22), a quintessential discursive construct located in the nineteenth century's preoccupation with defining the human and one with roots in the Enlightenment, the Renaissance, and earlier. However, the nineteenth century saw the rise of industrial technology and its transformative effects on human beings, society, and the environment; these effects have led to the proliferation of imaginary and then realized worlds at the same time the human was being drawn with such limiting precision.

As with modernity, varying definitions of humanity conditioned by space have been fretted over by philosophers, artists, writers, politicians, theologians, scientists, etc., rarely with consensus or a final word. Even within the context of modern humanism, such thinkers as Rousseau wrote about the move from the country to the city and Marx about environments conditioned by relationships of production and whose instruments, he argued, the bourgeoisie must constantly change. These environmental responses to the rise of technology led the twentieth century into an abstracted modernism that flattened perspective, ranges of thought, and notions of the human, often offering dangerous totalizations, most clearly seen in the limited view of Futurism, the obvious repulsion of machine romance, techno-fetish gone wrong. Such missteps hint at how to rethink limited notions of the human. What must be challenged is the factory mindset, the machine mindset, environments that reduce people to cogs rather than agents with, at least, some sense of autonomy.[54]

Avoiding this pessimism fuels much of the modern fantastic, rather than finding its ground in the consciousness of a political-cultural modernism and its crises. Weber's mistrust of social institutions and cultural values devoid of higher spiritual calling, even more so than a mistrust of individuals who suffered behind the bars of economic instrumentalism, still inspires much thinking in explicating the problems of modernity. Yet, even in the face of the most stringent anti-humanist inflections, be they fretful or hopeful, the persistent human subject

[54] See Berman 1988.

returns to be refashioned again and again. Modernism's abstraction-of-the-self acted as a precursor to the many later assaults but can also be framed as a signal that we should now look at the spaces in which selves emerge within a modern context. When we do, we see a need for humanized spaces that affirm embodiment and materiality. A common critique of modernity is that it is separated from a sacralized, enchanted past and, thus, lost or disenchanted. Realized spaces, be they magic circles, heterotopias, or game tables offer such reworking as a type of enchantment, or ironic magification (see below).

Within critical theory, the recurrent dethroning of 'man' (i.e., humanity) misrecognizes the true challenge in drawing the human: the tyranny of mundane reality to define the real and, thus, the human. The Copernican revolution from the Ptolemaic to a heliocentric universe often symbolizes a tectonic reorientation of Western Europe's medieval understanding of humanity's place in the universe. Darwin's dethroning of biblical 'man' as the privileged species is often touted as another scene in this displacement drama. Other insults to humanity's exceptionalism have followed, Nietzsche and Freud both offering major comments that demonstrate our irrationality.[55] A nascent change in fashioning a new understanding of ourselves is already occurring, and we see it when we view the realized as the proper space of investigation for modern subject formation. When we chart these realizations, corresponding figures emerge, variegated imagined types of humans that flourish (or not) within it.

While the modern fantastic's realized worlds describe the rise of playful fantasy spaces, they also demonstrate how their theorizing invigorates the discourses of critical (post)humanism—the conception of a thinking subject beyond the constraints of Cartesian dualism. *Dread Trident*'s focus on analog/digital fantastic spaces proliferating in today's technologized culture intervenes in the discourse of posthumanism by shifting the focus from bodies to spaces. Within the context of a 'gameist' modern fantastic, our natures as technologized persons rely on the creation and consumption of game settings that offer systems and spaces of narrative in addition to the narratives themselves. Such spaces begin as gametexts, a backdrop for the deployment of analog game systems, and expand to become imagination engines for other media: books, TV shows, video games, LARP (live-action role-playing), and memes.

---

[55] Bruce Mazlish suggests that a fourth 'discontinuity' may occur if human-like artificial intelligence arrives, arguing we reassess ourselves in light of non-biological intelligences (see Mazlish 1995).

The discourses of trans-and-posthumanism provide a theoretical base in this book's examination of TRPGs because they are predicated on the curious admixture of analog/digital gametexts and tools: the process of *posthumanization*.[56] Posthumanization acts as a primary cultural mechanism within the modern fantastic that builds analog/digital subjects in our complex technosocial world. Critical posthumanism, i.e., the professional discourse of posthumanization born of critical theory, seeks agency for persons transformed by sophisticated technology. As noted earlier, in its most distilled form, critical posthumanism rejects abstracted Cartesian notions of the normative human, while accepting Renaissance humanism's particularism. Just as the idea of modernity reaching beyond the Cartesian definition to a literary influence a century before Descartes is valuable, if flawed, we should see the modern fantastic's form of posthumanism defined by its creation of realized worlds, encouraging within them humans to be humans in a posthumanized fashion.

Material objects, like gametexts, act as tools of such agency. The posthuman subject is not lost or disoriented but located, often in realized worlds of a person's own creation. TRPGs frame us within these technologized settings, and posthumanization is the most helpful cognitive configuration that describes such a process. It may seem too narrow within the established context of modern studies, but it carries its weight when we add technology and fantasy.

The professional discourses of trans-and-posthumanism have been in motion since Donna Haraway argued that the cyborg was more than a science-fiction trope.[57] Haraway reinterpreted the standard notion of the cyborg, detailed as early as 1960 in an attempt to theorize how humans might live in space.[58] Instead of such an instrumental approach, she challenged old dualistic separations of the human vs. machine, as well as influenced theorists who followed her into articulating the complex relationships humans face in today's technologized world. Likewise, N. Katherine Hayles argued in *How We Became Posthuman* (1999) that imagining a self without a body is a techno-fantasy. Her target was Hans Moravec and others who championed scenarios of radical mind

---

[56] For a look at *Dread Trident*'s use of the term 'trans-and-posthumanism,' see *Post- and Transhumanism: An Introduction* (Ranisch and Sorgner 2014). It reverses the terms to post- and transhumanism. But it recognizes a competing field of discourses under the umbrella concept. Also, see the introduction, where Sorgner and Ranish write of the terms' "inter-relationship" (7) as a way to rethink both terms pointing "beyond humanism" (7).

[57] See Haraway 1991.

[58] See Clynes and Kline 1960.

uploading. Since her response, much of critical posthumanism seeks ways to challenge the Enlightenment project's traditional categories of the human, nature, the self, and so forth through the discourse of the corporeal or somatic. One focuses on the importance of actual bodies affected by actual technologies.

In moving away from the posthuman body toward conceptualizing the process of engineered posthumanization through fantasist spaces in which new subjectivities emerge, *Dread Trident* alters historian Michael Saler's term, 'virtual' worlds, for 'realized' worlds to foreground in analog terms the democratization of agential, systemic, and creative thinking, changing discourses away from bodies toward those of space, that is: world-building and play in those worlds.[59]

---

[59] Saler explores contemporary society's compulsion for fantasy in *As If: Modern Enchantment and the Literary PreHistory of Virtual Reality* 2012. He argues that the imaginary worlds of late nineteenth-century writers, such as Sir Arthur Conan Doyle's 221B Baker Street, overcame early devaluations of the imagination and developed into virtual worlds far beyond the authors' control. He focuses on the Victorian London of Sherlock Holmes, the Middle-Earth of J.R.R. Tolkien, and the Cthulhu Mythos of H.P. Lovecraft, arguing that these later genre exemplars influenced the explosion of virtual worlds from those of Star Wars to the Marvel Universe, Star Trek, Dr. Who, etc. Interestingly, he dedicates space to the often maligned but misunderstood TRPG D&D, recognizing its historical debt to its predecessors like R.E. Howard, Lovecraft, and Fritz Leiber, as well as its influence on later multi-user dungeons (MUDs) and massively multiplayer online role-playing games (M.M.O.R.P.G.s) (2012, 101). For Saler, virtual worlds are fantastic, with mimetic/realist attributes in which readers contributed to these worlds through letter writing, clubs, conventions, etc.; these are fantasy worlds constructed in a realist manner, replete with all the mechanisms of modernity: from indexes, maps, and tables, to detailed historical descriptions and ethnographies, cultural statistics, and character backgrounds. Saler argues that as readers of fictions identified with, say, Sherlock Holmes of 221B Baker Street, they enhanced their reading experiences by dressing like him, investigating the texts for discrepancies, meeting together, taking walking tours, etc. While these new phenomena emerged in force at the end of the nineteenth century, the Age of Technology, at the end of the twentieth we have both digital and, not surprisingly, analog forms that encourage such engagement in even greater degree. *Dread Trident* would depart from Saler's concept of the virtual for the realized. His use of the *virtual* in this description may raise some eyebrows. While Saler is insightful that the virtual in his sense does have a broader context beyond video game studies, my use of realized worlds avoids confusion by foregrounding the idea that these fantastic settings approach the real in varying degrees, while reminding us how unreal is the actual world.

Gametexts and tools are analogues of this broader process in a literal analog sense. They do more than entertain; they refract technologies of posthumanization, like those in the digital world, creating spaces in which emerge new discursive subjectivities between humans and nonhumans, and these relationships are vital in understanding notions of the human in our networked and distributed societies. Even more incredibly, these new identities manifest in a variety of new spaces, many realized. This relationship among technical artifacts, discursive subjectivities, and new spaces is a complex amalgam foundational in understanding contemporary subject formation and what it means to live today in highly technosocial societies.

Posthumanism is also one of the most important concepts that describes humanity's location in contemporary cultural theory. Why worry over such a term? One early describer retreated from the discourse because of "lost faith, even blasphemous faith, in posthumanism" (Badmington 2010, online). We also know of Haraway's retreat from the concept and her adoption of companion-species theory in its replacement. The reasons, according to those who've distanced themselves, vary from disciplinary oversaturation with the concepts to annoyance at the stigma of their association with transhumanism to simple exhaustion. In its place Haraway focuses on companion species, while Cary Wolfe argues for a vibrant form of posthumanism that is ethically admirable by extending personhood to animals.[60] This wider species-centric approach continues a project of decentering human exceptionalism that has been underway since the Romantic critique of the Enlightenment, and one that stands on the shoulders of twentieth-century anti-humanism: the idea that the borders separating the human from nature, from machines, from the alien, what Elaine Graham calls the 'ontological hygiene' of the human is not just under pressure but has been fully eroded by science and technology.[61]

The terms used to describe this process, especially within the trans-and-posthumanism discourses, tend to revolve around a few consistent axes.[62] *Critical* posthumanism vs. *popular* posthumanism (i.e., transhu-

[60] See C. Wolfe 2010.
[61] See Graham 2002.
[62] A few introductory approaches within the discourse help in teasing apart important differences. In the context of medical enhancements, Andy Miah's helpful "A Critical History of Posthumanism" (2009) views the term through three lenses: *political, cultural,* and *philosophical.* The political focuses on issues of biopolitics—in particular, how society will be shaped by concerns in medical ethics, social policy, and bio-enhancement. Cultural posthumanism is another term for critical posthumanism, but for Miah,

manism) is the most common way to differentiate the approaches, the
former attacking humanism's core dualism as its primary aim, while the

he broadens his perspective so that the genealogies of Haraway, Hayles,
Graham, etc., are less about disciplinary discourse-making in critical theory
and more about how posthumanism works in a wider cultural sphere. He
sees that these political and cultural trajectories also have philosophical
influences, which he locates in the literature of SF's precursors like
that of Mary Shelley and later through the work of Aldous Huxley, on
to actual philosophy of technology via Heidegger and his interpreters.
Another helpful schema breaks posthumanism into *dystopic, liberal, radical,*
or *methodological* categories (Sharon 2012). Dystopic is a term for biocon-
servatism, or the insistence that technology used to enhance human beings
is potentially dangerous. Liberal, on the other hand, would use technology
in a democratic way to enhance human beings. Radical is similar to
critical posthumanism in its challenge to such notions. And methodological attempts a formalistic description of posthumanism, especially in
how human and nonhuman elements work in complex networks. Moving
toward more specific configurations within the discourses reveals elements
of weight, but also their idiosyncrasies. Commonalities exist among the
differing approaches, but, like humanism itself, managing such a slippery
concept proves difficult. Some of the more interesting approaches prove to
be the most creative. Haraway is a key figure. Her notion of the cyborg as
a trope of resisting ingrained Western categories has outlived its ability to
shock, while the project even if abandoned by Haraway continues within
critical posthumanism as a consistent attack on Cartesian dualism (see
Grebowicz, Merrick, and Haraway 2013). Hayles's investigation into how
information lost its body at the crossroads of philosophy and cybernetics
offers an approach that continues to inspire. For Hayles, posthumanism must
be embodied, rather than the nightmare scenarios of disembodied living
argued for by certain technologists in favor of SF-styled mind-uploading
scenarios (see Hayles 1999). David Roden's *speculative* posthumanism sees
itself outside the standard schema of critical vs. popular because "it is not
a normative claim about how the world ought to be but a metaphysical
claim about what it could be" (2014, 9). His concept helps, he claims,
because of philosophical failures on both the critical and popular sides in
admitting ontological possibilities outside of ethical formulations. Roden,
in particular, makes these moves, not to avoid ethical responsibility, but to
allow for positive posthuman possibilities. Stefan Herbrechter has provided
much material in clarifying the concept of posthumanism and posthumanization. In particular, Herbrechter's critical analysis works through most of
the key elements, while arguing for a revitalized critical posthumanism,
via deconstruction, by focusing on the process of posthumanization. This
focus reveals a series of crises with many phases over the nature of the
human hastened by technology (Herbrechter 2013, 76). For Herbrechter,
this process of posthumanization perennially foregrounds the inhuman and
how humanism has always contained elements of its own demise.

latter describes how technology can be used to enhance human beings. Critical posthumanism takes much of its inspiration from critical theory, while popular posthumanism grows from SF and its proponents' dreams of making fiction into reality.

Of core importance to many thinkers in the discourses are bodies inscribed by technology. Rosi Braidotti offers one of the more nuanced interpretations based on readings from heavy-weight philosophers such as Deleuze and Derrida. She sees posthumanism emerging after the many 'posts' within critical theory to offer a type of monistic explosion of subjectivities contrary to normative dualities in Western thought. With both the evolutionary model of organistic growth that Deleuze championed, as well as the discursive model of Derridean *différance*, Braidotti suggests that posthuman subjectivities are relevant in demanding new humanities to reflect them. She does this to map new references for human beings in our current moment, as a feminist and posthumanist philosopher.[63]

A constant concern of much critical posthumanism is the notion of normative humanity and, in many cases, how discourse inscribes this normalness on bodies. This concern is not unique to posthumanism; nearly all of Foucault's work takes this subject for his complex canvas, as does the work of many feminist theorists interested in the combination of discourses and bodies.[64] But posthumanism, as Foucault said about the coming century being Deleuzian, looks to how technology creates new, unexpected subjectivities through the technical and discursive manipulation of bodies (both oppressive and empowering).[65]

In theorizing the modern fantastic, *Dread Trident* follows Hayles's insight that we are already 'posthuman' as we interact with digital worlds behind screens. But we might also consider that we were never human in the Enlightenment sense (much less posthuman), as Latour has said about our modernity, that each articulation of the human is part of a constructed discourse etched at a certain time, an earlier Foucauldian insight that explains not just the recent appearance and disappearance of the modern human, but the mechanism of our continued articulations.[66] For example, persons today must contend with modern networked technology, and do so with embodied modes of experience. Selves multiply. Identity over-saturation (or confusion) often follows. The calls

---

[63] See Braidotti 2013a.
[64] To take one recent example from feminist critical theory of how discourse 'writes' bodies, within the context of SF, see Vint 2007.
[65] See Buchanan 1999.
[66] See Latour 1993.

for an informed, ethical posthumanism are expected continuations of projects in the refinement of drawing the human.[67]

Dread Trident's aim in theorizing the modern fantastic as driven by a posthumanization of realized space (rather than bodies) is not to challenge critical posthumanism, just to frame their articulations as intellectualized forms of the *posthuman modern fantastic*. These theorizings of critical posthumanism are as much a part of the technologized modern fantastic as are imagined aliens, the dream of spacecraft, and the seduction of intelligent robots. Posthumanization proves to be the process of creating realized worlds and selves, not just a drastic reorientation of borderless subject formation or even freeing the political body of its humanist constraints.

Intervening in the discourse of posthumanism ultimately widens the focus from individual subjects and bodies to the spaces constructed for them, their realized worlds. Yes, the subject is the shifting self framed through discourse, a steadfast definition that reminds us that subjectivity exists in a world of ideas that must emerge in some material manner from a spoken or written word to an image or set of complex cultural codes, and objects, many of which have degrees of agency. And, yes, we must recognize the importance of continued work in interrogating the political drawing of bodies inscribed by discourse. Both concepts remain critical.

However, challenging the tradition of the liberal humanist subject, or providing another description of transgressing a coherent stable self, or demonstrating how power structures and discourses dominate and manage us, be they disciplinary or hyperreal, or even imagining what a post-biological or post-anthropocene humanity would look like—all valuable and rich fields of inquiry—blur once we understand that technologies have always framed discourses of the human, that we use these to embed ourselves in the world, and that our uses of these technologies have always changed ourselves and the world around us. In this sense, even language is a technological tool.[68] Yet, a curious

---

[67] Such an approach argues against the most radical forms of posthumanism in this redrawing—for example, those that rely on the extreme univocalism of Deleuzian rhizomatic imaginings, utopian configurations that decenter every aspect of the human.

[68] From a modern, gameist perspective, *language*, we might consider, could be seen as the first technological attempt at such systematized yet imagined play, rather than simply communication. Wittgenstein's language games speak to this inherent quality that defies the logical positivism of some philosophy. See Wittgenstein 1968. Poststructuralism celebrates this ludic quality, articulated in Derrida's seminal essay, "Structure, Sign, and Play," in

configuration appears as we mix analog/digital forms. The result? We now have the ability to turn imaginary worlds into realized worlds for extended periods of time, fantasy worlds that challenge the mundane world for our attention due to their sophistication and verisimilitude.[69]

Hayles's argument on materiality and embodiment inspires *Dread Trident* to rethink negative aspects of posthumanization. She imagines the terror and pleasure of becoming posthuman. And she notes that

which he writes of a structure's inherent tendency to allow for infinite play. Derrida inaugurates poststructural critical theory's critique of formalism with this essay's argument that play is inherent in any structuring of thought, or a text. His use of gameist language is telling:

> The concept of centered structure is in fact the concept of a play based on a fundamental ground, a play constituted on the basis of a fundamental immobility and a reassuring certitude, which itself is beyond the reach of play. And on the basis of this certitude anxiety can be mastered, for anxiety is invariably the result of a certain mode of being implicated in the game, of being caught by the game, of being as it were at stake in the game from the outset. (Derrida and Bass 2001, 352)

And postmodernism foregrounds language that slides atop the surfaces of things, an endless cascade of play, an understanding that commodifies nostalgia into mass-produced products that redefine the past. See Umberto Eco's seminal ideas in The Return of the Middle Ages section of Eco 1990. These become mechanisms of new subject formations, rather than mechanisms of subject erasure; they become positive agents for the construction of realized fantasy.

[69] Jean Baudrillard, as well, is concerned with space. In fact, his entire project of defining hyperreality as movement precession between the orders of simulation, simulacra, and the real deserves comment. The 'real' for Baudrillard is disappearing. What precedes the real are simulacra, copies of the real, that should come after it. And we are dominated by the process of simulation that creates the simulacra, the real only emerging as vestiges. This immense pessimism speaks to the continued need to understand how the modern fantastic is changing our perceptions of ourselves and the world around us, especially in the naive acceptance of the real vs. unreal or imaginary as an accepted binary. Baudrillard's conception of simulacra as a dominating mode of understanding the world is fantastic, in that it is hyperreal, or something other than defined by standard, naive realism and its supposedly stable representations. The classic example Baudrillard gives focuses on the U.S.A., a favorite target. He claims that Disneyland is neither imaginary nor real. It is hyperreal. He wants us to resist thinking of it simply as a fantasy land. Instead, we are to think of it as real, so that the world around it is revealed to be fantastic. He believes Disneyland is needed as a tool of reason to shore up its own falsity, that by presenting Disneyland as a mere fantasy, the world around it will seem to be made real (see Baudrillard 1995). Also, see Umberto Eco's views on Disneyland in Eco 1990.

we can conceptualize the posthuman along intellectual or literal lines, excoriating a literalist posture that encourages a disembodied machinic fate for humanity. She sees the posthuman flexible enough to contain other meanings that, for her, are embodied.[70] Like many critical theorists of the posthuman, Hayles's hope is mistranslated by some thinkers into a radical understanding of the posthuman, a type of intellectual fantasy itself rooted in critical theory: the escape from dualism, the core of Western thought, especially since Descartes began his rational process of framing the human along his narrow path.

The process of posthumanization steps center stage within the cultural logic of the modern fantastic. Even in our rush toward digital life, positive forms of the human are emerging that are inclusive yet retain necessary borders, are flexible yet mostly stable, and are imbued with strong senses of social justice without jettisoning recognizable metrics of behavior. Sidelining pure, discursive subjectivity forces us to refocus instead on these spaces in which selves emerge. This complex process of posthumanization, in which we are entangling ourselves with digital spaces and selves, condenses highly imaginative and visible forms (i.e., the fantastic imaginary worlds in which so many humanist tendencies reform) into realized space.

While critical posthumanism's primary aim has been to continue the philosophical critique of the Enlightenment project's liberal, humanist subject, the posthuman is also a literary trope with a represented fictive historiography in SF, if not a fully theorized one. In today's world, the post(modern)human is still located within Jameson's cultural logic of late capitalism, yet often emerges haunted by a nostalgia for a rational subject that was never stable but has accelerated toward radical transformation. The distribution of the self across networks and assemblages is already a fact of the mundane world, as is the invasion of the machine (or the artificial) that now crosses critical boundaries between the human and its environment.

In many ways we already have such incipient posthumans, their identities distributed across a wide range of networks, their bodies beginning to be changed by wearable and implantable technology, their selves ever shifting. We are, involuntarily, on this road. Untangling the varied articulations is difficult because critical posthumanism rubs shoulders with the popular form in its focus on technology. Transhumanism, a type of hyper-humanism, would entrench the normative identities detailed during the Enlightenment, and would do so to such a degree these persons would be advanced over unenhanced

[70] See Hayles 1999.

humans. In its discourse, it posits posthumans as the ultimate endpoint
of such enhancement. We see this most clearly in SF and in real-world
policy-making, bio-ethics discussion, and engineering circles. Of primary
concern for many is the fate of our planet as a sustainable place for life,
as well as the fate of ours and other species.

Critical posthumanism associates the failures of humanism with more
than Cartesian constraints on how discourse inscribes bodies; it sees
material misuses of our planet's environment as an extension of the
philosophical shortcomings derived from the continued influence of the
Enlightenment project. With a focus on the material world it extends its
reach beyond discursive subjectivity. Braidotti clarifies such a charged
position: "Posthumanism theory is a generative tool to help us rethink
the basic unit of reference for the human in this bio-genetic age known
as the 'anthropocene,' the historical moment with the Human has become
a geological force capable of affecting all life on this planet" (2013a,
5). For Braidotti and other critical theorists like Cary Wolfe and Claire
Colebrook, *anthropos* is the primary target because of its negative effects
on the environment and non-human living creatures. Braidotti urges that
even for progressive individuals sensitive to how humanity poses threats
to its ecologies, interaction between humans and non-humans still tends
to create humanized spaces. Our humanism is entrenched, she would
argue, to the disadvantage of the planet and its non-human creatures.

A new materialist philosophy has emerged in the work of thinkers
such as Karen Barad, Braidotti, DeLanda, and others that offers a
reworking of metaphysics away from standard notions of discourse and
subjectivity located within humanized spaces.[71] Alongside this focus
on materialism, a curious discourse has emerged under the rubric of a
speculative realism representative of how fruitful a 'speculative' turn can
be within philosophy.[72] Quentin Meillassoux, Ray Brassier, Graham
Harman, and Iain Hamilton Grant are associated with working through
these core ideas. Without parsing the different positions of its primary
thinkers, whom Ian Bogost calls the "four horsemen of anticorrela-
tionism" (2012, 5) we should note that such speculation has been
used before within fantastic fiction that tried to broaden vistas beyond
standard tropes within modern SF.[73]

---

[71] See Braidotti 2013b; Barad 2007; DeLanda 2015, as well as Coole and Frost
2010 for a representative anthology of professional articles, and Dolphijn
and Tuin 2012 for interviews with important thinkers.
[72] See Bryant, Srnicek, and Harman 2011; Shaviro 2014 for good introductions
to speculative realism.
[73] See Damien Broderick's approach in 2000, which exemplifies a comment
within SF theory.

Speculative realism tries to solve specific problems in philosophy, rather than fiction, one of which concerns the nature of reality, others with representation, others with Kant's continued influence. Of note here is one of speculative realism's most important thinkers, Meillassoux, who clarifies a key tenet of its thinking with the concept of correlationism, the idea that we come to know the world (and the things in it) as a correlation between ourselves (a human-oriented subjectivity) and outside objects.[74] Because of this inherent correlationism within Western thought, we are linked to the objects of this world through our perceptions of them; and, because of this bond, they exist in so far as we can perceive or understand them.

The calling for these thinkers is the removal of human-centered subjectivity as the driving locus of knowledge within humanized spaces.[75] At its heart appears to be the sort of self-actuated extinction that posthumanism scholars like Claire Colebrook see attached to a move beyond human subjectivity. Of course, a critique of correlationism doesn't mean the human is eradicated. We are objects in this world of many things. Yet, converging threads of thought within a broad coverage of modernity that has reworked humanism continues a process of reducing human exceptionalism, one that leads to the foregrounding of the material human as but one of many objects. Subjectivity, beleaguered as it may be, must accept this displacement and, as a palliative measure, we can accept an ironic enchantment of living, breathing, and playing in embodied fantasy spaces for its continued articulation.[76]

Posthuman discursive-and-material practices, Braidotti's ideas about rethinking humanized space with respect for *zoe* (life force) and *bios* (biological life), the rethinking of Deleuze's assemblages as examples of posthuman subjectivity so that 'becoming machine' is more than cyborg existence, as well as Haraway's and Wolfe's idea of Deleuzian 'becoming animal' or of Braidotti's 'becoming earth,' have all moved the conversation beyond the exhaustion of earlier tropes and into its most frightening form of posthumanism, i.e., erasure discourse. Extinction is being theorized, both as a phenomenological

---

[74] See Meillassoux 2010.

[75] See Bryant 2011.

[76] In its most extreme form of thought, a post-anthropocene-posthumanism would see an extinction for the human as a subject and object, as the result of human action upon its environment, as accidentally self-inflicted through technological change, or as intentional, the last often encouraged by critics of humanism in the hopes that the posthumanism of a post Anthropocene Age would be other than humanistic.

and material aspect of subjectivity, but also as a literal event, or series of events.[77]

But a pre-critical version of posthumanized thinking can also be found within SF that transforms these nuanced philosophical postures into a literary metaphor: ultimate erasure. Such extinction threats are common elements in much SF, from the alien invasion made famous by Wells in *War of the Worlds* (1897) to more recent near annihilations by Cylons hunting humans in *Battlestar Galactica* (2004–09). We also see the erasure of the human in cyberpunk/biopunk variations, such as vengeful replicants and their executioners on the loose in *Blade Runner* (1982) to zombie plagues in a host of films, TV series, video games. An analogue of human erasure also finds complex representation when we look at the cosmic horror of a writer like H.P. Lovecraft. In literalizing the process of posthuman extinction with tropes from SF, he posits a post-anthro-pocene universe prior to the discourses of trans-and-posthumanism. His response is horror.

When a critical posthumanist such as Colebrook asks, "How might we imagine a world without organic perception, without centered points of view of sensing and world-oriented beings?" (2014a, 23),

[77] Colebrook explores the nuances of extinction in a two-volume set (Colebrook 2014a; 2014b) while Transhumanists such as Nick Bostrom consider the potential for actual extinction of the human species in Bostrom 2009. Organizations have been formed to avoid potential threats to life on this planet, such as the Lifeboat Foundation, who approach technological change with hope and concern. Both critics and enthusiasts for technological trans-and-posthumanism have infused the discourses with a degree of immediacy beyond academic conversations about discourse and subjectivity. While many thinkers like Colebrook note the long conversation of the modern subject's erasure and see in modernity's lavish encouragement of spectacle and surface a point of critique, she is exemplary because she rethinks ecological space (i.e., the environment or climate or planetary milieu) to note that a consideration of the environment as a circumscribing space is part of the anthropocentric problem that both feminism and posthu-manism challenges. Such delimiting of space complicates simple notions of progressive environmentalism to suggest that we should approach the natural world with more understanding of its ontological validity outside of ourselves, and less selfishly both as a space for resources and as a space of objects. Colebrook's nuanced critical theory of extinction ultimately asks us to "consider all the ways in which 'we' are now reacting with horror to our own capacity not to be ourselves" (2014a, 19). Such a drive for discursive self-extinction finds roots in the posthumanistic critique of Cartesian dualism and its requisite enshrining of 'man' as a foundational concept for Western thinking—one that we realize is either disappearing or being rewritten, and will continue to be so.

she recognizes that these questions about peeking beyond the veil of our own extinction-as-erasure have a long, unsuccessful historiography, and that with the supposed exhaustion of theory, a return to the materiality of things sparks interest along several academic lines into this ultimate mystery. What emerges is the idea that discourse, the subject, reading, writing, texts, language, thought, etc., are still being theorized but done so within embodied space that values the material and seeks, ultimately, for survival. *Dread Trident*'s use of the modern fantastic attempts no such answer. It asks only for relief from the mundane.

Embodiment and Materiality

Posthumanized embodiment in the context of *Dread Trident* derives from groundbreaking work pioneered by thinkers such as Francisco Varela, George Lakoff and Mark Johnson, Andy Clark, and numerous others who have reworked the computational theory of mind for one that views the material mind inherently defined by bodies and environments.[78] Yet, for decades, philosophical embodiment and materiality have been situated within the purview of cultural philosophers, such as the phenomenology of Maurice Merleau-Ponty or the genealogical work of Foucault locating the body as the central domain of disciplinary power.[79]

A consistent problem emerges that our examination of technology and its social effects on material persons are often reduced to discourse; thus, the confusion over terms such as actual, virtual, real, etc., not to mention posthuman, posthumanism, posthumanization, posthumanity, the modern, etc.[80] We use language to understand ourselves

[78] Embodiment as a concept within the science-of-mind popularized by Andy Clark in monographs such as *Supersizing the Mind* (2010) and *Natural Born Cyborgs* (2003) means that the body 'extends' mind into the world; thus, the tools we use become part of this embodiment process. See also See Lakoff and Johnson 1999; Varela, Thompson, and Rosch 1992.

[79] See Merleau-Ponty and Smith 2002 and any of Foucault's major works. See the introduction to *Discipline and Punish* (1977) and its detailed and horrific description of the execution of an attempted regicide.

[80] In posthumanism, following initial work by Haraway, Hayles fired a shot over the bow of techno-fantasists when she critiqued how "information lost its body" (1999, 2) to challenge the idea that selves can exist in disembodied form. For Hayles, and others, embodiment is necessary for any hopeful construction of the human, especially those mediated by technology (Hayles 1999, 288).

and the world around us, as well as use mathematical symbols and other inscription devices to flatten the material world. Deleuze in particular was interested in the realm of experience before linguistic formations, a realist's instinct that his philosophy of problem creation attempted to redress. Yet, he did so primarily through the writing of monographs.[81] This aspect of discursive practice acts as requirement for *Dread Trident*'s analysis of analog gametexts, tools, and the entire assemblage of material elements, from things to persons.

What we see with the resurgence of TRPGs in the face of digital video game dominance is that the material matters, that embodiment matters. Who you have at the table matters. What has always been a detriment for TRPGs, i.e., trying to find living people with whom to consistently play, is solved with communication tools via the Internet: virtual tabletop software and chat environments, social networking communities, online forums, etc. These new spaces allow for embodied humans and intelligent machines to engage in an activity that is often overlooked with the rise of video game culture. Digital realized worlds, by far, dominate in popularity, from *World of Warcraft*'s (2004–present) earlier successes to current console-based video games such as *Eve Online* (2003–present). Yet, the analog world provides curious examples that better illustrate the broader posthumanizing process. The actual books, manuals, the gametexts, are important not just as texts but

---

[81] Others have noted this conundrum, such as Hayles's comments in the foreword to Mark Hansen's *Embodying Technesis: Technology Beyond Writing* (2000), or when he argues that technology exists prior to our attempts to represent what he calls the "materiality of technology" (2000, 4). His term "technesis, or the putting-into-discourse of technology" (2000, 4) limits technology to its explanation through thought and its discursive expressions. He sees problems in discursive half-steps toward a material world replete with Nietzschean and Deleuzian forces that exist before the collapsing of the world through discussion or analysis. Writing in the context of Lyotard's examination of technology, Hansen argues that to retain the human in the coming posthuman age requires critics to grapple with the possible displacements humans encounter in the face of the complexification of matter and technology (2000, 63). He urges us to develop "more concrete, locally attuned deployments" (2000, 263) of technologies within an accepted mimetic frame to make living in our posthuman moment more acceptable. Hansen's call to engage the material world demonstrates the sort of understanding of discursiveness's limitations, and the power of embodied materiality. His physical monograph functions as a concrete example of this process, a material and embodied written object critical for human beings seeking understanding, yet a discursive one.

discursive-material artifacts that provide tools for embodied play. And, thus, the analog mechanisms that gave us a variety of humanisms reassert themselves during this rise of the digital.[82]

One may protest that what is most at stake is how these games provide more than simulated agency—that they provide actual templates for agency in ways never expected. When medical science creates a somatic change such as scale-like texture to skin, or reshaped ears with pointy tips, it will be upsetting to bioconservatives who wish to retain normative standards. But before this imagined future happens, we can mine our textual and material constructions for clues to how these formations will function. We know from empirical evidence that our screened and written texts provide content for the imagination beyond sticking noses in books or sitting in theaters. Literature and film shape conceptions of the self and encourage their active construction. New, highly sophisticated forms that are played demand participation beyond reading and watching and do more than reorient (or reinforce) norms beyond those given by our humanist tradition. They form new cultures of identities with their own discursive properties.

The material as a site of embodiment is crucial even as digital screens proliferate, with many posthumanism thinkers like Haraway, Hayles, Wolf, Braidotti examining "better bodies-subjects" (Vint 2007, 182). These body-focused approaches argue that ignoring the body by those with a strong focus on the universal disembodied self leads to ethical problems or, worse. Just as problematic, though, material technological change that is embodied and body focused may exacerbate problems most critical-and-cultural posthumanism theorists hope to overcome. For example, cosplay (costume play) attempts with costumes, props, and make-up to imitate the heroes and villains of popular-culture novels, comic books, films, games, etc., even though these costumes often exaggerate stereotypical identities, sometimes sexist, racist, and warlike. Also, many LARPing communities engage in interpersonal and physical conflict scenarios that move away from notions of peace and inclusiveness toward ones that reflect, in non-dangerous situations, imagined forms of violence and domination.[83]

The question over embodied identity, like that of how to frame trans- and-posthumanism, is whether the discourses are fully articulated by

---

[82] 'Codes,' as Hayles calls them, are the pathways of signification and meaning in embodied space; see 2002. And discursive/digital codes need some sort of analog substrate to become embodied.

[83] For examples of well-documented, popular LARPs, see Stenros and Montola 2010.

critical theorists, philosophers of technology, bioethicists, policy makers, or even game theorists, etc. Any attempt, though, should describe the process in its most widespread form through its popular-cultural artifacts. At stake is deciding if embodiment should be encouraged to extend beyond the normative but limiting duality of liberal humanism to new embodied identities constructed through technologized change, many of which may be championed from non-critical positions in the popular sphere.

Physical experience is the giant leap that the digital world, and the posthumanization it facilitates, attempts to simulate or to enact, and to which analog forms return to add their somatic flavor. Realized worlds are emerging in more embodied forms, with TRPGs as a unique example of how a literary game mode (i.e., written) functions as a tool for both game simulation and narrative creation. Where Saler sees virtual worlds providing ironic re-enchantment, and Hayles sees embodiment as a way to enrich posthumanized lives, *Dread Trident* argues that analog gametexts prove to be critical tools that reflect a positive posthumanism resisting both nightmare forms and hyper-embodied forms.

Most radically, daydreams, the imagination, constructed fantasy games, etc., the alleged stuff of childhood, are the positive result of technology and humanity's embrace of posthumanization. These imaginative fancies prepare us for our posthuman future by prototyping through play the giving of agency to persons in a mundane world. And such an imaginative process reminds us that the real world, in many ways, is unreal. Such an awareness reorients us through popular culture's often overlooked ludic artifacts, such as complex gametexts. This process relies on digital high-tech. Yet, it begins with mundane, analog tech. The true posthuman emerges not as a cyborg, or biologically enhanced human, but as an analog/digital replacement within a realized world defined by its thrust away from the mundane and into the magical.

Gameplay

To understand the modern fantastic's gameist mode, we must understand its key mechanism: *gameplay*. The concepts of 'game' and 'play' function together because realized worlds aren't simply ones in which people play games, although in TRPGs play is a primary activity, yet not always required. Much time is spent within fantastic realized worlds, outside of time playing at a table. Consuming gametexts and utilizing their tools, when not occurring during table-time, is similar to the activity of reading, studying, creating, building, engineering, etc.[84]

Gameplay often comprises a mixture of forms, rarely in any stable configuration. Some game theorists today retain humanist notions of play by accepting that play occurs in social contexts.[85] They do admit, though, that the old divide of socially constructed vs. technologically

[84] Understanding the nature of play is beyond the scope of this project, as is understanding humanism, or technology, or modernity. Brian Sutton-Smith even begins his helpful *Ambiguities of Play* (2011) with, "In forty years of pursuing the meaning of play, it has become apparent to me that an understanding of play's ambiguity requires the help of multiple disciplines" (2001, vii). The theorizing of play finds a solid foundation with Johan Huizinga's powerful notion of play and can be found in an often-quoted part of *Homo Ludens*:

> Summing up the formal characteristics of play we might call it a free activity standing quite consciously outside "ordinary" life as being "not serious", but at the same time absorbing the player intensely and utterly. It is an activity connected with no material interest, and no profit can be gained by it. It proceeds within its own proper boundaries of time and space according to fixed rules and in an orderly manner. It promotes the formation of social groupings which tend to surround themselves with secrecy and to stress their difference from the common world by disguise or other means. (Huizinga 1949, 13)

One may pick and choose what parts of this statement are agreeable or disagreeable. I find the notion of fixed rules overly demanding, while the focus on boundaries works well with my use of realized space. Huizinga clarified this special place as a 'magic circle' that allows a new reality to be created based upon agreed rules of play.

[85] Most investigations into the concept of play must contend with Huizinga's notions in *Homo Ludens* (1949) that play is an analogue for how civilizations build themselves and how we become human by shaping a type of sacralized space in which to play. For Huizinga, "Play is older than culture, for culture, however inadequately defined, always presupposes human society, and animals have not waited for man to teach them their playing" (1949, 1). Such a suggestion at the time challenged long-held puritanical Christian notions that play is childish and frivolous. Even more so, for Huizinga, positive forms of contested play within language itself allow members of society to create identities and form social values. "The great archetypal activities of human society are all permeated with play from the start" (1949, 4). Sutton-Smith echoes this sentiment when he writes, "From contest power comes the development of the social hierarchies identity around which the society constructs its values" (2001, 78). For Huizinga, modern forms of play are often suspect because they fail to enrich society's civilization-building impulse. Such idealizing, as Sutton-Smith argues, is one major fault critics have with Huizinga, in its trivialization of many modern forms non-agonistic in nature.

determined persons is complicated by cybernetics and the resulting concept of the posthuman (Dovey 2006, 5). The posthuman, according to this reading, undermines humanist concepts that divide the human from technology, yet in this new configuration, agency emerges in gameplay. Yes, the digital realm of video games provides mileage in working through these new ways of understanding current personhood, but ignoring analog gametexts and tools disservices both their historical literary relevance and current importance in shaping posthuman agency.

These important concepts related to play, and the games that emerge from them demonstrate that the focus has moved from play as an idealized, structured behavior to games as a vibrant field of study. Debates over narrativist vs. ludic approaches demonstrate that internecine fighting can often be productive.[86] And continued scholarly work in game design demonstrates that the mechanics of gameplay are often just as vital in understanding experience as are narrative-based elements, like a game setting.[87] Game patterns emerge as important elements that designers utilize for specific reasons. For this reason, *Dread Trident* deploys *gametexts*, but also *gametools*, all of which affect *gameplay*. And the differences can be seen in the TRPGs detailed in this book, each one structured with certain mechanics that allow major differences in play.

To understand *Dread Trident*'s use of fantasy realized-worlds gametexts and tools, the best place to look are at its most detailed and complex game settings. For example, D&D's multiverse encompasses all of the combined worlds used with the game over its four-decade history. It is exemplary because of the amount of material developed and its ongoing status as a dominant game in the industry. The many campaign settings of its multiverse also work well as an example of a massive, shared, imaginary realized world because of the combination of analog/digital elements that help a player engage this archive. To understand the process of engaging such an archive, one must play the game for the experience rather than simply study the materials as discursive objects. One can begin playing with very little understanding of 'lore,' or the combined history (and redacted histories) of the settings. However, if one wishes to understand, say, the Forgotten Realms (one setting in the broader multiverse) in its entirety, one is faced with a daunting challenge comprised of many official gametexts, and countless unofficial

---

[86] See Harrigan and Wardrip-Fruin 2010.
[87] This leads some theorists to demand more from a term like gameplay and, instead, think about "game design patterns" (Bjork and Holopainen 2004, 4).

ones. Focusing on officially published material requires an ecumenical scope that encompasses game manuals, adventures, novels, comic books, films, online discussions, etc. That, and plenty of time.

Most importantly, TRPGs are both discursive and material objects. They are part of the modern fantastic because their systems are rational, organized, and embodied, and merge the digital/analog divide that characterizes the posthumanization process driving the posthuman. TRPGs typically begin on the printed page (or at least typeset page), are published in analog and digital forms, and in book form become studied objects in personal libraries for individuals who may never find a table to join. These hopeful gamemasters and players create new content, often posted to the Internet for free, exponentially expanding the megatext of imaginative TRPGs. Such new forms of gameplay are critical in understanding the increased emergence of fantasy in popular culture, as well as in understanding most TRPGs' fanaticism.

The most crucial step *Dread Trident* makes is to read the gametexts of these imaginary worlds as key texts in defining the modern fantastic. This gameist mode of contemporary culture, already on pace to supersede in popularity the cinematic and the literary, has roots in this book's particular case studies: i.e., the high/epic fantasy 'multiverse' of Wizards of the Coast's Dungeons and Dragons (D&D), the urban-Gothic World(s) of Darkness, the gametexts of H.P. Lovecraft's 'Cthulhu' Mythos, Games Workshop's 'grimdark' Warhammer 40,000 (40k) setting, and the far-future science fantasy of Numenera. It also provides a detailed reading and description of gameplay of the trans-and-posthumanist, hard-SF game: Eclipse Phase.

The analog gametexts of these imaginary universes are written manuals that give players the abilities to escape into realized worlds, and to affect them. The embodied materiality of the tabletop experience is critical. Physical gametexts must be read, outlined, annotated, as well as understood at an imaginative level. Gametools are critical as well.[88] The pen, paper, and dice combination, along with all of the rules and tables in the books, the maps, etc., function as material agents that augment the texts. Beyond the iconic dice, figurines on a battlemat are exemplary in providing analogues for this process, physical objects that abstract what they represent. Even more so, the use of online tools and

---

[88] These are similar but different to paratexts. See Gray 2010. With the extended worlds of TRPGS, each 'gametext,' rather than paratext, forms a part of a larger whole. Rulebooks, campaign settings, adventures, novels, comics, errata, etc., have different functions, yet all work together to facilitate gameplay.

virtual tabletops (e.g., *Roll20.net*, Fantasy Grounds, and a host of others) further embed players into the posthuman realm where intelligent machines work in their favor. In fact, the latest version of D&D—the 5th edition—has been noted for its rulebooks as hacking tools, as well as for their difficulty of use because they require a dungeon master (DM)[89] to jump back and forth between texts (a problem complexified by the supplement of third-party resources), one now assisted with online tools like *D&DBeyond.com*.[90]

Rich cultural products like TRPGs allow fans to expand story worlds for their own play. Buying a core rule gametext, tweaking it, adding material online, creating 'homebrew' rules, collaborating with others at the table, utilizing OCR–PDF versions, joining a virtual tabletop, adding a character-management app to your phone, and so forth, all correspond with the type of cultural transformation now informing an embodied material techno-game-culture. What makes the TRPG unique in this process is its mix of discursive and material components. These gametexts are important as guides for imagined realized worlds and characters—written records in both analog and digital forms. These material objects function as embodied entities enmeshed in dynamic human/nonhuman relationships.[91] TRPGs step beyond a reader's consumption, or even engagement via fan fiction, letters, etc., beyond the construction of virtual spaces. Instead, these realized worlds form a microcosm of the broader social-technical world emerging today.

These material tools provide us with new discursive postures (and, possibly, in the future, actual new material identities), as well as their containing spaces. Traditional literary tools like written texts act as fundamental elements in this process.[92] By default, a traditional game

---

[89] This is D&D's term for the game master, or individual who manages the content and narrative, as well as adjudicates rules. The Dungeon Master is a type of game and narrative organizer and controller. He or she 'runs' the game, while the players manage their characters.

[90] See https://www.dndbeyond.com/.

[91] For a detailed 'experiment' of how game materials function as actors, see Bienia 2016, 135. Bienia attempts to give game materials a voice, thereby adding a humanizing element to his deployment of Actor-Network theory, similar to what Latour did with his quasi 'novel,' *Aramis or the Love of Technolgy* (1996).

[92] D&D provides one of the most detailed and sophisticated systematizations of this process, with decades of material to mine: a prime example of the modern fantastic in the mythic mode. Also, the TRPG, the Call of Cthulhu, solidifies a Lovecraftian Cthulhu Mythos in game form, providing one of the most succinct and consistent ways of viewing this complex realized world in the modern fantastic's scientific/rationalistic mode.

like D&D cannot happen without the material analog elements. With no persons, there is no game. No table, pens, paper, dice: you simply have storytelling, as some TRPGs demonstrate. The use of the Internet and its digital tools have been marshaled to enhance an embodied experience. Virtual tabletops allow people to video chat and play a game as if sitting around a table. Within the context of the example above, discursive elements found in game manuals blend with embodied elements (such as pen, paper, dice, living people, etc.), ceding to quasi-embodied forms such as increased virtual verisimilitude via computers to more hyper-embodied forms such as LARPing.

Dread Trident asks what do TRPG gametexts and tools reveal in their clarification of the modern fantastic? They offer a rationalization-and-classificatory system of textual mechanisms in an analog substrate (pages in books, but also in a variety of non-textual tools) that prefigure the more sophisticated forms in digital video game environments. We see rudimentary technological tools that, when expanded with sophisticated technology, encourage the current interaction of biological humans and machines that so characterizes today's dynamic. We have 'paper' and 'pencil' for the writing of game details, twin pillars of human achievement that, coupled with language and mathematics, have given us a plenitude of wondrous artifacts. We also have dice to insert a touch of randomness. We have tables of information, 'stat' blocks, images, equation-like mechanisms. And we have bodies at a table both simulating and narrating a game story with physical voices and limited somatic movement.

Coupled with these embodied analog elements, we also have a digital array of Internet tools: online forums to discuss rule adjudication, virtual tabletops to allow games to be played at a distance, websites with resources for players and game masters, etc. Such game system elements function discursively in detailed written procedures and guidelines that organize the experience, forming a prototype for the information-rich environment of later digital games. The tables, the mechanics, the rules function like coded algorithms that work behind the scenes to run our highly technologized world. Except these elements from gametexts are hackable by anyone who can read, write, and imagine.

A perspective that theorizes the modern fantastic from the bottom-up allows for an examination of analog gametexts as foundational mechanisms, with literary histories, for the fashioning of realized worlds and selves through the use of analog/digital game mechanics. This fashioning is a rationalized-imaginative process rooted in our current posthumanized moment in which we navigate complex analog/digital terrain. While *Dread Trident* accepts ideas of personhood that are constructed through textual and material discourse, it moves out of these theorized frames into frames of sophisticated science, technology, and engineering where we shuffle between the imaginary and mundane.

Enchantment as Magification

Along with Michael Saler's *As If* (2012), Jane Bennett's *The Enchantment of Modern Life* (2001) takes modern enchantment as its topic. She argues against the idea that contemporary modern culture is disenchanted.[93] For her, technology creates wonders, nanotechnology, but one with a promise to encourage Deleuzian crossings of matter at the molecular level. Such enchanting technologies are the playful wonders that SF first championed as its themes in the years between Gernsback's first articulation of scientifiction and Campbell's solidification of SF into a well-defined genre. Bennett, though, demands a metaphysics of actual enchantment, which differs from my approach, because she rejects a distancing irony.[94] She demands this actuality so that it can lead to a Tolkien-like consolatory joy, and a subsequent ethics. Regardless of

[93] In Bennet's "quasi-pagan model of enchantment" (2001, 12) she channels Epicurus and Lucretius, Deleuze, Latour, a touch of Nietzsche, as well as Ilya Prigogine and Isabelle Stengers, to challenge the story of a modernity bereft of meaning, or one in which a purposeful universe must be predicated by the divine. Instead, she sees in the plethora of contemporary artifacts a "world that retains the power to enchant" (2001, 4). Of note for my study is her admission that certain strategies amplify this power, one of them being play. Bennett recognizes contemporary culture to be full of "the marvelous specificity of things" (2001, 12), a notion derived from Latour's philosophy of agential objects, as well as a positive view of object-oriented ontology. Likewise, Saler's thesis is predicated on the idea that the prevalence of imaginary, secondary worlds is best understood within the discourse of a disenchanted West, one he argues against. For Saler, "modernity is Janus faced" in that "modern enchantment often depends upon its opposite, modern disenchantment. A specifically modern enchantment can be defined as one that enchants and disenchants simultaneously: a disenchanted enchantment" (2012, 12). This double consciousness, this ironic imagination, then, is critical in the creation of imaginary worlds which, sometimes, blossom into realized worlds. It is also critical in any understanding of the processes that combine fantasy, SF, and posthumanization.

[94] Quite the opposite of my approach. She writes, "To be enchanted is to be struck and shaken by the extraordinary that lives amid the familiar and the everyday" (Bennett 2001, 12).

her insistence for such a metaphysics, her analysis of disenchantment as rooted in the Weberian concept of *Entzauberung* (disenchantment) provides a fitting frame for *Dread Trident*.[95]

Bennett's work in indebted to Latour, and he also helps in my study to clarify this notion of disenchantment/enchantment, as well as how demagification/magification function as false binaries. Latour upends conversations within modern studies by arguing in *We Have Never Been Modern* (1993) that our tendency to view nature and society as separate, or discrete, is unfortunate and, worse, false, because of the constant state of hybridized things. The instinct for separation, or differentiation, unfortunately encourages us to demand that the modern form another binary with primitive so that we can explain the fruits of our progress.[96] Modernity contains this great contradiction in its core, and Latour helps us see that such clean lines are illusory, even if sometimes seductive. Thus, we have never been modern, and we have never been enchanted or disenchanted. We are in a constant state, as Foucault would argue, of negotiating these postures.

Latour's refusal also clarifies how we can move beyond the idea of classifying the human vs. posthuman vs. nonhuman. The recent scholarship discussed above in the continued discourses of (trans-and-post)humanism has sought to understand Latour's 'parliament of things' outside of human perceptual constraints. This non-human world we wish to recognize exists separate from human understanding, yet, due to our inherent correlationism, is impossible to view outside of our own cognitive categories. For example, object-oriented ontology seeks a metaphysics that resists the privilege of human perception, while thinking in 'new'-materialist discourses also works against anthropo-morphic constraints to impart, as best they can, subjectivity to objects.

---

[95] As Bennett notes, its literal translation is "demagification" (2001, 57). This suggests a more fitting use for my study predicated on the use of the fantastic.

[96] Latour's 'great divides' thesis works against a variety of foundational narratives of the modern, from binaries such as modern vs. primitive or nature vs. culture to mind vs. body or, even, seemingly impossible, the real vs. the imaginary. Disenchantment vs. enchantment also reorients us to an important process within modernity. Secularism's rise as championed by Nietzsche's 'death of god' is supposed to have worked a dis-enchanting counter magic that challenged the waning of revelation even as fundamen-talisms in the West, and around the world, flourish. Latour resists such grand narratives. He sees categories such as religion, civilization, the West, modernity, etc., as delimiting attempts to segregate concepts into purified, discreet categories. A counter technique within modernity of Deleuzian chimerification also demolishes any such stable categories. See Latour 1993.

While *Dread Trident*'s theorizing of the modern fantastic briefly
touches on such a non-human object-subjectivity in terms of the cosmic
horror of Lovecraft, it sees in distinctions over the varieties of human
and nonhumans another example of discrete lines being problematic.
The differences in human, posthuman, and nonhuman are important
questions, yet often confusing.[97] These conversations are important
for an understanding of an 'enchanted' modern fantastic. This sort of
enchantment, though, seen with the rise of realized worlds as a type of
ironic magification, imparts a touch of thrilling experience with enough
distance to remain safe in an understanding of its fantastic/imaginary
quality. The process of how this occurs, as this introduction has argued,
emerges as a key component within *Dread Trident*, one that relies on
the use of literary gametexts, embodied play, and the mechanisms of
posthumanization.

Most TRPGs are arenas for the amplification of the magical over the
mundane, especially pure-fantasy games like D&D. And the acknowledgment of the standard modern crisis story that derives from thinkers
like Weber is one in which the rationalization process of calculation
and bureaucratization acted as mechanisms for the denuding of the
marvelous (or magical) from Western culture. Yet, in Bennett, Saler,
and the counter approaches of others, they offer alternative narratives
rich in a touch of the marvelous. *Dread Trident* argues that such marvels
are often engineered. Magic, in such cases, can be rational.[98] This
modernized magification is a type of ironic enchantment that utilizes the
methods and objects of modernity, those bars of Weber's iron cage, to its
advantage. In this approach, agency emerges from the very engineered
mechanisms once imagined encouraging a crisis. If *Dread Trident* could
argue for one comprehensive point in theorizing the modern fantastic,
it is that such rational tools as seen in TRPGs provide us with a touch
of magification, enough to live within modernity.

[97] For example, they encouraged Haraway to transition from focusing on
cyborg tropes to validating non-human species. She even begins *When
Species Meet* (2008) with a section, "We Have Never Been Human," to
further complicate the idea that a great divide exists between humans and
non-humans, such as animals. "The clean lines between traditional and
modern, organic and technological, human and nonhuman give way to the
infoldings of the flesh that powerful figures such as the cyborgs and dogs
I know both signify and enact" (Haraway 2008, 8).

[98] For example, D&D's entire system of arcane spellcasting is based on the
laborious process suffered by Jack Vance's wizards, such as the spell-seeking
Turjan. See Vance 2000.

'Dread Trident'

Regarding the title of this book, *"Dread Trident"* alludes to Shakespeare's *Tempest* and its mention of a 'magic item' wielded by Neptune and referenced by the spirit Ariel in Act 1 Scene 9, as he "flamed amazement" aboard the damned ship. It reminds us that in dramatic literature, especially in theater, we encounter spaces created for the representing of a variety of imaginary persons, effects, images, scenes, sets, props, etc. Shakespeare has been a touchstone for literary studies for successive generations, especially since praise by the Romantics cemented him as an imaginative cornerstone of the English language. Criticism of Shakespeare, though, has never been stable. Recent postcolonial reworkings of *The Tempest* demonstrate how insightful theories breathe new life into a text that was traditionally viewed as a comment on the New World.[99]

A realized reading of the play provides new insight as well. We see it first as a screenplay meant to be performed, each instance of the performance different, each embodied aspect of character something to be experienced as a spectator, the visual and aural materiality of the play as critical (i.e., the theater's location, plus its staging, its troupe, its seating, etc.) beyond the abstract concepts derived from words on a page. To imagine oneself as Ariel, or even Caliban, works within a literary frame. To become either, in some analog fashion works within a partially realized frame. And this materiality provides both the troupe of actors and the spectators degrees of experienced immersion into the realized world of Prospero's island. Such insights extend to the broadest effects in theater. Poor Yorick's monologue in *Hamlet* without a skull held aloft is less, rather than more. My title, then, evokes a fantasy trope of a shaking, dreadful trident held aloft by Neptune, a symbol of the creative imagination and its power to inspire.

---

[99] For a traditional reading, see Bloom 1999; and, for a postcolonial reading, see Loomba 1998. Also, for foundational studies of culture, fiction, narrative, and colonialism, see Said 1979; 1994. For a recent comment, see Rieder 2008.

Chapter 2

The Posthuman in the Schismatrix Stories and Eclipse Phase

This chapter argues that Bruce Sterling's influential Schismatrix stories of trans-and-posthumanity represent posthuman hyper-embodiment prior to the emergence of the professional discourses of trans-and-posthumanism. His representations of hyper-embodied materiality reinforces the argument that fantastic SF is just as important in understanding the posthuman as are the professional discourses. In fact, his representations prefigure playable character types in TRPGs such as the one examined in this case study, hard-SF Eclipse Phase (EP), and, thus, posthuman subjectivities.

This chapter insists on a rhetorical justification for foregrounding the modern fantastic within SF due to the prevalence of science fantasy in both fiction and popular technologized culture. In TRPGs of the posthuman we see clear examples of SF's mythopoetic power predicated on modern fantasies of world-transforming social change (i.e., imagined social singularities). However, this chapter avoids the arguments of technologists such as Ray Kurzweil and other transhumanist Singularitarians, as well as their detractors. Instead, it argues that the sort of SF exemplified by Sterling's Schismatrix stories is, in fact, a fantastic mode of fiction with a mythopoetic impulse and that even a hard-SF TRPG like EP also exemplifies this impulse.

This chapter uses Istvan Csicsery-Ronay to theorize a SF that provides the most consistent attempt of any fictional form at modern myth-making. For example, the 'Singularity' is one such problematic myth born of SF often argued for its inevitability by policy makers, bio-ethicists, technologists, engineers, etc. However, SF as modern myth has failed, the mode/form of SF balkanizing into a myriad number of sub-genres, and the Singularity derided as a techno-fantasy. It is in this recognition that SF's ineffectual myth-making impulse must accept its modern fantastic impulses.

Such fictions influenced EP, which provides mechanisms to play Sterling-like transhumans and, even, disembodied posthumans. It calls itself 'hard' SF because it works within a science-and-technology frame, yet the game is highly fantastic. To allow players a chance at playing a sentient octopus, or even a disembodied piece of information, regardless of the rational justification, infuses the game with the sort of fantastic tenor *Dread Trident* explores. In such an important sense, EP demonstrates how even a well-researched and detailed hard-SF game can also exhibit fantastic qualities. It does this to transport its players out of the mundane world and into one where the wondrous occurs.

A sustained critique of the representations of trans-and-posthumans in the Schismatrix stories thus allows a reading of EP as providing these imagined stages within SF for new subjectivities theorized by the contested discourses of trans-and-posthumanism. Its gametexts provide tools to imagine and play multiplicities of normative, trans, and posthuman ontologies that frame the posthuman not only as the possible problematic endpoint of unchecked transhumanism, but as a dominant SF trope for the coming century. Moreover, the experience of EP at the table reveals a game with complex mechanics that demand much out-of-table work from both game masters and players, but that also captures the realms of possibility such a posthuman future may possess.

Yet, even in EP a resurgent humanism remains. True posthuman subjectivity like that posited at the end of *Schismatrix Plus* (1996) can be imagined but can't be played because for the game to be enjoyable human beings at tables must encounter problems to be solved for some reward. Human agency is required. Even as players choose posthumans to play or as they encounter examples of posthumanity (e.g., a person evolved into a biological space-station), the players at the tables are still human beings with human desires and emotions. Without a vestigial humanism in EP, no game exists to be played. Such a realized world imagined when reading the Schismatrix stories or experienced when playing EP, again, reinforces traditional notions of the human through their uses of stable humanistic categories: like embodied and material people at tables using tools and discursive gametexts to enjoy play.

SF as Modern Myth-Making

One recent attempt to understand SF as a myth-making mode of fiction is Istvan Csicsery-Ronay's *The Seven Beauties of Science Fiction* (2008), a formalistic study that embeds SF within its respected disciplinary field as a discrete genre.[1] He helps in foregrounding how current thinking

---

[1] He follows Northrop Frye in seeing SF as a romance, but a rationalized one

by Singularitarians/Transhumanists represents SF's most recent attempt at modern myth-making, one *Dread Trident* views as an example of how both SF and SF-infused posthumanism are imbued with the imaginary. For this chapter, his theorizing the 'Singularity' introduces the science-fictionality of the concept as another example of the modern fantastic's reach.[2] Csicsery-Ronay also provides a foundation for my use of both the Schismatrix stories and Eclipse Phase as texts that represent the draconic-posthuman as, primarily, a fantastic trope.

For Csicsery-Ronay, and others who follow Suvin in demanding that SF separate itself from (in their views) the genre of fantasy, the *novum* is key, especially as a rationally explained material phenomenon. Such theorists use it to wrest SF away from fantasy, although the novum as an estranging device works within the broadest frame of the modern fantastic. In the most restricted notion of SF, Csicsery-Ronay sees such a novum as often the result of invention or discovery or new social arrangement, a mechanism for a change of perception of reality. He reads Suvin as focused on how the novum is addressed within a rational/cognitive framework as a paradigm for the imagined world distinct from the real world.

Csicsery-Ronay moves beyond Suvin, though, to frame the novum pointing toward a ludic relationship that isn't simply theoretical or critical, but representative of physical change and ethical change.[3] This focus on the novum makes SF a modern art form for SF scholars. Csicsery-Ronay would argue that in society, new inventions and their artifacts necessitate historical change and that literary SF reflects this social process, hence its mediating function. And, hence, its need to estrange to be effective.[4] Such a serious demand for literary SF, that it must separate itself from the less serious form, what Csicsery-Ronay calls popular sf, or sci-fi, the very bulk of material in the modern fantastic.

dominated by "science fictionality as a way of thinking about the world" (Csicsery-Ronay 2008, ix).

[2] And, even more critically, although my book does not investigate this, transhumanism represents a marked lack of irony in its construction. In fact, its program is very much predicated on the actuality of its SF fantasies. See Eden 2012 for a comprehensive examination. Also, see Raulerson 2013.

[3] He writes, "I shall refer to the novum as a device that creates a playful vertigo of free possibility in response to radical imaginary changes in readers' consensual physical and ethical worlds" (2008, 57).

[4] Such statements as "the sf novum is the stone thrown into the pool of existence, and the ripples that ensue" (Csicsery-Ronay 2008, 59) demonstrate the sort of lofty rhetoric Csicsery-Ronay uses in his theorizing, a sure sign to tread carefully, or to pay close attention.

Science fantasy falls under this unfortunate rubric, with film one of its most egregious forms. Such sci-fi film, as read by him, often concerns itself less with the novum and its requisite ideas and more with images and their effects: in essence, with performance instead of contemplation.[5]

For serious SF-theorists like Csicsery-Ronay, though, the often silly stuff of fantasy must bow to the more pressing themes born of techno-science: i.e., those within SF about invention and engineering. The demanding business of imagining and possibly constructing a "second nature" (Csicsery-Ronay 2008, 85) beyond our biological natures allows SF to be the literature that represents agency for humans in the face of a determining society and universe. Such is the rarefied themes of utopianism, which leads to its critique in anti-utopian or dystopian literature, key thematic trends in literary SF.[6]

In following Csicsery-Ronay toward a post-Suvin form of reputable SF, we find ourselves searching for ludic myths of how SF affects contemporary culture. For example, he mentions how a science-fictional consciousness emerged out of cyberpunk to affect real-world hackers. We can follow his analysis to view a similar analogue in which SF influences the construction of emerging modern myths in contemporary culture as discourse. Csicsery-Ronay even mentions Vernon Vinge, a fiction writer, whose ideas have been bolstered in an attempt to fashion the modern mythos of the Singularity. In this understanding, we can, thus, view the potential of convergent twenty-first-century sciences as fantastic imaginings from SF, from nanotech to advanced artificial intelligence and robotics, regardless of their actual states of technological progress or their potential.

Such a view of mythic SF sees it not simply as a mode of story-telling but a persistent cultural impulse attempting to actualize storytelling. We

[5] He reduces popular sci-fi film to spectacle even when it leans more toward serious SF in that it reflects the modern equivalent of myth-making and its plethora of archaic dreams, the stuff of "quasi-novums" (Csicsery-Ronay 2008, 74). In such screened and written texts, the jargon of modern science is used to tell tales of myth and fantasy, a nod commensurate with my use of the modern fantastic.

[6] The two primary twentieth-century dystopian novels in respected literary SF being George Orwell's *Nineteen Eighty-Four* (1948) and Aldous Huxley's *Brave New World* (1932). Much literary SF finds grounding in utopian/dystopian themes, Margaret Atwood's *The Handmaid's Tale* (1985) a valued literary text, one that has now been made into a TV series. For Csicsery-Ronay, such weighty concerns also utilize evolutionary tropes as alternatives to relying on techno-scientific tropes. Evolution and devolution are acceptable subjects for him. Again, the focus is always on proper SF as a literary form that represents agential possibilities for humans.

are to move from imagined narratives and their ideas and structures to view how these emerge in the world as hoped-for narratives. For example, with advanced robotics we see this attempted translation. In our 'science-fictional' world we now expect the creation of humanoid robots as depicted in SF film, video games, and novels. The successes have been slow in materializing, while other forms of robotics flourish.[7] Also, advanced nanotech is still very much far from the fantasy of Neal Stephenson's *The Diamond Age* (1995), as is the creation of general artificial intelligence far from the representations in films such as *Her* (2013). The tension between desire and reality is demonstrated in the N.B.I.C. (nanotech, biotech, artificial intelligence, cognitive science) document that Csicsery-Ronay mentions, especially when viewed as a fantastic text that presents nanotech as a fictional device yet to be made real. Finally, the "third nature" (Csicsery-Ronay 2008, 138) suggestive of the Singularitarians' hope for transcendence beyond our biological natures into something unknown foregrounds the discourses of trans-and-posthumanism as theorizing the ultimate novum: posthumans beyond our understanding.

The tropes represented in SF from such fantasies continue to conflate the imaginary with the actual. This is difficult ground to mine. Csicsery-Ronay recognizes that society is now often unable to differentiate between science and pseudoscience or technology and SF (Csicsery-Ronay 2008, 142). A hoax can sometimes be imagined as real, or even be attempted to be made real. Or SF can influence actuality (i.e., the drive by transhumanists toward the Singularity). Through this process flows the promise of the modern fantastic. For the type of SF espoused by Csicsery-Ronay to be seen as legitimate, the scientific materialism of modernity must be realized in its myth-making. This would replace the supernaturalism of prior myths of the marvelous or fantastic with SF-inflected ones. For a theorist like him, the supreme example of the modern myth of the Singularity would demand the incorporation of old tropes like spiritual disembodiment into a new framework of the material.

Such serious requirements ask much of SF. *Dread Trident* argues, though, that the modern fantastic drives much of this myth-making as hopeful fictions. Understanding that modern myths like the Singularity are fantastic in nature reminds us of their undeniably fictive, and imaginary, qualities. Nuanced critical approaches to SF reinforce the inescapable imaginary within modernity, even as it attempts the serous

---

[7] See Boston Dynamics' example of bipedal Atlas: https://www.bostondynamics.com/atlas.

business of myth creation. When looking at, say, the fantasy-inspired scenarios of Singularitarian discourse, we find imagined novums outside of traditional narratives (e.g., novels and films) and inside the minds of real-world individuals with real-world agendas (e.g., Ray Kurzweil, and others), but these narratives function in the same way Suvin suggests: they cause estrangement, which forces us to rethink possibilities that form from the imaginary.

The Singularity acts as one of these estranging imaginative ideas, even as its proponents proclaim its inevitable actuality. The problem here is that the fantastic aspect of the Singularity, born of SF, is not admitted by its staunchest proponents, even as the discourse reflects a sense of wonder, a key aspect of estrangement found in Suvin's SF. Like the use of Galileo writing about Jupiter's moons as an example of science wonder,[8] the estranging effect of Singularity discourse causes fear in some people, revulsion in others, excitement in some. This is because the encounter with the new and strange is fantastic, the key dynamic of our modern moment.

What is often ignored is that the posthuman (as well as the draconic) serves as a vibrant trope for contemporary society dominated by technoscience, especially in its recognized transhuman forms of cyborgs, mutants, superheroes, etc.; however, these technologically infused tropes fail to capture the essence of the older and more complex cosmic post-anthropocene posthumanism favored by professional critics, philosophers, and artists.[9] In popular culture, the opposing trope of the draconic (i.e., those seen within epic/high fantasy of the marvelous, supernatural, fantastic, etc.) continue to increase, often fusing with the posthuman in a supreme example of the modern fantastic's primary aesthetic, often blurring the lines between SF and fantasy. We see this with Sterling's Schismatrix stories and how he draws his posthumans.

Schismatrix and Posthumanity

Bruce Sterling's stories of the Schismatrix have been influential, although little acknowledged, as precursor texts for the discourses of trans-and-posthumanism. While later writers such as Iain Banks, David Brin, Charles Stross, etc., have added to the picture, Sterling's most impressive feat is in representing hyper-embodied posthumanity before the discourses became popular. A focused reading of Sterling's Schismatrix

[8] See Parrinder 2000.
[9] See Chapter 5 on Lovecraft.

stories reveals the posthuman to be a dominant trope in contemporary
SF's modern fantastic. This chapter works from a particular view of
trans-and-posthumanist SF as inherently fantastic, especially when
considering tropes like the posthuman. A place to begin is with the
stories themselves; a close reading of the novel *Schismatrix* (1985) reveals
its SF-inflected representation of hyper-embodied posthumans.

In terms of genre, most thinkers read Sterling's Schismatrix stories as
a SF blend of cyberpunk and space opera, with a focus on a near-future
earth.[10] Most criticism, though, sidesteps the fantastic posthuman for
genre or structural commentary.[11] Other thinkers see the Schismatrix
stories reflecting a natural process whereby human space colonization
splinters microworlds into differing environments much as evolutionary
mechanisms have splintered biological organisms into their differing
classificatory groups.[12] This evolutionary process, of course, is technological in the imagination of Sterling when representing humanity's
proliferation in a future world of space exploration, a fitting naturalistic
analogy that works well in the novel.

Dread Trident focuses on Sterling's imagined embodied subjectivities
as radical representations.[13] The type of imagined multiplicities of bodies
found in SF fiction like the Schismatrix stories foregrounds subject
formation as a key process in understanding the posthuman, one that
reflects an inherent modern 'fantasism' that Sterling refuses to admit
or adhere to because it would undermine his work as SF, rather than

---

[10] But Veronica Hollinger notes that "*Schismatrix* 1985 [is] one of the earliest
sf scenarios consciously to construct its characters as 'posthuman' and
to explore some of the implications of the term" (2009, 269). Hollinger's
recognition demonstrates that the genre of trans-and-posthumanist SF had
yet to emerge.

[11] Larry McCaffery calls *Schismatrix* "Sterling's radicalized antinovel" (1990,
211) because of its staccato style full of structured "disruptions" (229). In
an interview with McCaffery, Sterling provides a helpful way to conceptualize the novel as three mini-novels, each reflecting the major modes of
space opera. Part 1 is an adventure story in the vein of the pulps, Part 2
follows the tradition of social interaction, and Part 3 concerns a mystical
move into "Clarkean transcendence" (McCaffery 1990, 228).

[12] See Spinrad 1990, 132–3.

[13] Sheryl Vint provides an extended reading of the Schismatrix stories related
to the posthuman and embodiment. She sees Sterling's contribution as
valuable in positing a posthumanity focused on change. Her reading is
part of a project to insert an ethical understanding of how embodiment
embeds bodies in materiality. "Giving up old categories when they no longer
serve rather than defending them against inevitable change is the mark of
posthumanism" (Vint 2007, 175).

fantasy. Sterling's representations of hyper-embodied posthumans begin with "Spider Rose" (1982), the earliest of the Mechanist/Shaper stories, wherein Sterling has not yet defined the term 'posthuman.' Within the Schismatrix stories, he mentions 'posthumanism' in "Cicada Queen" (1983) where he defines it as "a metaphysic daring enough to think a whole world into life" (1996, 274). This conceptualization is framed within the discourse of technological transhumanism (a form of hyper-humanism) and, for Sterling, its imagining of future humans performing grand, planet-changing projects.[14]

Sterling's use of the posthuman, like those that derive from SF, often work outside these narrow parameters. For thinkers like Sterling, the posthuman is a technologically constructed subject rather than a philosophical posture. What we see with much of critical posthumanism are political positions on a continuum of antihumanisms; however, an actualized posthumanism like that seen in SF might function more like the nonhumanism of object-oriented ontology found detailed in *The Speculative Turn* (Bryant, Srnicek, and Harman 2011), an approach that seeks an ontology of things without the Kantian blinkers of the phenomenal world: a daunting task for any artist or writer wishing to draw such representations. Such challenges negate the traditions of Renaissance humanism and the articulations in the Enlightenment, as well as those of Jacob Burckhardt, Wilhelm Von Humboldt, and Matthew Arnold's nineteenth-century reimagined humanisms.[15]

We should note, though, that Sterling's Mechanist/Shaper stories maintain a stable humanist core that reaffirms the traditional preference of life over death. The novel begins with the most tragic of human literary themes: suicide. Sterling's young protagonist, Lindsay Abelard, is a Preservationist. He lives aboard a lunar orbiting world where he dreams of salvaging old-Earth culture prior to the fragmenting of humanity in

---

[14] Some thinkers, though, find Sterling's SF representations of these trans/posthumans dissatisfying. For example, Bruce Clarke challenges Sterling for encouraging a naive acceptance of the Western, liberal subject. Clarke focuses his critique on Sterling's use of aquatic posthumans who will inhabit the terraformed moon of Jupiter, Europa, claiming that these creatures are "anything but posthuman," (2008, 161) because, according to Clarke, they represent the ideal of the rugged, self-sufficient individual. In Clarke's reading, key tenets of humanism are strengthened and valued in the stories. What is happening here with Clarke, and so much of critical posthumanism, is a refracting of the concept into a specialized tool that challenges the Enlightenment project's constructed notion of the human and all its faults.

[15] See Davies 1997.

space. Sterling writes that Lindsay watches his love, Vera, who flies high above him in a glider. She nose-dives into the ground, ending her life in a grand existential gesture that agency is exemplified by taking one's own life. In a nod to *Hamlet*, as well as to *Romeo and Juliet*, Sterling writes of Lindsay's desire to follow his love to the grave. But Lindsay is sent to another orbiting world where he begins his journey away from petty human desires into a variety of posthuman existences. The tension, though, between normative human values and those offered within the new posthuman Schismatrix solar system emerges along a few key thematic lines.

Suicide also features in the final scene between Lindsay and the antagonist, Philip Constantine, Lindsay's old friend who once espoused Preservationist values but exchanged these for the thrill of conquest and human ambition. Constantine has been living as a wounded person since losing a duel with Lindsay. At this point, Constantine's life has been salvaged, but he exists in a liminal place between life and death. After years of recovery, he has forsaken his old ambition and is ready to die. He will take his own life, but not before stating that Lindsay will never follow the path of those who want to create aquatic posthumans. Lindsay will step aside at the last moment, which Lindsay does, choosing a much more mysterious path. The reason for Constantine's skepticism is that Lindsay has been a 'sundog,' a solar-system nomad, ever since he failed to kill himself, always surviving when danger crept too close. This adaptability is a key attribute of Sterling's protagonist, ultimately minimizing the thematic importance of traditional humanistic values in the novel for more radical insights.

Sterling maintains suicide as a key humanist concern. In the "Cicada Queen" (1983), he presents special rooms devoid of surveillance called 'discreets,' where people pass time in privacy. These discreets enter the narrative, though, as places where the distraught end their lives. Moreover, in the very last mini-narrative in *Schismatrix Plus* (1996), which combines all of Sterling's Mechanist/Shaper stories, "Sunken Gardens" (1984) sees the protagonist Nikolai Leng end his life due to ennui. What must be preserved by these characters who long for the ease of death is their sense of a humanity connected to a past. We have already seen this on the lunar world where the novel begins, and where Lindsay's love, Vera, has killed herself. The entire habitat has become a museum. We see its proprietor, Pongpianskul, in his office, with its cluttered papers and its imported mice, objects related to a vanished past. This cultural heritage is what is being lost as humanity transforms itself. And, for Sterling, a latent humanistic nostalgia and romanticism runs like a strong thread through the novel, never fraying or disappearing, even as he erects monuments to the imagination of the hyper-embodied.

In the novel, Sterling draws posthumans in a variety of forms. A cursory version is represented with mention of inhuman people living beyond a wall on a space habitat. They are inhuman in the sense of devolving, a common trope in SF, but one Sterling forgoes exploring. Instead, he provides iconic representations with a horrific image of the Yarite, a meatpuppet beyond the "limits of the clinically dead" (1996, 39). It possesses nerve impulses, some biological existence beyond the fully dead, even awareness, as Lindsay notices after he awakens it with a slap. In contrast, the genetically altered Shaper Kitsune is very human at this point (because of her sexual desire), but Sterling, in his inching toward a radical posthuman embodiment, has Lindsay reflect that Kitsune is also not human.[16] Kitsune is 'posthuman' in the sense of being altered, yes, but she is represented in a mode we now recognize as 'transhuman,' a word still in its nascent stage at the time these stories were written, and one Sterling does not use. She is transhuman because she is using technology to enhance what are, in essence, core human attributes. She is on the verge of becoming posthuman. When we meet Kitsune, her womb replaced with brain tissue, sweat that smells like perfume, a tongue with glands excreting aphrodisiacs, these alterations fail in comparison with Kitsune's later transformation.

The next time Lindsay sees her, a mechanical lamp swings his way, and two human eyes peer from beneath a shade. She is becoming a living habitat, the highly imaginative representation of a hyper-embodied being. She is alive, with massive cardiac pumping stations, sensitive walls and floors, and even a mind that has memory and volition. 'Kitsune,' in these forms, still lives. Yet, she must use one of her clone's bodies to communicate, to feel, to experience the everyday world. She has given herself to an ontologically problematic transformation that ends with her existing as an industrial being in the "emergent technology of the flesh" (1996, 212). Lindsay sees her as a person who has taken embodiment to its conceptual end. As much as I agree with this assessment, Sterling's refusal to go beyond is an unfortunate choice.

What is interesting in Sterling's Schismatrix stories is that his representations of the hyper-embodied are clear because they are drawn in stark relief with pitiful humanity. We have examples of genetically

[16] Kitsune is the Japanese word for fox. A comparative study reveals the deep connections within Japanese folklore. The fox is a type of trickster deity, which has parallels in other cultures. Sterling's use references Kitsune as a type of shapeshifter that moves from human form to a fully othered form.

altered Shapers transforming themselves into a variety of forms, from aquatic posthumans to big-brained Patternists. We also have representations of frail bodies ready for transformation. Sterling began sketching these sharp, hyper-embodied images early with the representation of an alien queen in the short story "Swarm" (1982). Descriptions of her "monstrous body" with "warm and pulpy flesh" (1996, 248) evoke disgust and terror. The alien queen is a factory for the colony that digests material and produces eggs, endlessly repeating the process like a biological machine.

Sterling also presents a tension between the dirty, virulent, smelly, human body and all of its crawling bacteria with a number of opposites. He juxtaposes frail flesh with the hyper-rationalized disembodied world of the 'wire-heads.' Like the character Ryumin, who Lindsay first meets when he becomes a 'sundog,' wireheads shed their bodies for the pure, disembodied world of data. Later, Lindsay meets Ryumin again, who is now a computer-generated face like William Gibson's super AI Wintermute at the end of *Neuromancer* (1984). Newly arrived on this particular space habitat, Lindsay is tainted with its bacteria. He is suffering a raging upper-respiratory infection. He has a runny nose. We can imagine rashes and eczema. We understand all the frailties that encourage Shapers to become radically embodied entities and Mechanists to discard the body.

On what side of the embodiment vs. disembodiment debate does Sterling fall? His representations of the hyper-embodied outweigh the disembodied in sheer numbers of representations and pages written. The physical world also has the most vocal advocates used as thematic mechanisms. For example, near the end of the novel, before Lindsay decides to create "aquatic posthumans" (1996, 232) on Europa, one of his 'admirers,' Gomez, asks, "What about the flesh? We are the flesh. What about the flesh?" (1996, 200). Here, by one of the founders of cyberpunk, and a forerunner for a later biopunk that foregrounds biotechnology and its effects on human beings, the flesh is valued, if acknowledged to be flawed.

Sterling is strongest as a writer when he is describing the material. One of the most descriptive passages comes when Lindsay has returned to Earth's seas to capture organisms for his Europa project:

> Life rose all around them: a jungle in defiance of the sun. In the robot's lights the steep, abrasive valley walls flushed in a vivid panoply of color: scarlet, chalk-white, sulfur-gold, obsidian. Like stands of bamboo, tubeworms swayed on the hillsides, taller than a man. The rocks were thick with clams, their white shells yawning

to show flesh as red as blood. Purple sponges pulsed, abyssal corals spread black branching thickets, their thin arms jeweled with polyps. (Sterling 1996, 227)

The language is like the best of Darwin describing the 'entangled bank' at the end of the *Origin of Species* (1859). Other thinkers have noted this connection. For example, Brian Stableford writes that

posthumanists see the future evolution of humankind in terms of a dramatic diversification of types, partly accountable in terms of adaptive radiation and partly in terms of aesthetic impulses. [...] the first significant popularizers of the notion of posthuman evolution in science fiction included Bruce Sterling, in the Shaper/Mechanist series. (Stableford 2006, 401–2)

Furthermore, Tom Maddox in *Storming the Reality Studio* (1991), writes that Sterling is a writer with a firm notion of both evolutionary theory and complexity theory and how these sciences portend a possibly frightening future for human beings. In this way, Sterling's stories of the Schismatrix solar system and its contending Mechanists and Shapers are ontological before anything else. Maddox notes that Sterling is aware of the tradition of representation within SF in which humans evolve beyond our current evolutionary history. He mentions Olaf Stapledon as well as Arthur C. Clarke's visions as precursors, not to mention Frank Herbert's use of transformation in the Dune series. Maddox argues that no one has provided such intensity or style to these representations as has Sterling (1991, 324–30). Maddox's reading, as well as that of other SF critics, writers, fans, etc., demands that the posthuman, as a concept, must be considered within the context of SF studies and its representations of the human and/or the posthuman instead of automatically attuned to the discourses of critical posthumanism.

The connection with evolutionary theory only skims the surface of the novel and short stories, rarely exploring theoretical nooks and crannies. These tales of biological evolution in the solar system imagine human societies splintering and evolving rapidly via a technological process similar to artificial selection, rather than natural. Sterling writes more than once: "Life moved in clades" (1996, 225). The representation of radical human evolution stems not just from the sciences of evolutionary biology but from complexity theory.

Throughout the stories, Sterling references 'Prigogenic levels of complexity,' a concept he formed from Ilya Prigogine and Isabelle Stengers's Nobel prize-winning work into self-organizing systems, *Order out of Chaos* (1984). In Sterling's stories, he refers to four levels of complexity, each building on the last to emerge into a new mode of being. Of course, like Sterling's ideas of evolutionary theory, these imagined levels are under-theorized. We must piece together what these levels mean to see how they relate to the hyper-embodied posthuman. The first is 'ur-space,' a vague reference to whatever undergirds space-time itself, which comprises the second level. The third level in which complexity emerged is organic life, and the fourth, that of intelligence. He constructs these so that he can postulate, then back away from, a mysterious 'fifth level.'

One can imagine this new level to be nonhuman/posthuman similar to the speculative posthumanism postulated by David Roden in *Posthuman Life* (2014), a term that defines posthumanism as completely other from the human and, thus, beyond our comprehension. Sterling details in his introduction to *Schismatrix Plus* (1996, vii) that when Prigogine was offered the stories to read he said they had nothing to do with his work. And nor should that be a requirement. Sterling's novel is a work of the imagination, fantasy-SF that blends cyberpunk and space opera. Even better, it is an early text that uses the terminology of the posthuman. Some of the clearest representations of posthumans make them an extreme other: as different from us as is a human from a butterfly. For example, in *Schismatrix*, one curious example can be found in the Lobsters (294). These posthumans live encased in form-fitting metallic armor. Like lampreys, they attach themselves to the sides of ships where their extra-human senses commune with the universe.

You would imagine that achieving this fifth level of being is what Lindsay desires above all else. But, no, the main narrative rushes toward another dream: "Life-spreading. Planet-ripping. World-building. Terraforming" (188). This grand plan is "humanity's sublimest effort" (283) akin to the civilization building documented in our literary epics.[17] We see the project underway by the brightest of the Shaper posthumans, called Cataclysts, a neologism that blends cataclysm and catalyst; they attempt such world-building on Mars and Europa to further their "biomorality" (190) and "bioaesthetics" (302), two aspects of a worldview the novel suggests is the true outcome of a worthwhile posthumanity (170). Again, Sterling's humanism surfaces with such hubris to reinforce the idea that a latent transhumanism colors many of his posthumans.

Besides Kitsune or terraforming as defining factors, what representation could Sterling have drawn of posthumans that are truly othered?

[17] See Frederick Turner (1988) for a 10,000-line epic poem about terraforming Mars.

Such an imagined fantastic ontology might be impossible to represent. Here the tension between the embodied and disembodied demonstrates the possibility of representing the former, while the latter proves difficult. In an article on "Cyberpunk and Posthuman Science Fiction," the authors compare Sterling's *Schismatrix* with Gibson's vision of our posthuman future, arguing that Sterling sees human nature as highly flexible in such a way that denies Gibson's ambivalence. The authors derive this interpretation from the fact that Lindsay refuses to be bound by the ideologies of either the Mechanists or Shapers (he's had Shaper conditioning, but also sports a prosthetic limb). Lindsay accepts his ultimate transformation at the end of the novel when he abandons his body with the aid of an alien Presence. The authors see his resistance to ideological ossification, as well as the abandonment of a body, as an "optimism and openness to new experiences and forms of embodiment" (Booker and Thomas 2009, 114). While this interpretation is fair, Lindsay's final choice of alien living is a negation of embodiment. It is a passive narrative choice by Sterling and, worse, one unwilling to usher its SF-inflected fantasism to its proper end.

Hyper-embodiment has been represented with sophistication and could have been exemplified in detail with Lindsay's final choice of becoming an under-water-living posthuman (an 'Angel'), or with some other embodied being. Lindsay's jaunting off with an alien Presence into disembodied life leaves the reader with a sense that Sterling balked when he should have delivered. Fantastic precedents of the ineffable are present in hard SF (i.e., Clarke's Star Child), but this tradition of foregrounding the fantastic within a hard-SF frame (and Sterling's refusal) demonstrates how difficult it is to represent the truly transcendent.[18] Moreover, with Sterling's imaginative transformation of Kitsune into a living, biological space station, we see a representation of hyper-embodiment begging for more exploration by the novel's protagonist. Sterling shies away from the implications of hyper-embodiment on an industrial scale to reveal this alien Presence that ushers Lindsay to the Fifth Prigogenic Level— in essence, relieving him of the tyranny of Descartes's dualism and ushering him into the truly fantastic realm. Sterling refuses to explore this other realm.

Granted, Sterling has company in his retreat. Edgar Allan Poe is criticized for failing to narrate the end of the *Narrative of Arthur Gordon Pym of Nantucket* when his narrator is faced with the transcendent but refuses to embrace it (Panshin and Panshin 1989, 35). H.G. Wells, while

[18] Frederic Jameson went so far as to say that Greg Egan, who has attempted to map this difficult terrain, is "relatively unreadable" (2005, 68).

known for venturing far into the imaginary realm of where science might take us in the universe, far beyond anyone before him, hesitated at imagining how humans could live in those horrific gulfs of space. We should also not forget that H.P. Lovecraft's alien/deities cause madness with even a glimpse. Here at the precipice of imagining where all of these fiddling posthuman technologies might lead us, Sterling backs away from true alterity. He avoids warping the genre of the new space opera in the direction of mythic fantasy to avoid radically altering his novel. Or maybe he refuses because of the difficulty. Moving beyond such categories, yet not retreating to traditional myth, has been a daunting challenge for modern science, one addressed by numerous SF writers, as well as in the text often considered the first true SF novel: *Frankenstein; or, The Modern Prometheus* (1818).

What then does *Schismatrix* reveal about the posthuman as a state of being? When Lindsay is challenged by the alien Presence to forgo becoming an aquatic posthuman and, instead, to take a leap into the Fifth Prigogenic Level, the Presence says this entails experience, not answers, and that the result will be "eternal wonder" (1996, 236). SF began its modern incarnation, after the science romances of Verne and Wells and the science fantasy of Burroughs and Merritt, to become a literature of wonder. This emotion was touted by Hugo Gernsback in *Amazing Stories* and later in the bedrock of John W. Campbell's *Astounding Science Fiction*. However, in the end, the wondrous still proves difficult to represent.

Sterling's representations of posthumans defy theory's attempt to dictate the discourse of trans-and-posthumanism. SF-and-fantasy studies, therefore, provide a ripe field of investigation with such fruitful artifacts, many of which are undervalued. My analysis has attempted to show that his most complex representations are of hyper-embodied, technological posthumans, a trope that far exceeds others in SF when defining the modern fantastic. In fact, such representations may be foundational for new articulations of the posthuman in the coming century that will rely on discursive formations tied to materiality. At this point, such imaginings are fantastic yet not purely imaginary. They retain their potential for SF extrapolation by remaining within the realm of the possible. As such, Sterling's Schismatrix stories play an important role in the modern fantastic and its continued articulation through science fiction and fantasy texts.

Eclipse Phase and Posthuman Subjectivity

Several TRPGs are also representative of SF's drawing of the posthuman after Sterling's Mechanist/Shaper stories, such as *Cyberpunk* (1988), *Cyberpunk 2020* (1990), *Transhuman Space* (2002), *Cyberpunk V3* (2005), and *Nova Praxis* (2010). These fall within the adventure-SF camp, while, for example, Warhammer 40,000's series of grim TRPGs—menacingly titled *Dark Heresy* (2008), *Rogue Trader* (2009), *Death Watch* (2010), *Black Crusade* (2011), and *Only War* (2012)—blend a SF-horror-fantasy that pushes genre boundaries by marrying science and magic (see Chapter 6).

In the TRPG Eclipse Phase (EP), however, magic is minimized to oblique suggestions that alien intelligences may have been the cause of inexplicable events, "phenomena that seem to defy certain physical laws" (Boyle and Cross 2009, 42). EP expands its hard-SF-game universe with a number of supplements beyond the core rules: *Sunward* (2010), *Panopticon* (2011), *Gatecrashing* (2011), *Rimward* (2012), *Transhuman* (2013), *Firewall* (2015).[19] In these, supertech for readers and players functions in the same manner as the marvelous in fantasy role-playing games: nano assemblers, sapient AIs, uplifted animals, synthetic life, mind uploading, immediate information access, ubiquitous augmented and virtual reality, rapid cloning, egocasting, mind and body duplication, wormhole travel, etc., each one a perfect example of Clarke's supertech-as-modern magic. These are not mythic motifs found in traditional fantasy texts. Thus, the game distances itself from science fantasy. However, its use of hard-SF motifs proves just as functional in the creation of a contemporary trans-and-posthumanist myth for the future: the Singularity.

With EP we have a hard-SF yet imaginary trans-and-posthumanist-flavored game that provides a schema for playing trans-and-posthumans, rather than merely providing representations in a novel or on a screen, or even in real-world performance (as does LARPing).[20] With EP, we also

---

[19] At the time this book was being finished, EP released a second edition of its game rules.

[20] What we see here is a key concept in game studies that argues we need to move from mimesis to simulation if we are to understand how such games work. In fact, Espen Aarseth argues forcefully that traditional hermeneutics based on representation fails to describe the mode of gameplay discourse (2004). Certainly, a text-based, analog game like EP does more than entertain through telling collaborative stories. Its game mechanics allow for analogous subject formation that prefigures the dreams of often less-than-critical transhumanists who one day hope to create actual, technological posthumans, while also refracting more complex ideas from

have systematized subject formation in a creative crucible. My use of it demonstrates how a TRPG can illuminate a process like posthumanization and the trope of the posthuman intervening in the discourse by upsetting the notion that our future will be disembodied or that technoscience is erasing material embodiment. Yes, screens are increasing, as are myriad selves across distributed communication networks. But bodies push back.

In EP, the campaign setting determines the tone and type of play. It occurs "in the not-too-distant future" (Boyle and Cross 2009, 24) and is very similar to Sterling's Schismatrix stories, in which the Earth has suffered a series of ecological and martial disasters, a diaspora has occurred, and now humanity has expanded into the solar system and beyond to survive.[21] However, EP is laced with a horror element minimized in Sterling. A section titled "Things that Should Not Be: Horror" channels the pulps and Lovecraft (Boyle and Cross 2009, 389). The game even mentions Lovecraft's quote regarding fear of the unknown as the oldest emotion. By highlighting horror, EP suggests a basic humanist tendency to fear our posthuman future; thus, viewing the transhuman slide into the posthuman as pessimistic.

Other games as well have utilized Lovecraft within a high-tech milieu, such as *Cthulhu Tech* (2007), a far-future scenario where eldritch magic exists alongside giant anime-inspired mechas in a battle against Lovecraft's space deities and their cultists. However, instead of nebulous Outer Gods like Azathoth and the Great Old Ones like Cthulhu, EP imagines tech-created monsters such as the handiwork of an insane AI that fuses transhuman bodies into a "gigantic, centipede-like abomination" with the goal of also merging their minds (Boyle and Cross 2009, 88). Oddly enough, a section at the end of the core rulebook detailing references lists key texts from fiction, comics and graphic novels, non-fiction, other TRPGs, movies and TV, without mentioning Lovecraft (an odd oversight). The direct links to contemporary transhumanist thinking, though, are obvious.

Most importantly for EP's setting, "humanity as a concept has been replaced with transhumanity" (Boyle and Cross 2009, 38). EP's setting is detailed within a post-Singularity narrative of technological marvels after (trans)humanity's fall that began when ecowars between nations facilitated the creation of military AIs called TITANS. These sentient TITANS turned a war of nations into a theater that utilized

critical theorists and philosophers, such N. Katherine Hayles, Gilles Deleuze, Manuel DeLanda, Rosi Braidotti, Stefan Herbrechter, etc.

[21] More recently, the TV series *The Expanse* (2015–present) explores this scenario of the solar-system at war.

every weapon imaginable, a war that destroyed the environment with nuclear fallout, biochemical waste, nano swarms, etc. The TITANS forced the mind-uploading of millions of humans and then disappeared. But wormholes called Pandora Gates appeared in the solar system, suggesting the TITANS may have used them to flee after achieving a new level of intelligence and may have even had the help of extraterrestrial intelligences. Ten years after the Fall, transhumanity survives in factions, filling the solar system with new forms of existence, both embodied and disembodied. Some strive for a form of hyper-(trans)humanism favored by 'ultimates,' while others strive for posthumanity, such as the 'exhumans' who wish to be "godlike superbeings" (43).

The cover of the core rules markets the game as transhumanist and posthumanist, calling itself "the roleplaying game of transhumanist conspiracy and horror." In a section titled "Enter the Singularity," the rulebook identifies a series of themes:

> EP takes all of these themes and weaves them together in a transhuman setting. The post- apocalyptic angle covers the understanding of all that transhumanity has lost, the fight against extinction, and how much of that is a struggle against our own nature. The conspiracy side delves into the nature of the secret organizations that play key roles in determining transhumanity's future and how the actions of determined individuals can change the lives of many. The horror perspective explores the results of humanity's self-inflicted transformations and how some of these changes effectively make us non-human. Tying it all together is an awareness of the massive indifference and the terrible alien-ness that pervades the universe and how transhumanity is insignificant against such a backdrop. Offsetting these themes, however, EP also asserts that there is hope, that there is something worth fighting for, and that transhumanity can and will pave its own path toward the future. (Boyle and Cross 2009, 19)

This should be no surprise if one imagines a post-Singularity solar system of transhuman technology as post-apocalyptic with conspiracies about the nature of the Fall and humanity's best way to face the future.[22]

---

[22] Such weighty themes of the Singularity, as Istvan Csicsery-Ronay writes, "may be the quintessential myth of contemporary technoculture" (2008, 262). For many transhumanists, the Singularity is an unacknowledged "existing science fiction, the consensual hallucination [...] sf's imaginary empirical prophecy" (Csicsery-Ronay 2008, 264).

The game, though, doesn't admit this modern mythopoetic element. Its acceptance is tempered by claiming that its transhumanism, as a primary theme, actually leans toward a pessimistic posthumanism, one in which the hyper-humanism of human enhancement has derailed. In a section titled, "What is Transhumanism?" EP's core rules differentiate two standard definitions: (1) human enhancement and (2) the transition to the posthuman. In the game, number one proves beyond our ability to control, thus leading to a dystopic number two. This tension runs through the game and is expressed as if 'transhumanity' is a character providing instructions: "We humans have a special way of pulling ourselves up and kicking ourselves down at the same time" (Boyle and Cross 2009, 18). More instructions take the form of direct messages from Firewall (a clandestine organization dedicated to protecting transhumanity), providing both narrative flavor and campaign information, as well as taking the form of a nameless, tough-talking character willing to provide "the real deal" (29).

In fact, the rulebook is peppered with these separate pieces of fiction: e.g., a transcript of an audio file and other random messages. In the end, the game counters its pessimism by claiming "that there is hope, that there is something worth fighting for, and that transhumanity can and will pave its own path toward the future" (Boyle and Cross 2009, 19). Such an appeal proves it follows Sterling and has, ultimately, a humanist foundation, which will please most players whose characters act as sentinels, secret agents of Firewall. Yet, the game is flexible enough that a player could create a character dedicated to overthrowing transhumanity or to the exploration of playing within a truly posthuman ontology.

Along with its detailed narrative universe, the core rulebook is a gametext that begins with a dash of fiction, as do many TRPG rulebooks. The early placement of the short story, "Lack," orients players toward the major themes and elements in the game. We are introduced to several key concepts: resleeving, mesh inserts, Firewall, cortical stacks, muses, morphs, ecological disaster, the TITANS, forced uploading, rep, factions, etc. We learn that death isn't the end. One character blithely shoots another when escape proves impossible. No worries. A new body can be had for the right price, as long as your ego (mind) has been preserved. You can choose to be any imaginable form from uplifted animals such as sentient octopi called octomorphs, to hyper-intelligent genetically altered humans called mentons, to new forms of synthetic life called pods, to mechanical life within robotic shells, or even to the pure intelligence of a disembodied infomorph.

EP demonstrates a concern for Bakhtinian "carnivalesque" (Mackay 2001, 72) subject formation in the most imaginative manner because bodies (morphs) are plasticized. Such flexibility allows for a major reorientation toward basic ontological categories. The diaspora didn't just cause a space-opera-like jaunt into the solar system. Many people escaped a ravaged Earth by choosing the in-between state of disembodied existence, creating digital backups of their egos (minds/selves), hopefully to regain bodies in the future.

> Most people now alive left Earth as infomorphs and were subsequently resleeved into new morphs. Bodies are things that can be modified and replaced, much as someone can alter or exchange a suit of clothing. Identity is centered in the mind, which can exist as a disembodied infomorph living in virtual worlds or dwelling in a vast array of strange and exotic morphs. (Boyle and Cross 2009, 38)

This hyper-embodied flexibility allows for delivery from "non-permanent death" (Boyle and Cross 2009, 50). Like Sterling's imagining of Kitsune as a biological/industrial being, such resleeving demonstrates the most radical posthumanism imagined. In the supplement *Rimward* (2012), EP even details a biological habitat called MeatHab, a piece of performance art by a transhuman that developed into a population of 500 religious acolytes. "MeatHab is an ego that has sleeved into a habitat" (Boyle and Cross 2012, 198), a clear indication that an intelligence still exists. The game allows one to play "exhumans [who] seek to take the capabilities of self-modification to the absolute limit and become posthuman" (Boyle and Cross 2009, 80). However, MeatHab is represented, not as the most extreme form of posthumanity, but as retaining its humanist core: "Exhumans wrongly interpret him [MeatHab] as being in their camp, when in reality MeatHab is a very humane soul who happens to enjoy having his insides full of a lot of other transhumans" (Boyle and Cross 2012, 198).

The game reinforces the Cartesian split of mind and body because players, like most people, have a dualistic conception of themselves. However, in EP, the traditional self is under pressure. While the game recognizes the potential problems in capturing a disembodied mind, you still have an ego. Yet, this ego isn't stable. The process of 'forking' allows you to back up your mind—in essence, the combined experience of yourself. "People use forks of themselves to get work done in everyday life, and almost everyone has at least experimented with forking at some point" (Boyle and Cross 2009, 275). You can create mini-selves that enter the world to complete tasks. Or, just as incredibly, you might egocast your ego/self, thereby gaining rapid travel through the solar system in a disembodied state. It even allows for the existence of neurodes, an extreme form of hyper-embodiment that eschews a standard sleeved body "in exchange for a multi-pedal neuronal shell that is both body and brain at the same time" (362).

In such a world in which resleeving into multiple morphs, where egos can fork themselves into multiplicity or remain disembodied, where brain-beings exist, identity is a problem the game exacerbates. Thus, EP provides an arena for the "experimentation with other bodies" (34), while also providing the expected cyberpunk entrance to the disembodied virtual world, thereby reinforcing a standard Cartesian humanism in its attempt at creating a trans-and-posthumanist game. It even states that "EP's setting dictates that a distinction must be made between a character's ego (their ingrained self, their personality, and inherent traits that perpetuate in continuity) and their morph (their ephemeral physical—and sometimes virtual—form)" (121). This decree occurs because players demand it. For the game to be posthumanistic it would eschew such a foundation and would be unplayable.

In an email conversation between the game creator, Robert Boyle, and myself, Boyle states that he sees these "transitional identities" (2016) as critical to understanding the game's mechanical and thematic flexibility. These transitional identities allow players at a table to construct their identities in a complex manner, but one that poses gameplay challenges. Boyle writes that

> it opens up possibilities for behavior and roleplaying that many other games don't. It also challenges people's concept of self, as their mind can be altered, sometimes willingly, sometimes not. I get the sense that some players really grapple with the idea that they are the same person if they die and are copied to a new body, at least at first. I've heard stories of players that go to great lengths to have their characters physically relocate around the solar system, rather than egocasting their minds and downloading in a new body, partly for gameplay reasons (to conserve gear), but also partly out of uneasiness or unfamiliarity with the concept of willingly vacating the body you're in. (2016)

According to Boyle, the challenges faced by players revolve around key decisions that affect gameplay, such as whether to simply resleeve a body after being killed (or doing everything to avoid such a fate) or choose to fork one's ego into multiple copies to increase their agency. Boyle states that power-gamers lean in this direction. Players may also become disembodied infomorphs, a choice for those seeking freedom of movement

(Boyle 2016). These choices affect gameplay, and EP's complexities allow for such flexibility, even though the strain on the gamemaster demands attention and the options for players can be daunting.

How does this flexibility emerge during gameplay? The mechanics, or game design patterns emerge out of demands engendered by the setting. Boyle, as well as an EP gamemaster Anandraj Singh, both describe the pessimistic horror setting as something prevalent but not all-encompassing. Boyle states he "would contest the idea that EP is completely pessimistic" (2016), but that hope can be found through transhuman technology, while Singh as well sees the game providing a "dark, grim side of fallen Earth and the affect it has on the population" as complex but not limiting (pers. comm. Singh 2016). Singh details a process of gatecrashing, or jumping to foreign worlds, as one that alleviates this pessimism. Also, another key aspect of the game's hopefulness is its focus on player agency—in particular, the dynamic between consistent egos and flexible changing morphs (bodies).

Within this optimistic humanistic impulse, the game's particular setting and flexible gameplay provide sophisticated social critique. The varied discourses of critical posthumanism can be seen in EP's positing a world in which natural categories have been superseded by tech. It reflects potential problems in human capital when the poor are not only disenfranchised because of technological developments but are forced to inhabit inferior morphs designed for menial labor, or even live as disembodied infomorphs. The game states that non-human morphs, or uplifted animals, suffer prejudice. Some characters in the game even challenge the ideological notion that they should be "anthropocentric" (Boyle and Cross 2009, 81). After the diaspora, these new types of persons are given second-class citizenship among the solar system's habitats, this game element reflecting a political agenda in animal studies that wishes to grant rights to non-human persons. Such non-democratic uses of technology run counter to thinking by those in critical theory eager for egalitarian answers to our current technosocial lives. Embodiment and disembodiment, both of which are still framed within a Cartesian theater so that a player can give his or her character agency, allow for multiplicities of being within the traditional categories of race, class, gender, sexuality, etc., but also in fantastic categories like new forms of personhood and modes of being. It is a game of Deleuzian becoming in which even death has been vanquished. You simply need to resleeve your ego into a new morph of choice—if you were prudent enough to create backups.

EP reflects this social tension in its two major systems: the versatile hypercorps' controlled authoritarian inner system of Martian dominance and that of the less authoritarian, post-consumer-capitalist, autonomist outer system beyond Jupiter. The outer systems reflect the sort of radical political entities often argued for by contemporary critical posthumanists as open, borderless, decentered societies. The concept of the hypercorps also reflects the idea of the corporation as posthuman, a reflection of a process that is happening today as corporations are afforded more agency yet rely on automated processes without direct human action. "Some hypercorps are in fact entirely 'virtual'" (Boyle and Cross 2009, 70), with very few personnel, such as Solaris, a hypercorp with "no offices or physical assets; each banker is a mobile virtual office" (73).

The system and the setting both affect the experience at the table. Boyle notes that players often gravitate toward play within enclosed spaces out of a lack of understanding how survival in space works (something the game designers went to great lengths to detail). "It helps them to focus on enclosed spaces like habitats and ships, because these are a bit more like the cities most of us know so well [...] also, the enclosed nature of ships and habitats lends itself very well to survival horror scenarios" (pers. comm. Boyle 2016). Boyle notes that these limited spaces also encourage "small-town interpersonal drama, where everyone is crowded up against their neighbor's affairs" (pers. comm. Boyle 2016), seeing in these demands reasons why a GM might want to begin the game in an isolated setting as he or she introduced more complex elements at a consumable pace. Singh argues that the gamemaster faces the greatest challenges when contending with so many variables "to not get overwhelmed" (pers. comm. Singh 2016). EP is a "crunchy" game, meaning it requires "a lot of math," and that one of the most demanding parts of the game is character creation; yet he recognizes that, even more difficultly, "getting people into the frame of mind of transhumanity [is ...] a very difficult concept to explain and get thematically right" (pers. comm. Singh 2016). These setting choices, then, prove critical in understanding the constraints needed for the game to work.

Ultimately, EP exemplifies SF as rational with its game mechanics, classification system, world building details. However, it is fictional, and those who play, regardless of their hopes and fantasies and fears of such a world, understand it to be so. Drawing the line between the fantastic and the mundane, though, is difficult because real-world advocates of transhumanism often argue with no sense of irony for a posthuman future. The debates often center on the bioethics of human enhancement, on the social policies of creating new types of persons, on whether the Singularity (or Singularities) is a fantasy, on whether a mind can exist without a body, on whether a posthuman metaphysics is even possible.

Complicating the matter, often behind the scenes, actual science and technology provide new insights, techniques, and products that look little like what we see in SF but are no less amazing. For example, Juliano Pinto, a paraplegic, used an exoskeleton to kick a ball at the 2014 World Cup in Brazil. Advances in gene therapy, nanotechnology, 3D printing, robotics, etc., all occur with enough impact that, in the least, imaginations are spurred to think new fantasy worlds into being, regardless of their potentials for becoming real. EP reflects both the hopes and fears of such SF fantasies. In this sense, it falls within the discourse of transhumanism and its hopes for the posthuman. But it is a game, and, as such, should be understood as one because its gametexts provide the basis for the realized worlds they create.

Chapter 3

Dungeons and Dragons' Multiverse

Of seminal importance for *Dread Trident* is the examination of complex realized worlds and how they are detailed in archives of gametexts. Dungeons and Dragons (D&D) occupies an important place as one of the most popular and under-theorized realized fantasy worlds created, a stellar example of the modern fantastic in its discursive yet engineered mode. For the last forty years, numerous authors, players, game-masters, novelists, film makers, etc. have expanded the multiverse of D&D. It began in the early 1970s as an attempt to alter wargaming with fantasy elements, along with a touch of role-playing. By the early 1980s, D&D was a worldwide phenomenon, exploding in the U.S. with such vigor it entered the culture war as a misunderstood target of conservatives. Its resurgent popularity in the last decade has reinvigorated the TRPG industry, as well as helped spawn a number of other media from live twitch streams to game play in front of audiences.

What makes D&D interesting for *Dread Trident* is its massive amount and different types of gametexts and tools representative of the modern fantastic: source-books, novels, adventures, manuals, maps, game journals, etc., especially fan-created content dispersed by the Internet, as well as a variety of gametools, from iconic figurines and dice, to battlemats and tabletop settings props. The amount of textual content alone is far beyond any one scholar to absorb in a lifetime, especially if one considers the amount of fan-generated content. It outstrips even that of Star Wars, maybe only rivaled by the Marvel universe. D&D has a player base that has been actively creating content in its imaginative universe to fuel shared experiences within TRPG settings. Fan fiction and films abound for the most popular imaginary universes, but D&D has provided a consistent archive of material for the creation and experience of its realized worlds, what it calls the campaign settings of its multiverse. Players create or alter these to participate in the realized worlds, rather than simply consume them.

This chapter covers D&D's expansive multiverse through a historical account of D&D as a realized fantasy TRPG. It examines key gametexts to demonstrate how complexification has been added through the editions, as well as the need for harmonization so that they form a cohesive playing field. The development of this multiverse cosmology reveals how a shared, imaginary world becomes realized through the use of official and fan-created material as mechanisms of expansion. This chapter details a few of the most popular campaign settings, some of which foregrounded its initial generic setting, such as Greyhawk, while others, such as Planescape, revealed how a fantasy setting can resist clichés and tropes found in high-fantasy. This chapter focuses on the Forgotten Realms (D&D's current default setting) because of its publishing history and its use of seminal harmonization elements, such as a 'godswar' and its 'grand' history to further both its narrative and marketing needs within a comprehensive whole. This chapter's history of D&D gametexts details how the 'planes' of the multiverse also act as harmonizing mechanisms for the settings of Greyhawk, Ravenloft, Krynn, Spelljammer, Planescape, etc. With harmonization, all the campaign settings of D&D, back to its earliest, form this grand multiverse that allows players to use any published material.

Knit together, these analog gametexts and tools function in the same way as Eclipse Phase's (EP) wild posthuman imaginings do for that SF game. Both the high-fantasy inspired D&D and the hard-SF EP offer frameworks for the creations of subjectivities within fantastic realized spaces that occur at tables during games. Genre distinctions appear when juxtaposing D&D and EP, yet what binds these case studies is a focus on experiential play that occurs within their particular imaginary, realized worlds. With such distinctive genre elements that range from disembodied information or sentient non-human synthetic creatures to dragons, demons, devils, aberrations, and a host of other mythic creatures, embodied experiences flourish without genre prejudice, a welcome surprise in our increasingly digitized lives.

This chapter ends with a comment on the rise of digital streams of tabletop games as a new form of entertainment within the modern fantastic that continues to expand the imaginary archive of this intricately textured realized world beyond those found printed in sourcebooks. We increasingly see that the traditional literary mode of working through words on pages must contend with a variety of different digital media that encourages play across a wide spectrum. Watching the actual play of recorded sessions expands the archive of gametexts, as well as the type of consumption. In this curious way, such new forms demonstrate how the modern fantastic is not limited to its traditional literary mode.

D&D and Fantasy Gametexts

The most famous TRPG, Dungeons and Dragons (D&D), is also one of the modern fantastic's most influential yet overlooked realized worlds. Far beyond those shared universes rooted in fiction, D&D's fundamental gameplay elements demand that players engage the materials beyond reading or viewing.[1] What is evident, though, when analyzing how gametexts function in the creation of realized worlds, is that as their numbers grow so do the complexities of their realized worlds. D&D's combined shared universes, its *multiverse*, more than any other TRPG's, provide years of shared world creation ripe for scholarly investigation.

The most comprehensive and extensive archive of gametexts can be found in the forty-year development of this single game that has developed over several editions. D&D has been through multiple revisions to its rule-sets, and has accrued an immense amount of material that describes its imaginary worlds—what it calls campaign settings, in which gameplay occurs. The current developers of the game, Wizards of the Coast (WotC) published D&D's fifth edition (5e) in 2014. It is the latest version that began when Gary Gygax and Dave Arneson published an original box set in 1974. It has evolved from a war-game to a flexible role-playing system through its successive editions, the game changing in significant degrees, while retaining core aspects that have been with it from the beginning. It has weathered cultural criticisms that have 'demonized' it as a tool of Satan worshipers and that have relegated it to the juvenile fantasies of prepubescent boys or super nerds.

Negative association with earlier niche 'nerd' culture have reversed. 5e has become inclusive in its reach of players, after years of focusing on a white, male demographic. The latest edition is constructed as an inclusive environment for fantasy role-playing that includes options for players to choose genderless characters.[2] At its simplest, the game system now encourages different types of persons to form a party not just to combat evil in the form of monstrous creatures, tyrants, demons and devils, cultists, elementals, villains, etc., but to engage in any number of

---

[1] Of course, simplifying these three activities to flat playing, reading, viewing fails to describe their reach. Reading is not passive. It allows for the construction of subjectivities based on engagement with a text, as does viewing. And play isn't simply daydreaming or frivolity.

[2] "You don't need to be confined to binary notions of sex and gender [...] you could also play a female character who presents herself as a man, a man who feels trapped in a female body, or a bearded female dwarf who hates being mistaken for a male. Likewise, your character's sexual orientation is for you to decide" (Wizards RPG Team 2014a, 121).

adventure scenarios. In mature play, dice are rolled but sometimes rarely, players with well-detailed characters engage in complex role-playing scenarios, and difference is understood to be nuanced and interesting. In less complex play, the world of pulp fantasy is embraced with vigor—in many cases, expected frivolity and fun the defining factor.

The game's core appeal is still one of exploration, role-playing, and combat, as states one of its primary gametexts, the *Player's Handbook* (PHB) (2014).[3] These three pillars have been with the game from the beginning, and while its gametexts have been updated through the editions, the rules expanding, sometimes changing drastically; often retaining much that went before, the game has grown to contain within its complete shared multiverse an insurmountable amount of official and unofficial material.

A key part of this literary complexity is the proliferation of gametexts created via digital means and distributed through the Internet. From its beginnings, a gaming community was always central for the game's success. Digital versions called multi-user dungeons (MUDs) have existed since the 1970s, as well as bulletin boards used to develop like-minded communities. However, prior to the browser revolution of the early 1990s, the amount of actual gametexts pales in comparison to what can now be found.[4] Fan-generated material from campaign journals to 'homebrew' rules to adventures have been with the game from the beginning—not to mention fan-fiction, artwork, forum discussions, magazine articles, etc.

With the PDF publishing revolution and the *Kickstarter.com* platform, amateur game developers have mechanisms for producing material that generates income, if not a profit. With the latest content-generating mechanism, WotC's *DMsGuild.com*, fans can sell their own D&D creations, thus increasing exponentially the content for D&D's multiverse. How has such a game generated such a wide impact? A look at its historiography reveals how the modern fantastic's realized worlds function as both analog and digital elements. Imaginative world creation combined with a dynamic rule-set has structured gameplay. In the beginning of the wargaming/TRPG industry, though, world building had yet to emerge as it has today.

As both Shannon Appelcline and Jon Peterson have noted, the path to popular-cultural penetration began when the wargaming industry

---

[3] See Wizards RPG Team 2014a, 8.
[4] With today's democratization of information via the Internet, one can attempt to create an archive, as I have of digital content of just official type-set published materials. This is quite a task. It is only a small percentage of the massive whole.

of the 1950s combined with the Tolkien phenomenon and fan-created scenarios of the 1960s to form a new type of gameplay in the 1970s: the fantasy role-playing game. TRPGs are a unique form of simulation-and-narrative text-based games, peaking in the U.S.A. in the early to mid-1980s with the success of TSR's D&D and since then expanding and collapsing at different times. D&D had been published in a variety of forms since 1974, only in the critical year of 1977 forming into the two versions of the game that would dominate the 1980s: Basic and Advanced.[5]

At this point, the epic fantasy of J.R.R. Tolkien found its first popular imitation with Terry Brooks's far-future *The Sword of Shannara* (1977), and a host of others soon to follow in the 1980s. A curious coincidence in publication dates also sees John Eric Holmes's version of the *Dungeons and Dragons Basic Set* (1977), as well as the first offering of the *Advanced Dungeons and Dragons* books, the *Monster Manual* (1977), both appearing in the same year as George Lucas's groundbreaking *Star Wars* (1977), a film that would thrust science-fantasy into the public imagination and create an immersive story world through merchandising of licensed products. Ultimately, these gametexts comprise milestones in the modern fantastic's move toward the creation of sophisticated realized worlds.

D&D is as expansive as is the human imagination, with a system ready to deploy its mechanisms on behalf of any fantasy. When Gygax and Arneson first collaborated on creating the new type of wargame that would become D&D, they called it "The Fantasy Game" (Appelcline 2015, 12). D&D itself was never stable. In the beginning, original D&D was open to hybrid science fantasy, comparable to Star Wars. Arneson's adventure, "The Temple of the Frog," included "battle armor, a teleporter, and even a scout craft" (Appelcline 2015, 20). One of the early adventure modules for AD&D, *Expedition to the Barrier Peaks* (1981) presents a buried spaceship that functions as a dungeon.

Furthermore, D&D performed a bridging role between these gonzo fantasy scenarios and the sober business world. *The Dragon* magazine became the first professional magazine dedicated to fantasy and science fiction games (Appelcline 2015, 23), and D&D's science-fantasy influence is clearly admitted in the "'Appendix N' of the *AD&D Dungeon Masters Guide* (1979)" (Appelcline 2015, 349), where references are made to the works of fantasists such as E.R. Burroughs, Lin Carter, L. Sprague

---

[5] While the *Monster Manual* was published in 1977, the other two books that comprise the Advanced game were published in the next two years, the *Player's Handbook* (1978) and the *Dungeon Master's Guide* (1979).

de Camp, August Derleth, Lord Dunsany, R.E. Howard, Fritz Leiber, A. Merritt, Michael Moorcock, Tolkien, Jack Vance, and Roger Zelazny (Gygax 1979b, 224). The modern fantastic leans on the classic fantastic to deliver.

While D&D would become famous as a refined example of sword-and-sorcery tabletop role-playing, the industry would expand into all major publishing genres, hybridizing, fragmenting into a variety of systems and gaming styles. Science-fantasy, though, would prove to be a favorite of later games interested in dragons and spaceships, demons and detectives, broadswords and handguns. For example, Chaosium's groundbreaking publication of *Call of Cthulhu* (1981) demonstrated how a change in focus from sword-and-sorcery and mythic fantasy, as well as from space-opera SF to science-fantasy horror, changed both the mechanics and tone of a game from dungeon crawling, killing monsters, and gaining loot to investigating cosmic horrors. Such imaginative blending of supposed opposite science-fantasy tropes also defined later gametexts like *Shadowrun* (1989) and *Rifts* (1990). These would harness the genre mechanisms of both magic and science to enhance their game worlds, as well as the player and GM imaginative possibilities. Interestingly, two of the most recent popular TRPGs—Monte Cook's Numenera and, along with Bruce Cordell, The Strange—both utilize a science-fantasy approach.

A look at some of the most content-rich fantasy D&D campaign settings reveals an incredibly detailed series of imaginative realized worlds that far exceed those of any one writer, even Tolkien. Yet, early campaign settings of D&D were abstract and only managed a few sketches and brief descriptions.[6] Gygax's company, TSR, showed an ability to expand from its initial world, Greyhawk, with the publication of *Ravenloft* (1983), an example of a mixed-genre adventure, this one fantasy and horror, as well as an adventure that focused on problem solving instead of simple dungeon delving. This adventure module would, itself, inspire an entire setting later. The Dragonlance series of adventures of the 1980s are examples of the turn toward in-game narrative sophistication already seen with Ravenloft, not to mention the attention paid both to its campaign setting and other product tie-ins, like the popular novels by Margaret Weis and Tracy Hickman.

Dragonlance's more cohesive approach to its campaign setting and adventures, though, were later superseded by the Forgotten Realms.

---

[6] A notable exception at the time was M.A.R. Barker's Tékumel, from *Empire of the Petal Throne* (1975), a more socially and culturally detailed game world at the time.

In particular, the *Forgotten Realms Campaign Setting* (1987) "was the first TSR setting that was truly and exhaustively detailed—thanks to a line of gametexts, rather than just adventures" (Appelcline 2015, 73). TSR would eventually release other detailed campaign settings: e.g., Spelljammer, Ravenloft, Dark Sun, Al-Qadim, Planescape, Eberron, Birthright, Mystara, etc., a trend that now defines the industry with 5e's multiverse combining all of these into one grand fictional universe.

D&D's Multiverse

D&D's widest imaginary world, the cosmology of its multiverse, has proven to be flexible yet sturdy enough to contain all of its intellectual property in a harmonious whole. 5e's *PHB* (2014) and *Dungeon Master's Guide* (DMG) (2014) provide the framework, the former offering critical gameplay information, while the latter develops the details. In 5e's DMG, an entire chapter is dedicated to 'Creating a Multiverse' with an understanding that its own cosmological historiography is complex and that players may have differing preferences. One may want a world with high magic and powerful, almost superhero-like characters; another may want a world of low magic with a quest for a single enchanted item; another, a world of commoners struggling to survive the night. All three of these scenarios are predicated on different cosmologies, or ways divine beings and magic work.

We are told, "Sages have constructed a few such theoretical models to make sense of the jumble of planes, particularly the Outer Planes. The three most common are the Great Wheel, the World Tree, and the World Axis" (Wizards RPG Team 2014b, 43–4). The Great Wheel, though, is the default cosmological system detailed in the PHB:

> Incredibly vast is the cosmos of the Dungeons and Dragons game, which teems with a multitude of worlds as well as myriad alternate dimensions of reality, called the planes of existence. It encompasses every world where Dungeon Masters run their adventures. [...] All the worlds of D&D exist within the Material Plane. [...] The best-known worlds in the multiverse are the ones that have been published as official campaign settings for the D&D game over the years—Greyhawk, Blackmoor, Dragonlance, the Forgotten Realms, Mystara, Birthright, Dark Sun, and Eberron, among others. [...] But if your campaign takes place on one of these worlds, it belongs to your DM—you might imagine it as one of thousands of parallel versions of the world, which might

diverge wildly from the published version. (Wizards RPG Team 2014a, 300)

This last idea, that the dungeon-master's (DM) version of the published settings is a unique world, speaks to how realized worlds emerge, each one a reflection of the individuals who engage it through play. This flexibility is required because the entire cosmos of the game is hackable by DMs and players. Any homebrew—or custom-built—setting can fit into the cosmology.

D&D's shared multiverse today consists of a series of campaign settings/worlds in which the game can be played. At first, though, the shared universe was much more manageable. The Basic version of the game offered the original 'Known World' of Mystara and for the Advanced game (AD&D), Gygax's Greyhawk. With the transmedial success of fiction in the 1980s, Krynn (the Dragonlance novels' setting) saw traction as TSR developed a variety of settings-related materials flexible enough to handle the needs of the publishers. Just these three settings, alone, complexified the choices for players. They had to juggle different places, pantheons, heroes, legends, lore, etc. Later came Barovia, the Gothic-inspired demi-plane world of Ravenloft and the sun-scorched world of Dark Sun, Athas. With the publication of the second edition (2e) version of AD&D, more and more appeared. The multiverse of 2e detailed varying ways to understand the supernatural worlds beyond the material planes of each campaign setting. TSR even created a successful setting, Spelljammer, that allowed for space travel between the settings (see below).

When Gygax lost control of TSR in 1985,[7] the company saw an opportunity to move beyond Greyhawk and introduce a new default setting. D&D fan and DM Ed Greenwood created his own fantasy world in 1968 as a setting for fiction, the Forgotten Realms (FR). He also developed it for running D&D games. He would soon start publishing articles in *Dragon* magazine,[8] beginning in #30 (1979), where he introduced material from the FR. From the beginning, Greenwood created his world with the idea of a multiverse in mind:

> The "Forgotten Realms" derive their name from the fictitious fact upon which play in my campaign is based: that a multiverse exists, of countless parallel co-existing Prime Material Planes (including

[7] For a succinct account, see Peterson 2014.
[8] The publication was originally titled *The Dragon*; its first issue appeared in 1976.

the world presented herein, our own modern "Earth," and any other fantasy settings a DM may wish to incorporate in play), all related to the Known Planes of Existence presented in the AD&D system. Travel betwixt these planes was once far more common than is the case now (when few know the means of reaching other worlds, or even believe in the existence of such fanciful places); hence, the Realms have been "forgotten" by beings of Earth. (Greenwood and Grubb 1987, 4)

When TSR presented the idea to find a new default setting, game-designer Jeff Grubb suggested Greenwood's FR. The FR became the official setting for D&D products in 1987. At the same time, they published a novel in the FR, Douglas Niles's *Darkwalker on Moonshae* (1987), instituting a dynamic that would remain to this today in which its fiction often drives its setting (see the Avatar Series below as an example). A year later, R.A. Salvatore's popular Drizzt series of novels began with *The Crystal Shard* (1988), a book that introduced the FR's Underdark and its intrepid drow adventurer to fans.

Both official gametexts and novels educate players in increments to the FR through 'lore,' the history of a setting. Organizing all setting information from the FR's inception has proven to be beyond most players' time or abilities. This is no surprise because the FR is a shared universe, one in which Greenwood is the creative inspiration, but in which many individuals have added their ideas. The most powerful part of this dynamic has been the tension between the publication of core gametexts for the different versions of the game and the novels, which have expanded the lore. Harmonizing these is a challenge, as any shared universe of this complexity demonstrates.

With D&D, the versions of the core game that act as rule-sets for the different campaign settings like FR have seven official iterations. The original D&D was published in 1974.[9] Soon after, the first edition (1e) of AD&D (1977)[10] saw publication alongside a very popular Basic version of the game (1977), a simplified version marketed to younger players, and 1e maintained its sovereignty for twelve years, the longest stretch, until the publication of the second edition (2e) of AD&D in 1989. This version remained similar to the prior version, its revision goals to clarify rules, as well as to appease its critics after years of attacks in a

---

[9] This is often referred to as ODD. The other versions are 1e, 2e, 3e, 4e, 5e, plus Basic.
[10] Oddly, the AD&D's *Monster Manual* (1977) was published first. The *PHB* wasn't published until 1978.

cultural war that would see assassins disappear as well as demons and devils renamed to tanar'ri and baatezu.

In 1997, WotC bought TSR and soon offered a third edition (3e) in 2000. Version 3e quickly became 3.5e in 2003, with an open-source release, Pathfinder, finding much popularity, some players considering it 3.75e. A fourth edition (4e) soon followed in 2008. With a recognition that they had lost market control, as well as the confidence of many fans, WotC ran through a series of play tests as 'D&D Next' in the creation of the latest version. Edition 5e was released in 2014 and regained market control of D&D from Pathfinder.[11] An entire book could be written on the differences in versions and how these have been reviewed and accepted by fans and professionals. My interest, though, is in how another aspect of the game, its fantasy realized worlds, emerged while these versions were being developed.

The Planes

The planes of the multiverse, how magic works, how the gods function all receive varied treatments in the different settings. Over the course of D&D's publication history, these settings and their particular elements have emerged for a variety of reasons: some creative, some financial, some legal. The initial basic cosmology of AD&D was still quite vague in many instances, even though articles addressing aspects had appeared in *The Dragon*. As early as 1977, Gygax wrote an article explaining "for game purposes the DM is to assume the existence of an infinite number of co-existing planes" (*Dragon Magazine* 1977, 4). Soon after, in "Appendix IV: Known Planes of Existence" to the first *AD&D PHB* (1978), an attempt was made to provide the roughest of frameworks that would remain with the game to the present time. It expands on *The Dragon* information, presenting a visual representation of the Great Wheel Cosmology.

The need to address increased complexity of the game's various settings emerged quickly in the history of D&D. A fitting example can be seen, as early as 1979, after the arrival of AD&D, when Gygax wrote in *The Dragon* (#32) of the need to detail the planes. This may have been in response to another *The Dragon* (#28) article, written a few months earlier, that delves into the lore of imaginary devils, Satan, and the rise

---

[11] The newest version has been deemed a success, if one looks at the core source-books' standing in Amazon's lists or checks conversations in TRPG gaming forums such as *ENWorld.org*.

of Asmodeus, a supreme fiend who has lasted until the current edition as the ruler of D&D's version of Hell.

Even though this material is meant to be taken with a degree of humor and irony (the editor's note from T.J. Kask even addressing how gamers are viewed as strange and the fact they often revel in this), U.S. popular culture in the late 1970s was full of occult iconography often misunderstood by the mainstream. Considering this phenomenon now, music acts such as Alice Cooper or Black Sabbath, we see the contrived and comical theater behind the imagery. The fear in some conservative circles in the U.S.A. of Satanism demonstrates a ludicrous misprision, especially after so many of these elements have been co-opted, repackaged, and tamed within popular culture. Alice Cooper, Ozzy Osbourne, and Gene Simmons of KISS all have reality TV shows. AC/DC's "Back in Black" has been used in a Wal-Mart commercial. Threats of 'Satanic' cults are now understood to be isolated incidents of overblown fear-mongering. D&D is no more pernicious than Monopoly. However, at the time, TSR had yet to experience the backlash that would come in the 1980s. For lead creative thinker Gygax, detailing the planes was important, and those of the devils necessary. He also recognized the cosmological need of "Astral, Ethereal, and Elemental planes" (Gygax 1979a, 12) to harmonize the non-material worlds that housed such creatures.

Not long after, Greenwood wrote an important article, "Down-to-Earth Divinity: One DM's Design for a Mixed and Matched Mythos" (*Dragon* #54), that inadvertently challenged an earlier article by Craig Bakey where Bakey states: "it should be emphasized that the old gods are meant as background and as such have no real substance in the D&D universe" (Bakey 1979, 4). Abstractions over how to conceptualize old gods vs. new gods allowed Greenwood to counter Bakey with an approach that humanized deities by limiting their power so that they and their fates are agents of free will, like the characters, although immensely more powerful yet not omnipotent.

This humanization suggests a familiarity behind these flawed deities, one we recognize that developed through Western culture's Hellenic heritage via Greece and Rome. It also suggests a Hebraic conception of divinity framing these humanized instances, this one abstracted and universal. Greenwood leaves this "higher force" as a "Great Mystery" (Greenwood 1981, 7), later to be named Ao. He also mentions how to utilize the more humanized deities yet do so in a way that maintains the importance of the players' characters. "Another mechanism for keeping things under control is the 'Godswar.' This concept was also a justification to explain the changeover of a campaign moving from D&D rules to AD&D" (Greenwood 1981, 7). As early as October of 1981, these two primary aspects of this pantheon emerge in a dynamic that would define how D&D's most popular setting, the FR, was constructed: (1) the gods are distant—thus, removed from affecting the player characters in game, and (2) a godswar mechanism explains the complexity of the campaign setting and justifies changes wrought by new editions.

Greenwood's early 1981 *Dragon* article provides a list of deities that will become standard for the later, official FR campaign setting. His use of the godswar emerged in the creation of a pantheon in which he "found it expedient to have overlapping portfolios for the gods" (Greenwood 1981, 9). Why? "This allows strife among various priesthoods as the prominence of the gods within a community or society changes" (9). Greenwood follows the basic approach of TSR and AD&D that the gods themselves should rarely interact with the players' characters. The obvious reason is that these gods are so much more powerful and, thus, their servants should interact with characters. Yet, as the publication history shows, especially how it relates to fiction, the gods of the FR become interesting themselves as non-player characters (NPCs).

To make these humanized gods accessible, they became physical avatars of their primary characteristics. This scenario is fictionalized in a specially detailed godswar dramatized in The Avatar Trilogy (1989).[12] A key character in this narrative, a mortal thief named Cyric, ascends to godhood, becoming the god of strife. This reversal of deifying a mortal rather than humanizing a god reflects the game-focused impulse Greenwood detailed as an inspiration for how his pantheons work and how his campaign functioned: a human thief can ascend to the divine. This tension between humanized divinity and deified humanity is the fundamental bedrock of the FR campaign setting, as it develops into AD&D 2e (see below). Before such developments emerged in the fictionalization of a godswar, Greenwood's article listed all of the major deities, as well as provided descriptions that would become standard in the broader D&D multiverse.[13]

Greenwood also wrote a two-part article in *Dragon* (#75 and #76) that detailed his version of the Nine Hells, two documents sharply in

---

[12] Two more novels were added. *The Avatar Series* now also contains *Prince of Lies* (1993) and *Crucible: The Trial of Cyric the Mad* (1998).

[13] Of note is Greenwood's admission that Tempus, the god of war, receives the most detailed treatment for a game such as AD&D being combat driven, while the others have briefer descriptions. Most of the key deities who will later figure into the FR's godswar are here. For example, Bane is labeled the "big baddie" (Greenwood 1981, 52). Mystra, Bhaal, Myrkul, etc., all receive enough treatment to suffice at this early stage, while later editions detail them in a much more rounded manner.

contrast with the earlier one by Bakey and its emphasis on distant deities.[14] Greenwood mined disparate material from AD&D and shaped it into the cosmology for the FR, going so far as to note that his god of darkness, Bane, works in conjunction with lawful arch-devils like Asmodeus. Developing here in the thinking of Greenwood was a comprehensive use of the various published AD&D materials in the creation of the FR's cosmology. An instinct for harmonization can be seen as early as the second part of this article (August 1983) wherein Greenwood detailed how Asmodeus's palace in the Nine Hells contains a magical portal/gate that connects all the planes. In fact, from the prime material plane, where characters experience their adventures, one can travel directly to the Nine Hells. Greenwood, thus, provided an adventure mechanism for DMs to allow interested players a method to send their characters into the hells, if need be, as well as provided an exit. This gameplay mechanic also signaled a broader type of thinking to harmonize the bulk of the published gametexts and gameworlds. Of course, with Greenwood relinquishing his control of the FR, such harmonization became a more difficult problem to solve.

At first, the idea of a multiverse received only intermittent comment in *Dragon*, working like an understood, if less-than-thoroughly detailed framework. Later, attempts were made to harmonize the various elements that had been published by coloring AD&D's cosmology in increased detail, a canvas that would stretch across numerous campaign settings. For example, like Greenwood's portal to the hells, the World Serpent Inn featured prominently in a 1e multi-adventure, *Tales of the Outer Planes* (1988). It served as a literal meeting place for characters to jaunt into the different planes. This mechanism from *Tales of the Outer Planes* would also emerge as a 3e web enhancement (2001), with a detailed explication, and later feature in a *Dragon* (#351) article (2007).[15]

D&D's cosmology was already detailed enough to suggest that these planes were navigable. This mechanism of an inn through which player-characters may jaunt to the differing campaign worlds emerged again in 5e, with the publication of *Tales from the Yawning Portal* (2017). This adventure gametext combines several iconic, previously published adventures from earlier editions. They have been reworked for the 5e rule-set, and a brief introduction provides a narrative framework.

---

[14] See "The Nine Hells, Part I: From Avernus through Stygia," in issue #75, and "The Nine Hells, Part 2: From Malboge through Nessus," in the following issue.

[15] For a direct link to the PDF, see Grubb 2018. For the article, "The World Serpent Inn," see Boyd 2007.

Characters can visit the popular FR town of Waterdeep, where an inn, the Yawning Portal, sits atop the ruins of a wizard's tower. An open, dry well drops into a massive dungeon, Undermountain, beneath the city of Waterdeep. "Adventurers from across Faerûn, and even from elsewhere in the great span of the multiverse visit the Yawning Portal to exchange knowledge about Undermountain and other dungeons" (Wizards RPG Team 2017, 6). A DM now has a place to begin any journey into the planes or to the dungeons of any parallel material plane. The Yawning Portal will provide the clues, guides, quests, etc., to begin the journey.

Making the imaginative leap from thinking about a material realm (plane) and all its concordant 'spirit' planes leads into thinking of many prime material planes, all of which share a common cosmology. But before this grand schema could emerge, detailing such a cosmology in a gametext needed publication. A year before *Tales of the Outer Planes* (1988), TSR released the *Manual of the Planes* (1987), the same year the FR 'grey box' was released. Project leader and designer Jeff Grubb wrote that "the term 'the planes' encompasses all the alternate levels of reality that may be encountered" (1987, 5), a recognition that D&D had grown beyond any one setting. It also reveals a shift in the historical locations where the game can be played (i.e., not just in the here and now of the material world of the campaign setting but faraway places whence come mysterious beings, angels and devils, spirits and fairies, etc.).

The attempt to manage this idea saw Grubb detail the schematization of the planes' requisite five areas: the Prime Material, the Ethereal, the Astral, the Inner, and the Outer planes. This basic structure is still used in 5e, with some changes that provide minor rearrangements and clarifications, such as the renaming of Olympus to Arborea in the Outer Planes, as well detailing the additions of the Prime Material planes' 'echoes,' the Feywild (the land of fairy) and Shadowfell (the land of shadow and darkness).[16] Grubb's approach demonstrated a need to codify, while still remaining flexible, that has remained as a primary aim of the latest edition.

Known World/Mystara

An examination of the most popular D&D campaign settings reveals their differences, as well as provides reasons for the current edition's approach to harmonization. The first supplements published for the original D&D

---

[16] See 5e's *DMG*, pp. 49–52.

game, *Greyhawk: Supplement 1* (1975) and *Blackmoor: Supplement 2* (1975), provided expanded rules with cursory setting information. The wider universe was still undefined.

Greyhawk was Gygax's own personal setting, while Blackmoor was Arneson's. Blackmoor's gametext contained an adventure, "The Temple of the Frog," with its Lake Gloomey, the Keepers of the Frog, and Stephen the Rock.[17] From the beginning, a flexible cosmology was imagined, even if at this point it was unstructured. While Greyhawk found traction because of Gygax's position in TSR, Blackmoor would find itself subsumed within the broader frame of what was called the 'Known World.'

After the original publication of D&D and its supplements, D&D became two different yet similar games for most of its history: Basic and the AD&D versions. The default settings for both also differed. The Known World for the Basic rule-set was a wide canvas that allowed TSR years of game development in which they developed this setting in piecemeal fashion. The first adventure modules for Basic, *B1: In Search of the Unknown* (1979) and *B2: Keep on the Borderlands* (1979), provided generic settings that were later placed within the Known World. By the time, *X1: The Isle of Dread* (1981) was published, many of the major locations were sketched, such as Alfheim, the Grand Duchy of Karameikos, the Kingdom of Ierendi, and the Empire of Thyatis. Eventually, these places of the Known World became Mystara.

Just as Blackmoor was incorporated into the Known World, Mystara was reworked into the broader multiverse. By the time the Basic rule-set was released as a single gametext, the *Dungeons and Dragons: Rules Cyclopedia* (1991), the setting was described in detail in an appendix dedicated to the game world.[18] Along with a plethora of information found in the Gazetters series, and the expansion of the setting into AD&D 2e and 3e, the Known World of the Basic game functioned as a realized fantasy world often ignored by any serious examination into fictional fantasy universes, even though it served a critical function in the experiences of many game players first introduced to D&D.

[17] "This fellow is not from the world of Blackmoor at all, but rather he is an intelligent humanoid from another world/dimension" (Arneson 1975, 24).
[18] See the comprehensive sourcebook for Basic (Allston 1992, 6). Blackmoor, Mystara, and the Known World are all mentioned together in a single paragraph.

Greyhawk

The codification of materials created by early D&D content creators like Gygax, Arneson, Tom Moldvay, and others often began in these designers' home games before being presented as campaign settings for D&D. As with Basic, the AD&D default setting developed as a patchwork that allowed players to stitch together many of the disparate parts of the game. A settings-jaunting mechanism was needed because the canvas of possible game worlds had grown over the years. Along with edition and rule changes, the cosmologies often conflicted, while core elements remained consistent.

Like Blackmoor, Greyhawk material was light on actual polished setting description, a characteristic that remained common until later publications. Greyhawk would have to wait until *The World of Greyhawk* (1980) and a subsequent boxed set released in 1983. A brief account can be found of the history of Oerth, the world of Greyhawk, where we learn about the Battle of Emridy Meadows, the Village of Hommlet, and the conflict with the Temple of Elemental Evil.[19] Earlier, the adventure module, *The Village of Hommlet* (1979) had already detailed many of the specifics. A pattern emerged at this time in which disparate information published in adventures or magazine articles found its way into an official gametext as canonical lore. In this case, such lore would re-emerge many times, later becoming part of the 'supermodule,' *The Temple of Elemental Evil* (1985) and the *Return to the Temple of Elemental Evil* (2001). Novels and computer games would follow, as well, with 5e's Elemental Evil storyline. WotC's designers repurposed this large adventure moved from Greyhawk to the FR, the *Princes of the Apocalypse* (2015), repurposing the old material for 5e, updating it, changing it where necessary, but retaining much of the core elements.

Ravenloft

The cosmologies of the numerous other campaign settings that emerged after Greyhawk are varied, even though they would be subsumed under 5e's umbrella concept of the multiverse. The pulp Hollywood, Gothic-inspired Ravenloft campaign setting, found in the core gametext *Ravenloft: Realm of Terror* (1990) pays homage to its "Gothic Roots," where we learn that "Castle Ravenloft lies deep within the ethereal plane, in a demiplane of dread and desire" (Nesmith and Hayday 1990, 8). The

---

[19] See Gygax 1980, 6–7.

Ethereal Plane functions as an anomaly where any stray setting can find a home. The flexibility of Ravenloft's 'demi-plane' is described in the *Realm of Terror* (1990) as a shifting, expanding, piece of solid physicality in the Ethereal Plane.[20]

Players are free to imagine a world unto itself, or, if they choose, connect it to the core world they use for their gaming. The gametext even provides information on how the mist, a mechanism for entering the world of Ravenloft, Barovia, connects to other campaign settings, such as Greyhawk, the FR, Kara-Tur, and Krynn. This development beyond the limited cosmological material in the original 1e module (an adventure without a larger setting), *Ravenloft* (1983), exemplifies how the designers stitched worlds from varying sources into a cohesive whole. Ravenloft would be detailed in numerous publications, revisited in 3e and 4e, and find a home as a non-FR 5e adventure in the *Curse of Strahd* (2016).

Krynn

Another popular world in the D&D multiverse, that of Dragonlance's Krynn, as well as the later-described Taladas, found a different path to popularity from Ravenloft. Where Ravenloft began as an adventure module, then developed into a detailed campaign setting, the Dragonlance materials began as a story in the minds of its creators. This story would see the creation of four adventures, starting with *Dragons of Despair* (1984), published in the same year as a novel *Dragons of Autumn Twilight* (1984). This novel became the first three of a series that spawned a massive production of fiction with nearly 200 published by 2012 (E. James and Mendlesohn 2012, 76).

Laura and Tracy Hickman wrote the first Ravenloft adventure (as well as others for TSR) and later joined with TSR book-editor Margaret Weis to write the first novel together. This attempt at transmedial publishing proved profitable for the gaming company, the trilogy spawning D&D's most popular early shared universes, this one with epic heroes and villains in a cohesive story.[21] What followed in the subsequent articles, gametexts, novels, etc., was a new world that fit into the wider AD&D

---

[20] "It is usually smaller than realms in the prime material plane, such as Krynn and the Forgotten Realms, but unlike them Ravenloft has no fixed size" (Nesmith and Hayday 1990, 9).

[21] "From the first scenes at the Inn of the Last Home to the terrible confrontation at the climax of the series, the story was plotted and out-lined before any other work was done" (Hickman qtd. in *Dragon Magazine* 1984, 45).

multiverse (i.e., a material plane with inner and outer planes, as well as demi-planes and what it calls the Grey, its own terminology for a type of transitive plane that the larger multiverse would see contain the Ethereal, Astral, Shadow planes, etc.).

Spelljammer

A unique gameworld within the D&D multiverse was published in the *Spelljammer: AD&D Adventures in Space* (1989) gametext. Like the mechanism of the World Serpent Inn, this entire campaign setting was designed around the concept of unifying the larger AD&D multiverse. It provided a D&D-meets-Jules-Verne, meets-the-Era-of-High-Sails-in-Space setting. It added a dash of medieval Ptolemaic Cosmological flavoring replete with phlogiston and crystal spheres, where players found a game framework with open ships that sailed through space via magic. The cosmology allowed travel between the different settings, an appendix even providing distances between the planets within the settings of Dragonlance, Greyhawk, and the FR.[22] Even Earth is detailed, suggesting that our own mundane world is part of this larger multiverse, if (sadly) bereft of its magic.

Some problems with harmonization occurred. Rather than Earth being the most inaccessible within the D&D multiverse, the Dark Sun campaign setting of Athas was designed to be isolated. It is a sun-blasted, post-apocalyptic world in which metal and water are scarce. The typical D&D gods are gone. Magic is a destructive force that defiles the land. Elves and halflings are unrecognizable. Spelljammer designers explained that "no spelljammer travels its [Athas's] skies; no ancient tome tells of the routes to its crystal sphere. Whether it is unreachable by spelljammer or merely so far from these worlds that any journey would take lifetimes is unknown" (Scott 1992, 13). Likewise, we are also told that Ravenloft, a demi-plane, is inaccessible, another admission that reflected the design constraints of a setting (Ravenloft's Barovia) into which you can wander but never leave. Spelljammer, though, solved more problems than it created with these settings—spanning ships designed as blatant science fantasy.

[22] See Grubb 1989, 90–1.

Planescape

The most complex example of the multiverse created during the
varieties of 2e's AD&D settings came with the publication of the
Planescape Campaign Setting (1994). A more nuanced and sophisticated
attempt at harmonization, Planescape provided an alternate way to
travel between the planes than Spelljammer's science-fantasy-oriented
approach. Planescape's sophistication marked it as D&D's answer to its
own simplistic medieval-European-inspired fantasy settings, a critique
often labeled at D&D's default settings as clichéd.

Planescape channeled the Weird before China Miéville brought the
'new weird' genre into focus with the publication of *Perdido Street Station*
(2000) and before it became the intellectual and creative ancestor of both
the video game *Planescape: Torment* (1999) and its successor, *Torment: Tides
of Numenera* (2017).[23] It also solidified the Great Wheel cosmology that
began in 1e and would later be reinstated in 5e as the dominant of three
theoretical models.[24] Planescape proved to be exemplary as a complex
imaginary world because of its systematic approach to harmonizing
D&D's multitude of campaign settings by fleshing out central gameplay
elements. The *Player's Guide to the Planes* (1994) explained that a character
must understand cosmology before entering Planescape's gate-way city,
Sigil, the center of the multiverse. It states, though, that "there ain't any
place in the whole multiverse that's more important than any other"
(D. "Zeb" Cook 1994b, 4) in a spirit of harmonization that this setting
embraced and the current edition champions.

In Planescape, the Prime Material Plane is comprised of many worlds,
like the FR's Toril or Dragonlance's Krynn, and spelljamming is offered
as a viable means to travel between the crystal spheres of these worlds.
Demi-planes are born in the Ethereal Plane, and "there's rumors of one
that's a place of absolute terror" (6), a clear nod to Barovia. The *DM
Guide to the Planes* (1994) reiterates that the multiverse is expansive and
contains all AD&D campaign worlds, as well as those created by DMs
(5). With Planescape, though, the tone is different; it recognizes the
epic tone of Krynn, as well as the dark, horror-inflected atmosphere
of Ravenloft. It also recognizes the FR and its massive canvas and the
world of Athas and its focus on survival.

Planescape's gameplay revolves around the players' ideologies and

[23] This video game combined elements from Planescape and the TRPG
Numenera. See Chapter 7 for my examination of Numenera.
[24] Along with the World Tree and 4th edition's World Axis, among others
(Wizards RPG Team 2014b, 44).

those of the NPCs he or she encounters.[25] This mandate encourages the setting's use of factions, groups, or organizations with ideologies that explain the different philosophical approaches to the multiverse.[26] These factions foreground into gameplay abstract notions so that they are lived by the individuals in the setting, as well as experienced by the players through their characters.[27] With Planescape, we have an attempt by an AD&D game setting to add layers of intellectual complexity to a game often driven by much more simplistic mechanisms. The greatest commerce isn't loot, treasure, magic items, etc.; it is belief so strong it can shape reality. In fact, belief is the ultimate currency. "Ideology is important because it can actually cause the borders of the planes to change [...] philosophy is more than just talk, philosophy is action" (D. "Zeb" Cook 1994c, 8).

This reference to action hints at the lofty aims of the game, reminiscent of Marx's ambitious call for an agential philosophy, even if it lacks any sense of the particular ideologies that have morphed into the varieties of Marxisms.[28] And while a Marxian critique of Planescape's differing factions would apply, I see the focus on ideology replacing the traditional currency of loot and magic items as a way to add intellectual sophistication to the game rather than valorize critical theory or social change, or even a particular political axis. What we see with Planescape is that the campaign setting is more than just a space for gameplay; it refracts the complexities of the multiverse as a concept by offering itself as a mechanism for harmonization that encompasses the entirety of the AD&D multiverse and one that offers new goals for players beyond the standard scenarios of dungeon delve, kill, loot, repeat.

This pattern of refracted sophistication is reinforced by other mechanisms. Sigil, a city at the center of the multiverse, functions in microcosm like the entire campaign setting; it plays a central role within the Outlands, a neutral plane with direct links to the outer planes associated with character alignment. Also, the Lady of Pain exists, a

---

[25] Planescape is about "ideas and philosophy, about the 'meanings of the multiverse'" (D. "Zeb" Cook 1994b, 7). Also, "A body's got to have a philosophy, a vision of the multiverse and what it all means" (14).

[26] The first three factions listed in the *Player's Guide* correlate to basic metaphysical postures: the Athar atheists, Godsmen theists, Bleak Cabal nihilists, etc.; also, the Doomguard focus on entropy, while the Dustmen think everything in the multiverse is already an afterlife. Factions dedicated to freedom, law, justice, and others all exist as well.

[27] These individuals don't "just ask the question, they live the answer" (D. "Zeb" Cook 1994a, 7).

[28] See Marx's "Theses on Feuerbach" (1845).

god-like governor of Sigil who no one prays to (or looks at) unless he or she wants to be flayed alive, who has no temples to be looted, who never speaks with anyone. She maintains the peace in Sigil, barring other gods from entering, and ensuring that the portals to the planes are respected. She functions as the ultimate balancing mechanism so that Sigil, the Outlands, and all the outer planes can co-exist. Finally, the Blood War acts as another important harmonizing element. It describes a cosmic battle between chaotic demons and lawful devils for control of the planes, with Sigil and its gates to the worlds of the multiverse's material planes the ultimate goal. This conflict rages eternally in the background, always available as a way to connect one setting to another.

Forgotten Realms

Just prior to the publication of 2e's *PHB* (1989) came the first official version of D&D's new default campaign setting, the FR, as well as the first FR novel, Niles's *Darkwalker on Moonshae* (1987). Over the subsequent years, numerous novels have been published and multiple additions to the setting published with official gametexts. However, with 5e, no comprehensive FR campaign setting book has been published. Instead, players find information about the FR in adventure gametexts, such as the extensive material on the FR found in Chapter 3 of *Storm King's Thunder* (2016) and the occasional narrow setting's gametext such as the *Sword Coast Adventurer's Guide* (2015).

A new D&D player hoping to understand the extent of the setting's scope across the entire planet of Toril, or even content about the main continent, Faerûn, is at a loss if he or she wants a single, definitive source. With the TRPG-PDF revolution, the prior editions' materials are available as reference. Parsing what is canonical for the new edition vs. what has changed can be a challenge. For example, the primary narrative mechanism of 4e, the Spellplague, imposed massive changes to the setting that proved less than popular and has been reworked for 5e (see below).[29]

As a realized fantasy world, the FR is a superb example because it combines the broad use of analog and digital transmedia and, most importantly, adds the continued expansive aspect of fan-generated materials beyond those of many shared universes. Because the core element of the FR is a game, this demands that individuals shape the world according to their needs. As I have shown earlier in this chapter, the complexity found in the FR's place in the multiverse has its roots

[29] For more on the Spellplague, see *Dragon Magazine*, 362.

in the beginnings of D&D's history and is now critical for the structure of the current edition.

With 5e, the choice was made to develop the game (and its default setting) with its iconic history in mind. The transmedia narrative-arc the Tyranny of Dragons was launched with the new edition's rule-set, its focus on dragons deliberate, being the most iconic. The first of these was the two-part *Hoard of the Dragon Queen* (2014) and *Rise of Tiamat* (2014), both of which focused on the rise of a dragon cult along Faerûn's Sword Coast and the cult's desire to raise the five-headed dragon Tiamat from Hell. They followed with the Elemental Evil arc, the adventure *Princes of the Apocalypse* (2015) a reworking of the *Temple of Elemental Evil* (1985), one of Gygax's most famous AD&D adventures. Here, the iconic aspect is elemental magic, rather than dragons. They followed with the Rage of Demons arc and its adventure *Out of the Abyss* (2015) set in the Underdark where characters confront the results of incarnated demon princes, such as Demogorgon, who have entered the material plane.[30] With the publication of *Storm King's Thunder* (2016), giants become the focus, the Sword Coast now drawn in plenty of detail across the adventures. Yet, the rest of Faerûn had been untouched until the *Tomb of Annihilation* (2017), an adventure that leaves the northern Savage Coast for the southern jungles of Chult.[31] Each of these massive adventures provides snapshot details of the FR, each a piece of a larger canvas.

A detailed examination of the FR proves it to be a shared, imaginary, realized universe spread across decades of published material, with no single definitive encyclopedic reference. This should be no surprise because of its construction as a realized world with multiple platforms of content creation. Anyone first introduced to the FR faces difficulties parsing all of the important gametexts for a comprehensive understanding of the published material. A fitting way to understand this lore is to organize it according to the in-game narrative dates of the setting as seen in the key gametexts.

The first official gametexts are the materials in the 1987 'grey box,' where internal dating of the setting is foregrounded. *The Cyclopedia of*

---

[30] Demogorgon has also been featured in Season 1 of *Stranger Things* (2016) as a key monster in the D&D game played by the protagonists.

[31] WotC continues to release large adventures that add official information to the setting. The only non-FR setting for 5e at the time of writing this chapter can be found in *The Curse of Strahd* (2016), a reworking of the Ravenloft material. *The Tales From the Yawning Portal* 2017 is much more of a generic adventure, presenting a series of non-connected dungeons. And even this sourcebook is framed in a way that players can begin in the FR city of Waterdeep.

the Realms (1987) begins its introduction in the Year of the Prince with the date 1357, Dalereckoning (DR).[32] The complexity begins immediately in this introduction because we learn it was penned by a scribe, Lhaeo, but that the most current events of the setting happened a year earlier, 1356, the Year of the Worm. What is critical to understanding a dynamic setting like the FR is that the published material not only has its own publication history, but the narrative is presented with a recorded past.[33] This mechanism of a past that reaches deep into the setting's history only becomes accessible for gameplay with careful investigation. What must be braved is separating what is happening currently in the setting (according to the most recent published materials), what has happened in the past, and what is happening at the table in an adventure.

The cosmology, though, of such a settings' wide-ranging materials has proven difficult to manage for D&D's game designers, a challenge the early designers faced. Gygax adopted design choices to solve these problems, one of which was a 'godswar.' Where the original Greyhawk publications saw little in direct detailing of the grand cosmology of Oerth, the 1983 publication of its boxed set provided a section titled "Deities of the World of Greyhawk" where we are told that, "in general, the greater gods are too far removed from the world to have much to do with humanity, and while they are worshiped, few people hold them as patrons" (Gygax 1984, 62) and "deities have weighty affairs to attend to, and in general they can not be bothered with the trivial needs of a party of lowly mortals" (Gygax 1984, 62). Gygax then detailed a conflict between the evil god Iuz and the good-aligned god St. Cuthbert, which provided a grand conflict that explains why distant gods might be interested in the world of mortals. This 'godswar' mechanism would be revisited more than once, as it was in the FR, the most popular and widely drawn of any D&D setting to date.

The FR's actual publishing history is the key to understanding its internal events, as well as its use of the godswar mechanism. Soon after FR's first grey box, AD&D 2e began in 1989. TSR adjusted the FR's internal narrative by advancing the setting one year, the Year of Shadow, 1358, where players' characters begin adventuring according to the new rules and where also begins the narrative framing device

[32] See Greenwood 1987, 4.
[33] For example, a player learns that in 1357 the fabled ruins of Myth Drannor, long protected by the elves of the forest, are now open to adventure. "And then, early this year, the last of the elves of the Elven Court passed over the sea to Evermeet, leaving the woods open to men for the first time. Since then, several bands of adventures are known to have entered the city. Not all have come out" (Greenwood 1987, 66).

of 'the Godswar' (also called the Avatar Crisis). This coincided with the first novel of the Avatar Series, Scott Ciercin's *Shadowdale* (1989).[34] Regardless of the marketing choices to use the Avatar's version of a godswar as a contrivance to sell 2e, maintaining continuity with its gametexts demonstrated the demands required to engage a realized world like the FR.

Following Greenwood's initial inspiration of humanizing his divinities, the Avatar Series details the Time of Troubles when the supreme deity Ao banished the gods to walk as mortals and to use avatars. It is a time in which magic is unreliable and chaos runs rampant, a splendid justification for designers eager to disturb the status quo both in the game world and at the table. Ao was angry that two gods, Bane (god of strife) and Myrkul (god of the dead), stole the Tablets of Fate. Until these tablets are returned, Ao decreed, the gods will be damned to the material plane, their powers greatly diminished. This godswar leads to the death of several important deities, such as Mystra (goddess of magic), who tried to return home before Ao gave permission (and whose death means magic is unreliable). Mortals, such as the thief Cyric (who would ascend to godhood), slew the well-established god of murder, Bhaal. Cyric's adventuring partner, the wizardess Midnight, also slew a god, Myrkul. She later ascended to godhood, taking the place of Mystra, before being killed by Cyric.[35]

The beginning of *Shadowdale* fictionalizes the confrontation between Ao and the gods in its first chapter. The remaining books in the series reflect the major events, as do the three adventures published in conjunction with the novels and release of the new rule-set. With the success of novels written in the FR, such as R.A. Salvatore's Drizzt series and Greenwood's novels of Elminster, as well as video games such as the Baldur's Gate series, the setting's complexity increased with each addition. With the publication of *The Forgotten Realms Atlas* (1990), an attempt was made to chronicle many of the more famous events, but even this is not exhaustive. *A Grand Tour of the Realms* (1993) provided a revised look at the setting, as well. Yet, none of these is comprehensive.

With the publication of 3e's *Forgotten Realms Campaign Setting* (2001), the FR's setting was only advanced from 1358 to midsummer of 1372, the Year of Wild Magic. After over a hundred products published in the FR, the 3e core rule-book provides a succinct yet detailed history of the FR.

[34] He and the other authors in the series wrote under the pseudonym Richard Awlinson.
[35] The series is comprised of four novels: Awlinson 1989c; Lowder 2003; Denning 1998; Awlinson 1989b; 1989a.

Because of the Time of Troubles, the FR pantheon shifted, with ascended mortals like Cyric stealing the 'portfolios' (powers) of other gods and causing conflict among his upstart followers and those of Bane, Myrkul, and Bhaal. With Bane's return, in particular, the balance between the original FR deities and those introduced with 2e was complete.

The FR, though, is a realized world in which players add to the setting, a phenomenon seen with the work of fan Brian James. He compiled online information that collated events in the FR according to their in-setting date. WotC eventually worked with him to publish it as *The Grand History of the Realms* (2007), a last hurrah for the setting before the major changes (such as the Spellplague) implemented with 4e. *The Grand History* is important because it represents how a shared, imaginary universe becomes realized through the combination of analog/digital tools made available to the public.

> This was something unprecedented for us; for the first time in my long experience with TSR and Wizards of the Coast, we accepted an unsolicited, fan-created piece of work, originally available on the Internet, and put it on our product schedule.
>
> *The Grand History of the Realms* is therefore not just an excellent Forgotten Realms resource, but also a truly revolutionary product and process for us. It's a sign that you, the readers and players of the Forgotten Realms campaign setting, are taking control of the creative process. Your interests and your collective experience with the setting that we all know and love have become just as big a part of Faerûn as any series of novels, gametexts, or adventures we've ever printed. The Realms are more than what we say they are—they're what you say they are, too. (Richard Baker, qtd. in B.R. James and Greenwood 2007, 3)

This reference-designed gametext represents the FR at its most robust, combining a history that stretches across three editions, and one that 5e has returned to in spirit. Compared to the rough sketch found in the *Cyclopedia and the Realms* (1987), a decade of material provided a truly age-spanning imaginative history for *The Grand History* to cover.

It also demonstrates what is required of any DM interested in a comprehensive understanding of the material. Such a DM will have to manage the FR's mythic history.[36] Many events in the past provide adventuring

---

[36] There are the Days of Thunder, some 35k years in the past, a time before humans, elves, dwarves ruled the FR, in which the fabled creator races like the saurian Sarrukh and the amphibian Batrachi dominate until a

scenarios that tie to the races of the characters. The Founding Time begins where the human-like species are ascendant. "This era signals the rise of all the humanoid civilizations, in a time when the many dragons and giants were long overthrown and the elf wars no longer loomed over everyone as a threat" (B.R. James and Greenwood 2007, 160). The dwarven nations are ascendant here, but the Age of Humanity sees the rise of human empires, such as the magic-using Netheril. A key event in FR history occurs when Netheril falls because archmage Karsus attempts to become a god and kills Mystryl, the goddess of magic (at the time). She is reincarnated as the first Mystra.[37] Dale Reckoning begins in 1 DR when the Standing Stone is erected in a land called Dale to show unity between elves and humans. The next 1,400 years provides a broad canvas for adventure, as well as moments of pivotal change.[38]

The pivotal year of 1358 is a milestone marker for the FR, both for its narrative and its publishing history, as well as to cement the default setting of D&D clearly within a romanticized view of an actual Late Medieval European history. Events either occur pre or post Avatar Trilogy.[39] Players who encounter Cyric as a god, or the struggle by cultists to resurrect Bane, are encountering post-Avatar elements. By 1372 DR, Bane has returned. The original fan-created *Grand History* ends in 1374 DR, while the published gametext ends in the Year of Blue Fire, 1385

devastating comet strikes Toril and creates the Sea of Fallen Stars in the center of what will become Faerûn. This climate-changing event sparks the hatching of thousands of dragon eggs and the rise of the avian creator race, the Aearee. At the same time, the giant-kingdom of Ostoria is founded, the setting ripe for the conflict that will come between dragons and giants for domination of the world. Such an intrepid historian of the FR will learn that the elves are the first of the humanoid races to flourish; this the time of their First Flowering. The great elven empires such as Aryvandaar are established. The first Sundering occurs at this point when elven high mages unleash powerful magic, splitting apart Toril's main continent and calling forth the island of Evermeet from the mythical land of the elves, Arvandor. Roughly, −12k Dale Reckoning (DR), the Crown Wars of the elven empires saw conflict among the elven empires, as well the elven god Corellon's curse on the drow, which creates the dark elves and damns them to the Underdark.

[37] This was mentioned in the original web document created by Brian R. James.

[38] For example, the Fall of Myth Drannor to the Army of Darkness occurs in 714 DR. Another key event occurs when good-hearted-drow Drizzt Do'Urden teams with Bruenor Battlehammer and others to reclaim Mithral Hall (1356 DR).

[39] See "Days of Future Passed: A Chronology of Published Forgotten Realms Fiction," by James Lowder in *Dragon*, #196.

DR. What is of important here is that the Times of Troubles are over but not their consequences. This is considered the Era of Upheaval in the FR, a time from the Avatar Crisis of the Godswar to the Spellplague. The Godswar continues. Shar, the dark goddess who covets Mystra's control of magic (The Weave), sets Cyric on a path to kill the ascended Midnight, who has taken the previous Mystra's portfolio. Midnight/Mystra's death in 1385 leads to the disastrous Spellplague, a 4e mechanism to justify its rule-set and setting's changes. Thus, begins the Wailing Years, a true alteration to the games' cosmology and the core game itself.[40]

The successes and failures of 4e are beyond the scope of this study. However, significant harmonization difficulties occur with 4e. The rule-set in 4e not only drastically changed the rules but changed the default setting. Its choice to switch to a generic default setting demonstrated a recognition that the combined megatext of D&D materials was a challenge for newcomers.[41] In an attempt to provide accessibility and flexibility, its simplified gameworld focused on 'points of light,' which is one of mystery, monsters, and ancient empires. The gods are distant again, exarchs (demigods) are their divine representatives on the material plane. And 4e offered the town of Fallcrest and the Nentir Vale as a default setting to begin such a game. This reduction offered the benefit of a contained and manageable avenue into D&D, rather than the very complexity related to the FR that seems do daunting.

The 4e's *Forgotten Realms Campaign Guide* (2008) describes a few of the key events that caused such narrative disruption and that would need eventually reversing.[42] The setting jumps roughly 100 years to 1479, the Year of the Ageless One. Nearly a century before, a devastating event called the Spellplague erupted in 1385, the Year of Blue Fire (the end of 3e's narrative). Abeir, Toril's ancient twin that exists in a parallel material plane, fused with Toril, causing cataclysmic devastation and change. The gods diminished; exarchs now represented them. Other changes to

---

[40] For another example of how the FR's realized elements add to the gameworld, see a fan-created continuation of the *Grand History* that continues where it stopped: "The Chronicle of Years: A Short History of the Realms after the Spellplague," by Christopher J. Monte.

[41] The revised setting explained that "wild, uncontrolled regions abound and cover most of the world. City states of various races dot the darkness, bastions in the wilderness built amid the ruins of the past. Some of these settlements are 'points of light' where adventurers can expect peaceful interaction with the inhabitants, but many more are dangerous" (Wizards RPG Team 2008a, 150).

[42] Of most interest is how 5e demanded that the FR be re-altered (some would say 'retconned,' or 'retroactively altered for continuity').

magic, nations, races, etc., also occurred, plenty of alterations to allow 4e to rework the game along its lines. "The timeline has advanced about one hundred years. That's quite a jump, but one that was necessary to widen the lens on a brand-vista of potential stories and adventures in Toril, and beyond" (Wizards RPG Team 2008b, 40): a narrative justification for design changes, and the presentation of a host of new books that must be bought.

5e has undone the massive changes to 4e's version of the FR. The Sundering Series of novels speaks to this reversal. It refers to a 'second' Sundering, the first occurring in standard FR lore when elves used high magic with disastrous effect. In 4e's alternate version of the FR's ancient past, the first sundering occurred when supreme deity Ao split apart the twin world of Aber–Toril (circa −31k DR).[43] In 4e, the planets were re-joined to explain all the turmoil. A new sundering was needed to return FR to its pre-Spellplague state. Such complexities are often beyond the interest of many players, but those who choose to unravel them face a historiography and an archive-building challenge of great magnitude. The latest articulation of FR, though, provides a workable solution because it has adjusted itself through the editions, enough so that even 4e can be situated into the multiverse under the guise that the veracity of these histories is difficult to determine, that in such a magical place as the multiverse, contradictory events can exist, due either to scribes and their faulty pens or to the unreliable nature of the multiverse itself.

Digital D&D

What makes the success of a setting like FR exemplary is its continued use as the default setting for 5e. Even more so what makes D&D's renaissance noteworthy is how it encourages new forms of entertainment beyond those found in sourcebooks. While the core aspect of D&D asks a group of people to sit at a table and play a game, or for DMs and players to read through gametexts, creating characters or game worlds, the Internet has allowed access to live *Twitch.com* streams, podcasts, *Youtube.com* videos of many 'actual play' campaign adventures or even 'one-shot' games.

In 2008, the creators of the web-comic, *Penny Arcade* (1998–present), Jerry Holkins and Mike Krahulik, teamed with WotC to podcast a few adventures in the previous edition, 4e. Long-time TSR/WotC employee Christopher Perkins acted as dungeon master for the group, and, along

---

[43] See Wizards RPG Team 2008b, 41.

with Scott Kurtz, created an adventuring party named Acquisitions Incorporated. The podcasts proved popular enough that the group began live-streaming sessions at PAX (Penny Arcade Expo) conventions, with the "The Prisoners of Slaughterfest" session at PAX Prime 2010. This successful live event was the first of many, with increasingly larger audiences. They seamlessly transitioned to the new edition. Along the way, guests joined the adventuring group. Host of the web-show Tabletop, Will Wheaton, remained until his character was killed under Perkins's direction, while other players' characters have survived longer. Novelist Patrick Rothfuss has maintained his presence with a dashing rogue character with a penchant for dangling from chandeliers.

Acquisitions Inc. demonstrated that fans were interested in listening to and watching individuals play D&D, enough so that the team began filming the sessions, replete with gaming table and miniatures, in a new series of adventures. This reflects a wider phenomenon made clear by numerous *Youtube.com* videos of individual gaming sessions by random groups, but Acquisitions Inc.'s contributions have provided an example of how digital D&D can become live entertainment.

A popular D&D stream on Geek and Sundry, Critical Role, followed Acquisitions Inc. by live streaming a continuous 5e campaign run by DM Matthew Mercer. He invited voice actors to join his table. This variant of D&D showcases individual performative talents by players, while skewing perspectives that D&D is primarily individuals sitting at tables doing voices. With increased subscriptions, Critical Role has proven to be a huge success, proof that voice actors are a perfect fit for streaming entertainment.

The confluence of these digital and analog streamed elements adds to the increasing archive of realized gametexts that can be consumed and analyzed within the modern fantastic. The adventures developed by Perkins and Acquisition's Inc. often have a ludicrous quality, while Critical Role foregrounds narrative drama to the point where the players seem genuinely riveted. The increasing archive of such material means that D&D's realized worlds continue to expand beyond the standard creative conventions of shared fantasy universes. The success of Critical Role encouraged Mercer to release a gametext for this campaign setting: *Tal'Dorei Campaign Setting* (2017). This can be purchased through a variety of methods, one of the easiest being through *Drivethrurpg.com*, an example of how the Internet's distribution of type-set PDFs has helped fuel analog gaming's success, as well as drastically increase the archive of realized worlds. No doubt, more forms such as virtual tabletops or LARP versions will emerge, the process broadening the gametexts, tools, and experiences.

Chapter 4

Worlds of Darkness
From Gothic to Cosmic Horror

From a gameist perspective that values experience over literary depth, *Dread Trident* has argued that imaginative posthuman elements within Eclipse Phase and harmonization elements within D&D both create unique experiences at the table, even if played from within the differing frames of hard-SF or high-fantasy. Another point of reference is that they both retain their ironic distance that encourages safe play. Critical to this understanding of ironic safety within the modern fantastic is the prevalence of the fantastic-monstrous, whether it be traditional 'draconic' motifs like vampires and werewolves or 'posthuman' motifs of technologically othered persons. Regardless of how they are represented as horrific, in TRPGs, they cross genre boundaries as key elements within the modern fantastic. They find homes in both traditional SF and fantasy, thus reinvigorating the fantastic impulse that informs these tropes.

The draconic as a fantastic impulse has re-emerged across a number of media as popular as ever, the Gothic vampire and the werewolf still the most representative. Likewise, the posthuman monstrous that emerges as a cosmic force of an indifferent or malicious universe, or as entities beyond human comprehension, also proves to be of critical importance because of the use of these motifs within a gaming context, not for fright, but for play.[1] What we see by viewing the Gothic-and-cosmic horror relationship through the lenses of TRPGs, though, is a refabrication of these images; they often operate at tables without players considering how monsters represent real-world others. They operate to encourage embodied play, a consistent theme throughout the examination of *Dread Trident*'s case studies.

---

[1] How modernity has treated its others, in the form of monsters, requires continued examination because of the real effects these have on the actual lives of individuals wrongly deemed monstrous, even as those forms are co-opted.

In working through the draconic and posthuman tropes in the TRPGs of the Worlds of Darkness, this chapter seeks understanding in the co-development of both Gothic and cosmic horror as major inflections of the modern fantastic. While in the Worlds of Darkness its vampires and werewolves are the most recognizable motifs descended from a Gothic sensibility, i.e., traditional horror fiction, this chapter views tales of witches, devils, and ghosts as provincial examples of the modern fantastic when compared to the emergence of a cosmic scale best represented by Lovecraft and those he influenced. For *Dread Trident*, they also prove to be of less interest than the God-Machine. This inscrutable entity represents the universe itself and one that this book sees as a posthuman trope, *par excellence*. The God Machine is a blend of SF and fantasy that attempts to represent the inscrutable, a consistent theme this book argues that gameplay sidesteps even as its sourcebooks and analog gametools represent.

Horror: From Gothic to Cosmic and Forward

A key moment in the construction of Gothic Studies as a coherent academic discipline occurred with the founding of the International Gothic Association in 1991 (Crow 2014, xviii), the same year White Wolf published the first *Vampire: The Masquerade* (1991) core rulebook. The TRPG settings of the Worlds[2] of Darkness foreground the modern fantastic in its Gothic and cosmic-horror inflections, as well as in their realized worlds. A look into the Gothic as a foundational concept reveals a transformation into a neo-Gothic that reuses standard tropes in original ways, as well as triggers new fantastic forms such as the cosmic horror argued for by H.P. Lovecraft and other thinkers of the Weird. It also provides understanding into how such a popular 'vampire' TRPG challenged Dungeons and Dragons (D&D) and offered an alternative model for fantasy role-playing.

At the same time that the discourses of trans-and-posthumanism began their articulation (see Chapter 1), the dominance of the vampire within Western popular culture as a primary draconic trope erupted with serious vigor. It can be seen in the novels of Anne Rice, in the

---

[2] My use of the plural for Worlds is purposeful. It suggests that this broad realized world of the combined settings work together. While differences are there for gameplay, an overarching frame does exist even between the Gothic-inspired world of Vampire: The Masquerade and the God Machine setting of the Chronicles of Darkness.

TV show *Buffy: The Vampire Slayer* (1997–2003), in many films such as *Blade* (1999), *From Dusk 'Til Dawn* (1996), and *Dracula: Dead and Loving It* (1995). Later, popular iterations emerged by Stephanie Meyer, such as *Twilight* (2005) and that of Charlaine Harris's The Southern Vampire Mysteries novels and the screened version, the HBO series *True Blood* (2008–14). Yet, these popular examples fail to represent the many other fictive texts that comprise the most recent vampire production.[3] At the same time as the re-emergence of the popular-culture vampire, the Gothic was being reimagined in a systematic way within TRPGs. Even more interesting, the Gothic's traditional challenger, a horror-infused cosmicism, was finding full representation as well.[4]

One recent examination into the motif of the vampire, Mary Y. Hallab's *Vampire God: The Allure of the Undead in Western Culture* (2009), begins by first asking, "Why is the vampire so popular?" (2009, 1).[5] Hallab views its undead aspect as a mythic metaphor. She is representative of the sort of treatment TRPGs garner in vampire scholarship when she mentions White Wolf's *Vampire: The Masquerade* in a note concerning people finding meaning in vampirism similar to religious belief.[6] Hallab provides examples of how people imbue these cultural elements with meaning:

> Most people who enjoy these imaginative works know that they are fantasies. [...] Examples include the fictional Narnia or Buffy's

[3] A quick look through Amazon's listing reveals a massive number of vampire-focused novels.
[4] Leading Lovecraftian scholar S.T. Joshi defines cosmicism thus: "Cosmicism is at once a metaphysical position (an awareness of the vastness of the universe in both space and time), an ethical position (an awareness of the insignificance of human beings within the realm of the universe), and an aesthetic position (a literary expression of this insignificance)" (Joshi 2001, 182).
[5] She dispenses with viewing the vampire as defined by its transgressive sexuality or its frightening foreignness; she locates its single most definitive quality: "the essential element that distinguishes the vampire—that of being living dead" (Hallab 2009, 4). This allows her to use the motif of the vampire to explore death as a universal for human experience, thus imbuing popular culture elements with moral significance.
[6] She writes, "For the modern vampire falls into the large group of well-known semi-mythical figures that are often referred to as though they were meaningful, even real, from Snow White to Darth Vader, who is, after all, just another reworking of Lugosi's caped Dracula. Associations accrued by the vampire throughout his long and varied history give depth and resonance to this modern sci-fi villain" (Hallab 2009, 70).

Sunnydale or life on the Enterprise and especially in the landscapes of popular role-playing games. In these worlds, groups of (usually young) individuals share a "pretend" alternative existence that runs concurrently with this world—like the games published by White Wolf, *Vampire: The Dark Ages* or *The Masquerade*, with elaborate rules for Gothic vampire fantasies. (Hallab 2009, 140)

Her suggestion that the young (rather than adults) enjoy the shared ('pretend') worlds of role-playing games demonstrates a typical misunderstanding by literary and cultural critics. The accusation of juvenilia removes any responsibility for extensive consideration. Archetypal motifs of the Gothic repurposed through the sieve of popular culture such as the vampire (and the werewolf) still find purchase in our collective imaginations because of their potency, and horror has developed new motifs beyond the Gothic that are broader in scope and surprising in their imaginary reach. We see this understanding of the Gothic's eclipse within Gothic Studies itself. Yet, within the context of gameplay, measured consideration is hard to find.[7]

Most 'vampire' scholarship in the last decade, however, has focused on its resurgence in popular culture along a variety of lines. One approach focuses on vampirism as a lifestyle, particularly predicated by a female perspective.[8] Such an account, though, ignores the importance of the vampire for TRPGs. Even more so, it does little to help our understanding of how fantasy is moving beyond traditional concepts of the Gothic, beyond reading and viewing consumption, even beyond lifestyles into the creation of fantasy-flavored realized worlds.

The transformation of the literary Gothic is fitting for an investigation into the Worlds of Darkness because of the slippery historiography of standard tropes and motifs that see vampires and werewolves superseded

---

[7] In contrast to Hallab, Paul Barber, in *Vampires, Burial and Death: Folklore and Reality* (1988), explores the idea of the vampire from an anthropological perspective. He distinguishes between the vampire of folklore and the vampire of fiction, the former drawn from a European peasant class rather than that of the fallen aristocrat—favored, traditionally, by the latter. He is most interested in how the concept of the 'undead' or revenant surfaces and how different cultures use this concept to handle the mysteries of death, 'vampirism' being a common term for the transformation of such a person who was often required to be killed a second time after already being declared dead. Barber's work, while helpful, though, leads away from the fantastic toward the actual misprision by people who believe in real vampires.

[8] See Maria Mellins's *Vampire Culture* (2013).

by new forms, a common tension *Dread Trident* locates between the draconic and posthuman. These tropes, though, were never stable. For literary theorist of the Gothic and horror Fred Botting, written Gothic produced in English is a literary form of excess that leads, in the twentieth century, to the cinema as a primary screened mode for the diffusion of Gothic figures.[9] He argues that within the sphere of popular culture we best understand its move from the margins to the center. He views this shift through a literary lens that would frame the Gothic as its own tradition, yet one that functions as a "darker undercurrent" (1996, 10) to dominant literary traditions—e.g., rather than an archetypal Byronic hero such as Heathcliff, we have the vampire, Count Dracula.

As the modern fantastic found its footing in the pulps and dime novels of the late nineteenth and early twentieth centuries, a challenger to the Gothic offered elements beyond the expected haunted houses, supernatural creatures, prophetic visions, etc. Cosmic horror emerged as a way to rethink limitations of an enervated Gothic. Today, it reflects a unique inflection of a posthuman perspective in both SF and fantasy that needs comment because it acts less as a prime driver within the modern fantastic and more like its unspeakable other. It is also a major component of the TRPGs in this study.

Fantastic-horror, rather than mimetic-driven horror (often thought of as evoking 'terror'), hearkens back to the supernatural horror of the literary Gothic as another pessimistic response to modernity. Fantastic-horror as supernatural, within a modern context, though, has been compromised, challenged, and denuded; outside of anomalies like the film *The Exorcist* (1973),[10] its effectiveness to scare recedes in the face of modernity's expanded knowledge of ourselves and the natural world, ceding ground to an inexorable cosmic horror, a posthuman worldview in which humanity diminishes in the face of an indifferent universe. Weighty stuff for philosophy, and perfect fodder for games that are safe behind a bulwark of irony.

Such a cosmic-driven worldview works within a few TRPGs as the ultimate horror: the complete dissolution of any human trace of

---

[9] Botting writes in an introductory volume on the subject that "the diffusion of Gothic forms and figures over more than two centuries makes the definition of a homogeneous generic category exceptionally difficult" (1996, 9). Outside of the initial period in the eighteenth century in which the key texts were written, he avoids focusing on the single term 'Gothic,' choosing instead to qualify it with descriptors such as: Gothic atmospheres/ landscapes/architecture; Gothic figures/villains; Gothic terms/texts/fictions/ plots/narratives; Gothic productions/styles/traditions.

[10] William Peter Blatty's novel was published in 1971.

existence. Yet, within the context of these TRPGs such dismal fare is rarely accepted by players, an unwavering humanist tendency standing firm by embodied players with embodied tools. This form of fantastic-cosmic-horror can be seen in screened TV, film, video games, etc., when humanity confronts its own obsolescence in the face of technological, biological, or supernatural threats. Such moments occur often, like that in the recent SF video game series *Mass Effect*, with their horrific Reapers, a race of ancient machines from the gulfs of space who harvest sentient life. Unhuman/inhuman threats drive the most interesting aspects of the modern fantastic SF/fantasy/horror beyond standard supernatural Gothic tropes.

In their place, we find a latent cosmicism that corresponds to a SF-flavored posthumanism, often with depictions of the weird and strange. Like the most challenging aspects of SF, these non-traditional conceptualizations of the fantastic align SF and horror within a curious fantastic frame. Even high-horror fantasy, often called 'dark' fantasy, finds a way to utilize these elements, such as the dominance of the God-Machine in the Chronicles of Darkness (see below). SF, fantasy, and horror prove to be a mixed bag of ingredients that, often, intermix to the point they are indistinguishable.

Such miscibility is important because it signals the success of modern fantasy. Its reach, though, extends into an imagined pre-modern past.[11] Romanticizing the past coincides with reconstructing it, and the Gothic encouraged such visions as an active reconfiguration of a medieval past seen through the lens of the eighteenth century.[12] Yet, at the same time, it developed through its Romantic beginnings into the Age of Technology as a response to the rise of 'mechanism,' as Roger Luckhurst has argued.[13] Thus, the Gothic found footing within a fantasy context that also inspired the weird and strange of the pulps.

The extension of Gothic tropes across a variety of modern modes of storytelling is labeled under the broad (and often unhelpful) 'horror' rubric, a literary genre that emerged gradually out of the Gothic. The

---

[11] As most scholars note, the date of Horace Walpole's *The Castle of Otranto* (1765) marked the beginning of the Gothic romance, to be followed by a number of derivations and innovations. "Gothic fiction is hardly 'Gothic' at all. It is an entirely post-medieval and even post-Renaissance phenomenon" (Hogle 2002, 1).

[12] Also, see how this proves to be a basic activity in postmodernism, one that Umberto Eco sees in how we rethink the medieval period through our own current period, romanticizing it in many ways. His novel *The Name of the Rose* (1983) reflects this process of reconfiguring the past.

[13] See Luckhurst 2005.

key moment in its history occurred as a response to the dwindling of the supernatural as a reality accepted by Western society, a society defined by the Enlightenment's attempt to secure Kant's *sapere aude* and the destruction of superstitions. The most influential of horror stories published in the late nineteenth century emerged at the same time a number of other fantastic genres were forming. Yet, as many critics such as Botting have noted, differentiating the Gothic from other forms that followed it is difficult, forcing us to ask "if post-Romantic Gothic can usefully be distinguished from adjacent genres such as science fiction, romance, fantasy, and horror" (Hurley 2002, 191). Rather than discreet classification, of interest is locating a common modern-fantastic thread that runs through these variations.

One way to parse the most complex forms of fantastic horror like those that emerged out of a general Gothic canvas is to contextualize them into patterns of representation. Philosopher of art Noël Carroll provides such a technique in his detailing of a philosophy of 'art-horror.' In doing so, he admits that such a philosophy is part of modernity.[14] The Gothic signals this appearance, but for an aesthetically inclined philosophy-focused thinker like Carroll, an understanding of modern horror begins with ideas about experiencing heightened emotion, an insight that stretches far into our literary past.[15]

Carroll situates contemporary horror within society's anxieties of its tempestuous present, even seeing in what he calls an American version of the postmodernist slogan, 'the death of man,' emblematic of the American individualist's dissolution (1990, 213). The Foucauldian 'death of man' seen at the end of *The Order of Things* (1970) is hailed by

[14] He writes, "horror is, first and foremost, a modern genre, one that begins to appear in the eighteenth century" (Carroll 1990, 4). And, "Art-horror, by stipulation, is meant to refer to the product of a genre that crystallized, speaking very roughly, around the time of the publication of Frankenstein— give or take fifty years—and that has persisted, often cyclically, through the novels and plays of the nineteenth century and the literature, comic books, pulp magazines, and films of the twentieth" (13).

[15] Carroll notes the common Aristotelian notion of catharsis, which suggests that tragedy works an emotional effect upon the viewer. We feel these emotions when we encounter 'art-horror,' artistic objects of horror. To do so he focuses on art-horror's inherent paradoxes. He asks, how can we be scared of what we know isn't true or, more difficultly, why would anyone attending a film subject themselves to such a viewing experience, echoing Rick Altman's insight that "definitions of the horror genre usually stress viewer experience" (Altman 1999, 86) over anything else. Horror, more so than any other genre, demands a reaction, a "mixture of fear, moral revulsion, and wonder" (Carroll 1990, 162).

critical theorists as signaling the end of the Enlightenment version of humanism so prevalent in modernity. If we use Carroll as a springboard to understand the tensions between the Gothic and cosmic horror, we see that art-horror reflects such fears as local anxieties, for sure, but the ultimate dissolution of humanity may be a literal one, seen in the cosmic posthumanism of Lovecraft and his descendants (see Chapter 5).[16]

Carroll's thinking demonstrates how complex art-horror reflects a philosophy of the present. Often, the genre acts as a way to understand the psychology of its consumers, usually as a mirror of society. Much of this thinking finds ground in the concept of the 'uncanny,' a concept that has been explored by a variety of thinkers from Freud to Todorov. The modern uncanny's continued use as a descriptor that the real has been compromised works even when embraced with irony. Through a lens that views modernity's uncanny others, we see it containing both mimetic and fantastic impulses in a broad canvas of forms, such as the Weird and the cosmic. Irony shields us from the most uncomfortable realizations of such insights, while the other extreme forces us to acknowledge a philosophy of erasure, the ultimate horror. Supernatural others, though, haunt our materialist tendencies, reminding us that they have not disappeared even as the canvas of the frightful has expanded.[17] These standard forms of the monstrous uncanny emerge as perennial tropes of horror. Yet, all of them have been co-opted to the point they often no longer scare. Count Chocula cereal is one example of this diminishment—or Casper the Ghost, shows about teenage werewolves, teenage vampires, etc.[18]

Where is one to look then, for the truly horrific, what Carroll calls the language of "natural horror" (1990, 12) or "tales of terror" (15)? Within a mimetic frame in which actual violence happens in the actual world, in which war ravages the innocent with machinery of destruction, or individuals commit crimes of hate against others, terror and horror exist

---

[16] Carroll understands this supreme form of modern horror when he writes that "the monsters of the horror genre [...] are beings or creatures that specialize in formlessness, incompleteness, categorical interstitiality, and categorical contradictoriness" (Carroll 1990, 32).

[17] For example, in *Danse Macabre* (1981), popular-fiction writer Stephen King provides a description of the horror genre as working at three levels of refinement (i.e., that of terror, horror, and revulsion). He examines a few dominant horror archetypes: the 'Vampire,' the 'Werewolf,' and the 'Thing.' He adds the 'Ghost' for good measure. King argues they work because of their proven successes, what he considers their archetypal natures.

[18] Botting would agree: "The uncanny is not where it used to be, nor are the ghosts, doubles, monsters and vampires" (Botting 2010, 11).

every day in full display on live and streaming news feeds. These acts, or the fictive texts that represent them from films such as *American Psycho* (2000) or *Natural Born Killers* (1994) or novels such as *Silence of the Lambs* (1998) are part of the modern fantastic, yet differ from those covered in this book in that they fictionalize what often happens in actuality rather than in their use of the fantastic imaginary. We are jolted by a continual tension that exists between the fantastic and the mimetic that can be seen in stark contrast ever since the rise of the realist novel in the nineteenth century. Without at least the appearance of the violation of natural law, or the assertion of the impossible, mimetic terror/horror fictions appear (often in some reprehensible way) to reinforce the possible, no matter how distasteful. Instead, the modern fantastic as imaginary fantasy, even when it operates as much as possibly within a mimetic frame, opens itself to vistas of the unreal, weird, strange, etc., that shield us with irony.

However, neither cosmic horror nor the Weird destroyed the Gothic. The most sophisticated thinking of the (*vampire*) *draconic* trope comes from theorizing within Gothic studies. After systematically working through the different frames for understanding the Gothic in a monograph dedicated to its subject, from its origins to its transformations, Botting ends his succinctly titled *Gothic* (1996) with a sub-section titled "The End of the Gothic." He provides a reading of Francis Ford Coppola's film *Dracula* (1992), seeing the film's attempt to portray the world imagined by Bram Stoker as less important than the film's softening of the Gothic vampire.[19]

Botting's critique suggests the film empties the Gothic of much of its ambivalent power both to embrace and transgress the values inherent in a challenge to a rational, secular world. "The vampire is no longer absolutely Other" (Botting 1996, 116):

> With Coppola's *Dracula*, then, Gothic dies, divested of its excesses, of its transgressions, horrors and diabolical laughter, of its brilliant gloom and rich darkness, of its artificial and suggestive forms. Dying, of course, might just be the prelude to other spectral returns. (Botting 1996, 117)

Botting's prophecy is prescient that the sentimental elements in the 1990s Coppola film signal a critical shift for the Gothic in which something

---

[19] He writes, "Dracula is less tyrannical and demonic and more victim and sufferer, less libertine and more romantic hero. [...] The new frame turns Gothic horror into sentimental romance" (Botting 1996, 115–16).

'spectral' might return in its stead. What could this be? *Dread Trident* sees an answer to this along two lines. The first is the resurgence of the draconic vampire motif seen in popular culture, such as that represented in Vampire the Masquerade (see below). It also sees an answer extending from a suggestion by Botting himself of what *Dread Trident* would call the *posthuman-draconic*, the vampire transformed within our technologized present.

Viewing Gothic tropes within a posthuman frame is just as acceptable as is viewing a cosmic posthumanism within a posthuman frame. Elements from both Gothic and SF-driven posthumanism prove just as emancipatory from humanist limitations. What is most interesting about the sort of cosmicism that Lovecraft popularized is how horror becomes the requisite response to humanity's knowledge of itself and nature. Viewing a vampire or werewolf within a posthuman frame suggests the variety of its forms in a posthuman world. Here the draconic and the posthuman merge as literary tropes. Both, of course, are very modern responses to the rise of scientific materialism.

What is significant is how even a fantasy-inspired posthumanism (rather than SF inspired) works within the discourse as a philosophical response to humanism, driven by technology's rise.[20] The cyborg or the technologically affected person is not the only modern form of the posthuman. The archetypes of draconic fantasy shed light on the posthuman as the ultimate other. Yet, viewing posthuman tropes of the cybergothic as a response to technology's impulse to create the inhuman still feels provincial in scope when compared to a cosmic posthuman vision. Such cosmicism has little to do with the proximate effects of technology and everything to do with conceptualizing the sort of deep time geologists utilize, time as a frame that minimizes, if not fully erases, humanity.

Yet, Botting hints that horror, itself, has within it a mystery of horrors to come in the forms of old and new monsters. What Botting calls 'horror's black hole' (see below) suggests that the spectral return may be more than a renewed Gothic vampirism for something much

---

[20] Botting writes, "monsters, ghosts and vampires become figures of transitional states representing the positive potential of posthuman transformation: they participate in a fantastic flight from a humanised world and towards an inhuman technological dimension, figures for developments in genetic and information science, cyborgs, mutants, clones" (Botting 2010, 4). Botting, here, is working within the discourse of Lyotard's use of the inhuman, his understanding of Gothicism's latent posthumanism allowing him to argue that the "Gothic cedes to 'cybergothic': cloaked in reassuringly familiar images, technology envelops humanity in a resolutely inhuman system" (14).

more ominous. *Dread Trident* reads this as the posthuman cosmic horror seen in the God Machine metaphor later in this chapter. Devils, ghosts, vampires, werewolves, or a malignant universe? What now scares us most? The issue of the ultimate horror monster arises, one that both traditional Gothic horror and Lovecraftian horror attempt to answer. We see the 'postmonstrous' Gothic thriving in bought-and-sold material objects such as novels, film, video games, etc., with no hint of its dissolution.[21] The TRPG Vampire: The Masquerade and its subsequent additions to the Worlds of Darkness attest to the appeal of such perennial (and comfortable) elements with so much lost in their ability to frighten.

In answer to the ultimate scare, Botting recognizes that

> Gothic fiction, which has served as modernity's black hole, serving up a range of objects and figures to solidify its various anxieties into fear and allow the pleasures of focused terror and expenditure, has become too familiar after two centuries of repetitive mutation and seems incapable of shocking anew [...] an object large enough to fill horror's black hole is wanted. (Botting 2010, 184)

This wanted 'black hole,' of course, was written about from a cosmic-horror perspective as a mindless divinity at the heart of reality:

> That last amorphous blight of nethermost confusion which blasphemes and bubbles at the center of all infinity—the boundless daemon sultan Azathoth, whose name no lips dare speak aloud, and who gnaws hungrily in inconceivable, unlighted chambers beyond time and space amidst the muffled, maddening beating of vile drums and the thin monotonous whine of accursed flutes; to which detestable pounding and piping dance slowly, awkwardly, and absurdly the gigantic ultimate gods, the blind, voiceless, tenebrous, mindless Other Gods. (From "The Dream-Quest of Unknown Kadath," Lovecraft 2008, 410)

This demon divinity serves as a literary hint of what a truly post-Gothic, posthuman universe would be like for standard humans, not simply the body transfigured or transgressed by technologies into the monstrous,

---

[21] Within the context of a renewed Gothicism, Botting calls the "postmonstrous" (2010, 45) a norm in a technologically driven society in which embodiment and materiality are plastic commodities, especially when these forms are shaped in spaces constructed for their flourishing or their reification.

but a world devoid of anything recognizable to humans. At best it is an indifferent world; at worst, it seeks our destruction. The 'other,' then, is the erased, or pulverized in the face of the 'boundless' dark.[22]

Like an oppressive universe dominated by Lovecraft's Azathoth, the ultimate fear for many contemporary media philosophers is not just an abstract, indifferent universe, but, more readily, the immediate dissolution of the human subject under the weight of a deadening techno-future, often representing in dystopian scenes filled with the imagery of the damned, that of a screen-dominated world.[23] This assessment of techno-modernity as a digital wasteland leans toward a pessimism familiar within the modern crisis, especially within a discourse of posthumanism driven by fear of Hayles's nightmare scenario of disembodied living. Yet, as Hayles demands, and *Dread Trident* tries to articulate, the embodied, material human pushes back against the domination of screens, or even against its ultimate erasure.

These varying theories of horror, when justifying them as a major part of the modern fantastic, foreground their importance within TRPGs, i.e., that across a broad range of these types of games, horror elements are typically present, even if sometimes muted or turned into comic relief. For example, in the high-fantasy of D&D exist monsters, traditional devils, demons, hells, abysses; furthermore, Lovecraftian mad cultists, evil grimoires, monsters of all types, etc., all feature in the game. These elements, especially horror monsters, do not define D&D as a horror game, as they do the Call of Cthulhu, which asks characters to investigate such unpleasantness as an incursion by Yog-Sothoth or Nyarlathotep and even adds a game mechanic for tracking the insanity gained by such exposure. Moreover, Eclipse Phase, which utilizes some aspects of horror elements, remains a fantastic, hard-SF game rather than a horror game. Warhammer 40,000 (40k), though, blends both fantasy and SF elements with a frame of galactic horror straight from a militaristic reinterpretation of Lovecraft. Yet, in all of them, players find themselves safe at tables with full knowledge that a game is being played, spells never trigger, and the worst nightmares the games offer are imaginary creations. No Shoggoth ever disrupted dice rolling. This

---

[22] From a literary perspective, such horror often remains unrepresentable, unnameable, or "untranslatable" (Harman 2012, 16), as the Lovecraftian tradition suggests, and taken to its extreme with the philosophy and fiction of Thomas Ligotti (see Chapter 7), even as some aspects find form within a game context cushioned by irony.

[23] Botting writes of "more and more ghosts gliding across the screens" (2010, 216), as well as "Negativity, machinic and inhuman, pulses beneath the fantasy" in which "no human hand is at the helm" (217).

is in marked contrast to the type of dread expected from a true Weird tale of horror.

The examination of monsters in the different games also reveals how to think of them in relation to horror. The monsters of D&D, though, are not designed to elicit the sort of "visceral revulsion" (Carroll 1990, 19) that Carroll says defines the emotional responses both of characters in horror stories and in viewers/listeners/readers of those stories.[24] This lack of revulsion is true even if such monsters are described in rulebooks as hybrids or unnatural creations, as legitimate horror monsters in Carroll's sense. For example, in D&D, even a horrid creature like a Beholder can be understood by players to be an in-game aberration within a mythic framework that produces such beings.[25] Many D&D heroes can look an abhorrent Beholder in its massive eye without pause or trembling. In Call of Cthulhu (CoC), on the other hand, for the characters (rather than for the players), the Lovecraftian pantheon exhibits horrific elements of the dissolution of natural borders that Carroll argues defines the horror genre (and these characters often go insane with the knowledge), while in Eclipse Phase (EP), such ontological assemblages can be horrific (if a gamemaster wishes to present them as such), or they can be presented as choices made by players to engage such posthuman monstrosities.

At this point, realized spaces within the modern fantastic must demure. They cannot (and probably should not) evoke a horrific tenor, only hint at it. TRPGs, as well, may use such frightening cosmicism as a background element without ever offering a true examination of its meaning. In the actual games that approach the subject matter such

[24] Carroll also writes,

> What appears to demarcate the horror story from mere stories with monsters, such as myths, is the attitude of characters in the story to the monsters they encounter. In works of horror, the humans regard the monsters they meet as abnormal, as disturbances of the natural order [...] Boreads, griffins, chimeras, baselisks, dragons, satyrs, and such are bothersome and fearsome creatures in the world of myths, but they are not unnatural; they can be accommodated by the metaphysics of the cosmology that produced them. The monsters of horror, however, breach the norms of ontological propriety presumed by the positive human characters in the story. (Carroll 1990, 16)

[25] A beholder is classified as an aberration, the very definition of the non-natural. It is a tyrannical and paranoid floating head with a single eye and a huge mouth of teeth. It has multiple stalks ending in eyes, each one capable of casting spells. It is one of a few original, iconic monster creations of D&D, and it features on the cover of the 5e *D&D Monster Manual* 2014.

as 40k, CoC, EP, and the Chronicles of Darkness (CoD), such inhuman posthumanity is given prominence as background framework for play, rather than understanding. In CoC, for example, it drives the adventures toward mysteries in need of unraveling (even at the cost of sanity), while in EP and the God-Machine of the CoD it acts as a background for the mysterious alien entities that exist. In 40k, more so than the others, such deep archetypes of chaos have their avatars that serve as the ultimate enemies, and ones that must be faced and defeated.

Vampire: The Masquerade

In the early 1990s, White Wolf Publishing, published Mark Rein•Hagen's original version of a fantasy TRPG, *Vampire: The Masquerade* (1991). This innovative game spawned a series of gametexts that developed beyond the initial focus of vampires, a series of settings that has come to be known as the 'old' or 'classic' World of Darkness, into expanded focuses on werewolves, mages, wraiths, demons, etc. This popular alternative to D&D continued to be published until support ended in 2004. It was followed by a reinterpretation of the game, the 'new' World of Darkness, which departed from the Gothic-punk themes of the earlier game for cosmic horror. This reinterpretation's core gametext, the *World of Darkness* (2004), provides general rules for playing in the setting, while the later revision of this, the *Chronicles of Darkness* (2015), updates these rules, as well as providing an intriguing example of the transition from Gothic to cosmic horror already seen in Lovecraft.

The popularity of Vampire: The Masquerade expanded into a variety of media. The collectible card game *Vampire: The Eternal Struggle* was originally published in 1994 as *Jyhad: Vampire, the Eternal Struggle*. A one-season TV show followed in 1996, *Kindred: The Embraced*, as well as a now bug-free video game, *Vampire: The Masquerade-Bloodlines* (2004). Fiction and graphic novels have expanded the shared universe, as expected. *World of Darkness: A Documentary* (2017), as well as a 5th edition of Vampire: The Masquerade, have kept the shared universe in the eyes of its fans. Following the successful model of Wizards of the Coast's *Dmsguild.com*, which extends the range of gametexts and acts as another example of how the analog/digital mix encourages the creation of realized worlds, the release of *Storytellersvault.com* allows players to create and release content within White Wolf's intellectual property and earn revenue.

As seen within fantasy and SF studies, the pattern of professional scholarly overlooking TRPGs continues within Gothic studies.

A few critical responses have emerged that counterbalance the lack of commentary, yet these focus on games as media or on game mechanics.[26] Representative approaches accept the challenges involved in understanding the impact of role-playing games even though gametexts as mass media are often misunderstood by digital game culture, enough so to also overlook their impact on the historiography of literary, cinematic, and popular-culture tropes like the vampire.

This case study follows the previous chapter's focus on high fantasy with a switch to the Gothic, as well as introduces a hybrid form of posthuman-inspired challenge to the Gothic. By looking at traditional tropes such as vampires and werewolves, and then looking at the inscrutable God Machine, this case study demonstrates how the Worlds of Darkness exemplifies a move toward a renewed Gothic within TRPGs. In fact, the vampire trope represented in this case study answers Botting's 'spectral return,' just as the God Machine presents a mechanized version of the 'black hole' within the Worlds of Darkness Gothic, an analog for the alien-deities that represent Lovecraft's cosmic void analyzed in the next chapter.

Before introducing the details of these two primary forms of the Gothic in the Worlds of Darkness, a brief comment is necessary on the primary mechanic that separates the White Wolf games from those of the dominant TRPG, D&D. White Wolf created a Storyteller System (SS) for its TRPGs. Rather than rolling a variety of oddly-shaped dice, the d20 being the most iconic, SS players utilize a dice pool of ten-sided dice (d10s) primarily tied to character descriptors (attributes and skills). The better your character is at a descriptor, the more dice

---

[26] Lars Konzack argues that the "role-playing game Vampire: The Masquerade, set in the World of Darkness shared universe, is foundational to the 21st Century vampire" (2015, 115). Konzack's article demonstrates the importance of both game mechanics and content, helping us see that without a history of TRPGs, we would lose the significance of a game like The Masquerade or CoC. He notes that both of these attempted to steer clear of the typical D&D scenario of delve, kill, loot, repeat, yet often failed to create a truly different experience beyond "brief combat simulations" (118). Konzack recognizes that such a game as The Masquerade is more than a simulation of, he suggests, Anne Rice's versions because "role-playing games as media have requirements and tendencies different from those of fictional narratives" (120). Recognizing the importance of what happens at the table, Konzack argues that these new requirements emerge in the amount of detail that must be added to the experience beyond those found in more traditional media. In fact, these new details emerge in gameplay through performance, through embodied experience within the creation and play of realized worlds.

you roll. Character creation is also different from that of D&D, with its focus on building a martial character who levels up and gains more martial powers. SS does allow increasing powers, often with a focus on aptitude in non-martial areas such as politics, intrigue, investigation, etc. While D&D can be played with a focus on intrigue, with few dice rolled during a session, and while SS games can devolve into simplistic combat, the rethinking of core game mechanics and character creation by Rein•Hagen reflected a trend in TRPGs to rethink the entire TRPG experience.[27]

The most recent version of Rein•Hagen's TRPG is the twentieth-anniversary edition (V20) of *Vampire: The Masquerade* (2011).[28] It stands as an excellent example of a game structured around sophisticated, systematized fantasy tropes within the mode of analog gameplay. V20 reflects a particular trajectory definitive in its use of punk-inspired urban Gothicism popular in the 1990s. Players begin with an understanding that their characters are outsiders, a theme structured into the primary experience of the game. The core gametext calls playing in this world "A Classic Experience" (White Wolf Team 2011, 5). 'Experience' in this case means the original effect Vampire: The Masquerade players experienced when it was first released. The new version encourages a nostalgia for its past (in which the energy of the urban vampire was exploding), as well as exemplifies the breadth of new life for its present. It also answers Botting's 'spectral returns' in which the diffusion of the vampire has exceeded anyone's expectations and now appears to be common acceptance within popular culture.

What is most intriguing for my study, though, is how V20's representation of a Gothic-punk setting demonstrates an effective, but narrow, version of the sort of fantasy/horror generated today. V20, at its core, is provincial fantasy in comparison with the cosmic horror represented by Lovecraft; it opts for an expected Gothic tone and imagery rather than a turn toward the unexpected. This is designed to root players in the recognizable. "The world of Vampire is a dark reflection of our own" (White Wolf Team 2011, 13), a nod to its gameworld located in cities, dark alleys, clubs, back rooms, sewers, cellars, etc. The use of shadowy imagery, of the liminal space between light and dark, finds roots in its reworked Gothicism, while another strain, that of soulless modernity, reflects a theme of resistance echoing cyberpunk. Both the ancient elements (supernatural beings) and the modern ones (technologies and

[27] See Harrigan and Wardrip-Fruin 2010.
[28] Other versions were published in 1991, 1992 (2nd edition), and 1998 (revised edition). A promised 5th edition was slated for release in 2018.

their social instruments like governments) have been corrupted and must be challenged.

Rather than global capitalism or oppressive governments, this focus on a fallen world in which the threats of darkness define the setting can also be juxtaposed with another reinterpreted baroque-Gothic setting, that of Games Workshop's Warhammer 40,000 (40k). Such a comparison reveals, again, V20's contained, narrow frame. Where 40k's gameworld spans, literally, the galaxy, with billions of human inhabitants and endless alien enemies, V20's is a personal, intimate setting designed for the intrigue that follows such interaction. These can be summarized as a focus on the conflict between the 'beast' nature of the vampire and the desire to maintain a core humanity. This inflection of the Gothic even becomes evident in the core rulebook when we are presented with an illustrative poem about the curse of Cain and Abel. It also focuses on the mysterious need to keep hidden such a damning secret, as well as to hide the stain that stretches from Cain's murder of his brother to every vampire.

This century-spanning mechanism presents an inherent hierarchy in which young vampires are weaker than older ones, and older vampires fear they will be murdered for their power. All of this corrupted mystery drives a continuous war that rages between elder and new vampires, as well as between vampires and humans, all of it promising a final, apocalyptic ending called Gehenna. It also utilizes a concept of the 'Jyhad,' or the endless battle between vampires for supremacy. Systematizing such a concept in which the young battle the old demands rigorous classification often glossed in other forms of vampire representation, such as novels or films.[29]

The original vampires are the Antediluvians, ancient and powerful beyond measure. This tension encourages a sense of timelessness, one that reflects a romantic longing for ancient aristocracies and past cultures. A customizable game like V20 separates itself from other fictive forms, such as novels or films, in its systematization of how to play such characters. Where Bram Stoker's novel *Dracula* (1897) provides a vampire aristocrat as an iconic character, one influential in subsequent conceptualizations, or where a movie like the *Lost Boys* (1987) redefines vampires within a popular sphere of punks and teenagers, V20 is designed for realized play of a variety of vampires, whether they be aristocrats, punks, artists, assassins, monsters, etc. It begins such flexibility by shifting the concept

[29] Kindred vampires in V20 begin as young Fledglings, become Neonates, then Ancilla before they become Elder, or possibly even a Methuselah. The hint for players is that their characters can follow this path.

from the generalized use of vampire to that of "Kindred, or Cainites, as they commonly call themselves" (White Wolf Team 2011, 720).[30]

Age as a rank in gameplay is less important than the clan a player chooses. This deviation from the standard race-and-class options seen in D&D reflects V20's particular mode of play. Each clan possesses different attributes that allow players to select from the variety of vampires he or she might have encountered in popular culture. V20 covers most options. One might choose the Toreador or the Venture, hoping to play an Anne Rice character dedicated to sensual pleasure and decadence or an aristocratic suffering ennui.[31] This initial choice is the first part of the core classification offered. A player must also choose a "sect—a vampire's political and philosophical affiliation" (White Wolf Team 2011, 20). The primary sect is the Camarilla, a choice encouraged by the game to introduce players to the Masquerade, which the Camarilla believes must be maintained.[32]

V20's character systematization relies just as much on methods of gameplay as it does on defining concepts. For example, the concept of the 'embrace,' or the initial act of turning someone into a vampire, exemplifies how mortal blood becomes a key resource in the game. It drives players to balance the ability to give a vampire character life and power with its abuse as a mechanism for encouraging dormant beast-like qualities to arise. Blood consumption is a resource a player must track on a sheet, and it is done under the guise of the Masquerade, the idea that vampires must remain hidden in plain sight.

Along with the sorts of roles characters can have in their clans, or the traditions players choose, V20 encompasses a wider world it hints at but allows other gametexts to cover, a wider gameworld populated with other supernatural beings, such as werewolves, magi, ghosts, and faeries. It also provides material that refines settings, such as playing in a Catholic, medieval past with neo-inquisitors, vampire hunters, etc. If a player is inclined, he or she may use the twentieth-anniversary

[30] These vampires are typically city goers because beyond the urban environment the wilderness exists where other dangerous, supernatural monsters roam, like werewolves.

[31] One might choose to be an Assamite assassin, or possibly a member of the Gangrel clan, whose members are "bestial and untamed" (White Wolf Team 2011, 20). The Malkavians are insane, while the Nosferatu are hideous and masters of secrets. The Tremere clan offers players a chance for their characters to meddle in sorcery.

[32] Opposed to them are the Sabbat, vampire zealots believing the apocalypse is nigh, that the Masquerade is a farce, and that humans should be ruled by their supernatural masters.

Vampire: The Dark Ages (2015) to explore this medieval game setting in the thirteenth century. Such additions add more detail and flavor to the broadest frame of the Worlds of Darkness beyond that of contemporary, modern society.[33]

Werewolf: The Apocalypse

The other core gametexts expand the game settings beyond the narrow alleys and underground clubs of Vampire: The Masquerade and the later V20. The twentieth-anniversary (W20) version of *Werewolf: The Apocalypse* (2012) provides another well-systematized setting connected to V20. The game focuses on werewolves called the Garou, physical and spiritual guardians of Gaia, "the soul of the world" (White Wolf Team 2012, 33). The shift here is from Gothic-punk to eco-consciousness.

The frame for this setting is more abstract than V20's biblical story reaching into modernity. In W20, "Gaia created the world and all living things in it. When time began, she released three primal forces upon the Earth: the Weaver, the Wyld, and the Wym [*sic* (Wyrm)]"[34] (White Wolf Team 2012, 48). The Weaver represents material construction; the Wyld is the life force driving the material world; the Wyrm balances the other two. The material plane is a battleground between these primal forces that once functioned symbiotically before the rise of human civilization and industrial modernity. A 'punk' aspect still drives this setting, as it does in V20; but in W20, the resistance is to the damage done to the wildernesses of the planet, and to the planet itself. A player must decide if he or she believes the horrific Wyrm is the ultimate enemy or the mechanized Weaver. This political choice between battling monsters or corporations, though, reflects a deeper spiritual battle in which the Garou must fight a losing battle that will end in the Apocalypse.

---

[33] The description I have provided ignores the interesting details that separate the editions, as well as ignores the details of its 'metaplot,' i.e., the timeline of major events within the universe. A helpful guide that details these can be found in the *Vampire: The Masquerade – The Storyteller's Vault Guide* (2017). Of interesting note is that it admits that V20 "deliberately eschews metaplot proper" (White Wolf Team 2018, 12). Yet, the metaplot of Vampire has proven popular enough that Onyx Path Publishing plans to offer a book dedicated to the details of the highly complex, published narratives. This will be another example of how realized worlds emerge at the intersection of the analog and digital domains.

[34] This appears to be a simple typo. It should be Wyrm.

The original *Werewolf: The Apocalypse* (1992) "described a war for the soul and body of the Earth itself, fought in countless gritty trenches and across truly cosmic backdrops" (White Wolf Team 2012, 30), presenting its mythic history to encourage players to embrace this terrestrial tragedy. Where vampires in V20 find their mythic beginning in the biblical Fall, the Garou of W20 are natural creatures of Earth who thrived as Gaia's protectors before the Neolithic, agricultural revolution. At this critical juncture in human and Garou history, two dominant types of Garou breeds emerged: the Homid, or human-born werewolf, who hides in plain sight, and the Lupus, or wolf-born werewolf that imprinted itself on humanity's psyche as the deadly hunter in the wild.[35]

Humanity's fear of the wolf was due to a period called the Impergium. "Humanity became terrified of the wilderness and wolves, in particular" (White Wolf Team 2012, 38), when tribes of Garou began the aggressive policing of humanity's new civilizations. Not only did the Garou inadvertently push humanity into the development of protective cities, but in the War of Rage the Garou destroyed many of Gaia's other were-animals, who also served as protectors. Such zealotry caused an internal argument among the Garou, many of whom believed they had gone too far. The Concord was created, which would see the Garou retreat into the shadows and leave the world of humanity to itself. This analogue to V20's Masquerade is a game mechanism that explains how the modern world exists in parallel with a secondary world of werewolves. It also explains that as modernity and industry grew, so did the Weaver's influence, the imbalance of cosmological forces gravely injuring Gaia.

While the theme of fighting a losing battle to protect the planet drives the ethos of the game, the most interesting part for my study analyzes how V20 represents werewolves in a systematic fashion designed for gameplay. The Garou can be juxtaposed with the vampires of the first setting. Unlike vampires, Garou are not cursed. Also, most avoid cities, where vampires flourish, preferring the ever-decreasing wilderness. But the wilderness is a reflection of a particular part of the Worlds of Darkness—the Umbra, or spirit world. The battle that the Garou fight is to protect Gaia, who is threatened by the Wyrm. These cosmological forces are imbalanced now that the Weaver has grown too strong. Players

---

[35] No two werewolves are allowed to mate, their offspring being a deformed and insane 'metis.' This condition is represented as doing much harm in making human society believe the Garou are monsters because these albino, blind, and mad beasts are, in fact, the most monstrous type of Garou, while a raging metis in Crinos form is also the archetypal monster-werewolf.

are asked to embrace this contest. They must choose sides. Typically, a player who chooses to be a protector-Garou embraces the duality inherent in the werewolf: "Everything about a werewolf is a study in duality: wolf and man, city and wilderness, duty and passion, Rage and Gnosis" (White Wolf Team 2012, 37). Rage functions as the battle cry, while gnosis is a spiritual passion. Garou, then, are spiritual warriors who rage against the disenchanting of the world (unchecked Weaver) and the chaos this unleashes (mad Wyrm).

What separates W20's handling of the werewolf trope from typical popular-culture versions, many of which rely on a person being bitten by a werewolf for the creation of a new werewolf, is in its systematization of the werewolf as a game character. This complex yet balanced array of details is necessary for players to build and play Garou. W20 begins by destabilizing the expected norm of werewolf origins: "The truth is, werewolves, are born, not made" (White Wolf Team 2012, 41), with genetic inheritance descending matrilineally. Such an offspring, called a 'cub,' won't know it is Garou until the first change occurs during puberty. This happens to a Homid Garou in human society as a regular human adolescent, while a Lupus Garou begins much younger as a wolf cub.

When a werewolf mates with either a human or a wolf, only one in ten has a chance of becoming a cub and undergoing a traumatic change. Those offspring of a werewolf who are denied this challenge are called Kinfolk, carriers of the genes. Just as real wolves declined along with the shrinking of the planet's wildernesses, actual Kinfolk wolves are prized because of their rarity. Shapeshifting between these forms allows players the freedom to explore different aspects of the game's dynamic tension between rage and gnosis. The Homid form looks human, while the Lupus form is the wolf running free in the wilderness. Crinos is a middle state between beast and humanity; it is the most iconic, and horrific, of the representations.[36]

A Garou also comes from a tribe, and a player may choose from thirteen options with associated attributes and mechanical elements. This comprehensiveness solves a problem of how to conceptualize a werewolf for new players, many of whom have read or viewed different versions beyond mysterious aristocrats. Players who want a werewolf

---

[36] The "adult werewolf in Crinos form is a killing machine, a massive, nine-foot tall monster plodding into battle on two legs. The very sight of one conjures up images of an age long gone, when massive shapeshifters stalked the Earth and herded their flock of breeding stock" (White Wolf Team 2012, 44).

dedicated to philosophy and lore with all of its contradictions might choose the Fianna, while someone who wants a warlike werewolf might choose the Get of Fenris tribe. Others cover a wide range of types, from those who justify the embrace of technology to those who wish to return to the time of the Impergium when humans feared werewolves.[37]

This game mechanic in characterization means players will focus on Homid Kinfolk and Garou dominating the gameworld, in terms of numbers. The game encourages conflict, both spiritual and physical, with the change only occurring after a traumatic event. This may begin early with a possible scenario in which a cub must protect other Kinfolk. He or she will be taken to a sept for the Rite of Passage, a dangerous test given by the particular tribe. Such an event will often precede actual gameplay, functioning as a way to determine character motivation.[38]

Other monsters within the Worlds of Darkness exist, from those that focus on wraiths, changelings, mummies, demons, etc. However, the only other major twentieth-anniversary edition (M20) that has been published is based on the original *Mage: The Ascension* (1993). This massive gametext reaches nearly 700 pages. It provides a different flavor from the two popular-culture tropes of the vampire and werewolf. In M20, players become mages who bend reality to their will. Its largest conceptual frame is simple to understand: the battle between reason and mysticism. Yet, the gameworld requires much work in understanding all of its elements because its systematization demands far exceed the other entries in the Worlds of Darkness.

Detailing these is beyond the scope of my study and would require its own extensive analysis. What is most interesting is how it admits an imaginative inspiration for magic rather than a literalist one, the latter embraced by real-world occultists without any sense of Saler's irony that defines the modern fantastic. M20's overt systematization and rationalization of the fantastic is similar to those found in occult books popularized

---

[37] A player may also choose to be from the Black Furies tribe, "the living incarnation of a woman's anger" (White Wolf Team 2012, 80), or maybe from the peace-loving Children of Gaia.

[38] Other critical choices beyond the breed and tribe provide more granular control of a player's character. Auspices describe the phase of the moon during the character's birth. Five possible phases correspond to mystical gifts that act as dominant characteristics, such as those of trickery and guile, of the mystical abilities of shamans and mystics, of the gifts of being a judge and caught in the middle of extremes, of those who keep traditions and lore, or of being spiritual warriors.

by Aleister Crowley,[39] yet because it is a gametext, its gameist awareness of these elements as imaginary demonstrates how followers of the occult misunderstand realized worlds. They lack the requisite ironic distance.

The original Gothic-punk, vampire-driven Worlds of Darkness expands the range of its realized gameworld with the addition of non-vampire material found in W20, and while the broader game does suggest a player might mine V20 to insert vampires in W20, it avoids any strict use. The two gameworlds do fit together, though, bound by their Gothic roots.

New World of Darkness: The God-Machine

The move beyond a Gothic literary sensibility in the most recent versions of the game point to its SF and fantasy tinged with the cosmic or the Weird, a vibrant development also seen in both fiction and gaming. Such a phenomenon is expected in a creative field that must explore new forms of the modern fantastic. For example, *The World of Darkness: Storytelling System Rulebook* (2004) updated the original core game to frame its gameworld as something other than our mundane world:

> Shadows are deeper, nights are darker, fog is thicker. If, in our world, a neighborhood has a run-down house that gives people the creeps, in the World of Darkness, that house emits strange sighs on certain nights of the year, and seems to have a human face when seen from the corner of one's eye. Or so some neighbors say. In our world, there are urban legends. In the World of Darkness, there are urban legends whispered into the ears of autistic children by invisible spiders. (White Wolf Team 2004, 17)

Such a setting foregrounds 'dark mystery' in which spiders whisper in our ears to broaden the narrower frames beyond the Gothic tropes of older versions, and the earlier game.

Representing such mysteries with language or at the table, though, is difficult. The use of fiction as a way to describe gameworld elements is common in many core TRPG gametexts, but instead of a detailed elaboration of the gameworld, fictive vignettes in the original gametexts provide mood and flavor suggestive of the types of mystery-imbued 'chronicles' (or stories) that might be played. The approach is generalized,

---

[39] See Partridge 2014 for an overview of occult practices and beliefs in the Western world.

rather than specific. In this sense, such core rulebooks function as the only required gametexts, although other more specific gametexts add specificity for the dominant tropes in the setting.[40]

The World of Darkness gametext was renamed by the new owner of the intellectual property, Paradox Interactive, with the publication of the *Chronicles of Darkness: Revised Storytelling System Rulebook* (2015). This revision continued the previous version's focus on an exploration of the dark mystery theme and its horrific cosmic horror hiding in the background. It even provides a list of influences, ending with *True Detective* (2014–present), a recent nod to Weird fiction in which a series of clues must be pieced together to understand a deeper mystery.[41] An underlying sense of incomprehensible dread works its way into all of the other sub-settings, many of which flavor traditional fantasy tropes grounded by these broader cosmic themes. The Gothic has been superseded by something quite different in this version.[42]

We see this switch with the God-Machine, a game mechanism that binds the settings so that a hidden horror behind the mundane world can be explored. This focus is detailed in a gametext that provides rule changes to the new revision, *The God-Machine Chronicle* (2013), as well as in a section of the later-published *Chronicles of Darkness* (2015) that utilized these new rules and material found in the 2013 gametext. This helpful mechanism introduces characters to the most mysterious and interesting aspect of the gameworld, a telling reason why it was added to the 2015 gametext. We are told that

> Something is out there, something bigger than us. It permeates our world and possibly even stretches into other worlds, other dimensions, and other times. Its power can be felt everywhere, the silent manipulator of all of human history. It has a plan, but we are not privy to it. (White Wolf Team 2015, 170)

This God-Machine is alien, and incomprehensible, "an entire ecosystem" (White Wolf Team 2015, 171), yet one, inexplicably, with interest in our material world, our universe, our solar system, our planet.

---

[40] *Vampire: The Requiem* (2004), *Werewolf: The Forsaken* (2005), and *Mage: The Awakening* (2005) all rework these standard tropes of the original World of Darkness within the new system and gameworld.

[41] See Chapter 7 for my comment on *True Detective* and its ties to Lovecraft via Thomas Ligotti.

[42] In describing how to fashion a chronicle in this gameworld, the gametext mentions incorporating a cosmic tier of gameplay by looking at films like *2001: A Space Odyssey* (1968) or reading Lovecraft (White Wolf Team 2015, 185).

Player characters in the new game, be they human or supernatural (i.e., vampires and werewolves) have a larger frame to explore than those found in the specific gametexts of the Worlds of Darkness, such as V20 and W20. Chronicles work from the local, to the global, to the cosmic scale. Inherent in such frames within frames is a design vagueness.[43] This inscrutable flexibility allows the gameworld to incorporate the supernatural elements from the other Worlds of Darkness versions, yet the focus here is with mortals.

Like Lovecraftian alien-deities that cause madness from a glimpse, this God-Machine represents the setting's attempt to systematize humanity's response to such a being through the mechanized metaphor of the sentient machine. Unlike most of the Lovecraftian deities who barely notice the doings of humanity, the God-Machine resembles the sentient emotions-made-flesh bubbling into material reality as do demons in the Warhammer 40,000 (40k) universe. The God-Machine is a being of cogs within cogs working toward an unknowable purpose across the Earth and into other dimensions. This distance allows players to formulate responses as either involved in uncovering the truth of this mystery or not. They co-construct the gameworld as joint storytellers, the most challenging goal being to interact with the mystery by delving deeper and having their characters experience the horror of directly access this mysterious entity.

The largest and most demanding drama is in discovering the nature of the God-Machine, learning its secrets, and posing a challenge. Such agency reflects a positive role for players in the face of monstrous power. Whereas a game like the Lovecraftian Call of Cthulhu (CoC) sees its players avoiding the greatest of enemies, less they be driven insane or killed outright, the God-Machine chronicles hint at a D&D-styled d20-like reinterpretation of the investigation-focused CoC.[44]

What the creation of the God-Machine as a game mechanism demonstrates is the sophistication of its gameworld's systematization through the development of horror themes. The God-Machine as a fantasy trope follows the trajectory of Weird writers like Lovecraft who worked beyond Gothic constraints to create new fantasy mythoi. The God-Machine is not divine in a traditional religious sense, like Lovecraft's rationalized deities who have alien-like qualities. The God-Machine is

---

[43] "What is the God-Machine? We'll state up front that we are not going to provide a definitive answer" (White Wolf Team 2015, 171).

[44] A d20 version even exists that foregrounds D&D rules that encourage players to engage in combat so that they can mount a challenge. See M. Cook and Tynes 2002.

not omnipresent, omniscient, or omnipotent. It uses intermediates. It is bound by the laws of physics, even if it has a much greater understanding of how to bend them than does humanity. And it is limited in its full understanding of material things, although its capabilities far exceed anything encountered by humanity. Like Lovecraft's uncaring universe, "the God-Machine has no concern for human beings" (White Wolf Team 2015, 172). This amorality has been explored in standard SF for decades.[45] Many other examples exist, especially of inscrutable aliens, like Q in several later *Star Trek* shows, an alien being with immense power who often appears to find humor in playing jokes on humanity.

CoD's use of the God-Machine is interesting because this inscrutability is systematized. The game provides the concept of 'infrastructure' to explain how the God-Machine works in the world. Exploring this system allows players to reveal the nature of the God-Machine; in particular, players seek 'lynchpins,' or the vulnerabilities in the infrastructure of the God-Machine's plans. These are reduced to key areas ripe for investigation by characters: 'suspicious fronts' are the physical areas like a gas station with out-of-date magazines or gas priced too low. These fronts barely hide their true natures as a concealment of the God-Machine's plans. Not only places, but 'unfaithful servants' accidentally reveal minor secrets of the God-Machine they may barely fathom themselves, also revealing their own roles as cogs in the infrastructure. 'Lazy scrubbers' work to keep the cogs functioning, while the most powerful parts of infrastructure can be found in politics, communication systems, corporations, etc. Finally, 'angels' are direct agents of the God-Machine, even if they are something other than the supernatural beings in traditional fantasy, while 'cultists' worship the God-Machine.

Like a complex investigative game, the goal is for players to locate these hidden lynchpins as a way for revelation to occur. The game system provides different tiers of play: local, regional, global, cosmic. In a local-tier game, the focus is on a single problem, in a single location, with a single agent from the God-Machine. This broadens the gameworld to connected chronicles on the regional level in which the stakes are raised and, thus, so are the consequences. This variable scope allows for varieties of organizations, which adds more complexities in terms of locations and agents. Where the local level might have a single cult, the regional level broadens this to a wider organization with wider aims, such as a government. The global tier works across

---

[45] For example, the short story "The Cold Equations" explores how the universe itself shows little compassion for human beings in need; written by Tom Godwin in *Astounding Magazine* (1954).

the entire world. Chronicles here focus on potential catastrophe or world-shaking events.

In a subtle nod toward harmonization, the core rulebook gametext suggests a global scenario in which "vampires decide to end the age-old practice [the Masquerade] of keeping their existence a secret" (White Wolf Team 2015, 184). Such a scenario might see the God-Machine intervene with characters caught in the middle. At the cosmic tier, we see epic-style play in which an "endgame [...] allows players to transcend global conspiracies to become part of the hidden system. [...] Players will stand toe to toe with angels, demons, and the things that exist outside our reality" (White Wolf Team 2015, 185). At this point, the game reiterates Clark's Third laws about advanced technology looking like magic and reflects how the modern fantastic utilize the impulse of fantasy:

> Stories set in the cosmic tier don't automatically equal science fiction, either. In the Chronicles of Darkness, magic is frequently more potent than science. It's entirely possible that the God-Machine is a magical construct, rather than an actual machine, and has promoted the use of science to blind humans to the reality around them. (White Wolf Team 2015, 186)

While the cosmic tier is the most expansive gameplay stage, many of the possible scenarios involving the God-Machine occur in the much more constrained areas of the local tier, while the intermediary tiers allow movement between the poles. The core gametext, *Chronicles of Darkness* (2015), details a number of these scenarios to aid gameplay in "Hagiography: Tales of the God-Machine." Most interestingly, these involve the 'Weird' as fundamental elements, rather than the supernatural elements of Gothic horror and, thus, are indicative of the move from a Gothic focus seen in the original World of Darkness to the more recent cosmic/Weird-inflected game. It demonstrates a natural development from the original, provincial settings of vampires and werewolves because it asks what might be hiding in deeper shadows than those of these Gothic monsters. It allows players to maintain their interests in these traditional tropes, while providing them a hidden layer to explore, one reaching beyond biblical frames or even those located within the earth itself. This frame is the cosmic. It points to the ongoing influence of H.P. Lovecraft and the Weird as a fundamental aspect of the modern fantastic.

This chapter's close examination of the Worlds of Darkness gameworlds associated the original World of Darkness with archetypal Gothic tropes of the vampire and the werewolf; this approach helped differentiate these gameworlds from their successor, the 'new' World of Darkness or what would later be called the Chronicles of Darkness, and its non-traditional trope of the God-Machine. This latest version demonstrates how complex fantasy often reinterprets traditional fantasy tropes, like those of the vampire, werewolf, ghost, thing, etc., and peers behind them for a deeper threat, like an inscrutable entity similar to the universe itself. This chapter focused on detailed readings from Vampire: The Masquerade, Werewolf: The Apocalypse, and the God-Machine of the New Chronicles. It did so to explore this complex realized world that encompasses reinterpreted Gothic tropes along with the more complex tropes of the God-Machine, a direct analog to the sort of cosmic horror later detailed in the chapter on Lovecraft.

Chapter 5

Lovecraft's (Cthulhu) Mythos

The central chapter of this book requires a case study that anchors the others. Howard Phillips Lovecraft functions as this foundation, and like favorite-target D&D has also been denigrated as tripe. This case study looks beyond the fact that Lovecraft often still suffers the accusation that he is a florid, hack writer of purple prose, although he has now been accepted by the academy as worthy of serious study.[1] This chapter examines Lovecraft's influence on popular-culture gaming, as well as on the settings of many TRPGs; this influence acts as a controlling element of analysis for *Dread Trident*'s methodology in theorizing the modern fantastic as a fantastic impulse creating common currency among the genres of SF and fantasy.

What is most helpful for *Dread Trident*, though, in Lovecraft, even beyond how his cosmicism and Weird materialism have captured the minds of current thinkers, is how his fantasy creations have influenced the expansion of realized worlds. The previous case studies have offered other aspects of how they contribute to the modern fantastic. The harmonization of D&D's planes, along with its 'godswar'; Eclipse Phase's representations of posthuman subjectivity; and the move from traditional Gothic tropes to those of the inexplicable God Machine in the Worlds of Darkness all demonstrate aspects of the modern fantastic's rush toward the creation of realized worlds within a gameist mode.

This chapter's case study examines Lovecraft from a number of angles that reveal his central influence. In particular, his literary materialism

---

[1] He has, of course, also been criticized rightly for his blatant racism and xenophobia, a fact that can be found throughout his prolific correspondences. Yet, the Library of America published an edition of his work: *H.P. Lovecraft: Tales* (2005), and the recent *Age of Lovecraft* (2016), from the University of Minnesota Press, demonstrates the sort of critical acumen that can be brought to bear. A stunning reversal.

and language of 'nerdy categorizing' emerge from analysis of direct readings within his fiction. These examples, though, follow what this chapter considers his greatest contribution to the modern fantastic: the Cthulhu Mythos. It began with the creation of a cosmic framework by Lovecraft and fellow writers who expanded the literary creations of Lovecraft. His crazed cultists, grimoires of dark magic, god-like aliens that drive humans insane, intrepid investigators, and fallen civilizations all figure into the most popular TRPGs. We see this in fiction, of course, but most clearly in the TRPG, The Call of Cthulhu. By taking the Mythos as its content, the game applies its need for systematization and constructs a gaming experience in which players directly encounter the cosmic horror of the Mythos.

Like the cases studies examined so far in *Dread Trident*, this central case study provides a theoretical foundation for the analysis within this book. Its central theme is that Lovecraft, the literary writer, understood the difficulties inherent within language in representing the ineffable. Because of this, he insisted on backing away from such attempts, relying instead on language to create a requisite sense of cosmic dread. Yet, the influence of Lovecraft within a gameist mode refuses such literary restrictions. The attempt to categorize and represent the unrepresentable, the undrawable, the unseeable, acts as a common thread within TRPGs. Lovecraft's "journeys to the penumbral worlds of the unutterable" (Houellebecq 2005, 33) led him to create a universe of alien entities, cults, evil books, etc., his Cthulhu Mythos. In TRPGs, we finally see them in full relief.

Lovecraft Scholarship and the Mythos

In helping define the Weird as a literary genre, as well as representing a sophisticated view of cosmic horror, Howard Phillips Lovecraft (1890–1937) has captured the minds of many leading twentieth-century fantasists: Stephen King and Guillermo del Toro being two of the more famous to argue for his merit. The long road of justifying Lovecraft from a literary perspective has seen traction in the academy.[2] Lovecraftians have argued for Lovecraft's literary merit because of a more credible

---

[2] His prolific biographer, the independent scholar S.T. Joshi, spent decades in undoing the devastating slight by literary critic Edmund Wilson and echoed by most professional literary scholarship that in Lovecraft's work "the only real horror in most of these fictions is the horror of bad taste and bad art" (1980, 47).

threat: the highlighting of Lovecraft as the creator of his 'Cthulhu' Mythos, rather than as a literary figure. This chapter, though, resists the project to foreground the Mythos as an exemplary realized world within the modern fantastic. In fact, it valorizes the Mythos as a stellar example of how a realized world crosses the divide from traditional literary texts into gameist texts.

Lovecraft's literary merit, though, still requires explanation. Others have also worked in favor of Lovecraft as a writer, rather than as the creator of the Mythos. Sword-and-sorcery pioneer Fritz Leiber wrote an early essay, "A Literary Copernicus," that demonstrated Lovecraft's worth as both a stylist and a proponent of cosmic horror, while Joyce Carol Oates wrote an article/review for the *New York Review of Books* in 1996, "The King of Weird," that recognized Lovecraft's importance as a purveyor of post-Gothic cosmic horror.[3] More recently, *The Atlantic* published an article about the 'reanimation' of Lovecraft. He "hasn't just escaped anonymity; he's reached the highest levels of critical and cultural success. His is perhaps the craziest literary afterlife this country has ever seen" (Eil 2015, online).

Leiber, Oats, and others have dissected Lovecraft's literary techniques, providing an ongoing fruitful addition for a literary understanding of his style. While my study recognizes Lovecraft as a writer, it focuses on him as an architect of the imagination; it sees his work as a prime example of how an imaginary world becomes realized through the complex interaction of both digital and analog elements—and a host of individuals who utilize them. One irony is that an obscure writer repulsed by modernity and mechanization, by most forms of liberalism such as sexual freedom, democracy, and multiculturalism, by progressive change he saw eroding his comfortable traditions, created an imaginary framework that has not only conquered the literary world but has exploded into Western popular culture as a part of the modern fantastic.[4]

---

[3] See Leiber 1980 and Oates 1996.

[4] In attempting to explain Lovecraft's appeal, French novelist Michel Houellebecq's extended essay *H.P. Lovecraft: Against the World; Against Life* (2005) describes Lovecraft's work as a virus that acts to shock a reader; in doing so, he is articulating that "there is something not really literary about Lovecraft's work" (Houellebecq 2005, 34). He captures this tragedy of both Lovecraft's life and his personal views that made him reject a world outside of his imaginary creations. Houellebecq recognizes that Lovecraft was driven by fear of the modern world and that this spurred him to respond to the dominance of literary realism with his own philosophy of dread: the cosmic horror of a material universe indifferent to futile, human aspirations Rather than arguing against Lovecraft as a literary writer, Houellebecq

Dread Trident places Lovecraft within the context of the modern fantastic, which sees him as a catalyst within both popular culture and literature. Novelist of the New Weird Jeff VanderMeer echoes Kathryn Hume when he writes of "impulses" (2008, ix) leading to a "shift" in the 1990s that saw a variety of writers channel the old pulps in a new fashion. He provides a working definition that situates the New Weird clearly within a modernized present.[5] While such a definition is helpful, professional scholarship has begun unpacking the concept in more detail. For example, a recent article in *Genre* articulates distinctions between 'old' and 'new' Weird to tease through the variety of definitions.[6] They avoid a focus on overt definitions or classification for addressing the concept as a response to what they call the "Lovecraft Event" (Noys and Murphy 2016, 119), which is located in his writing of "Supernatural Horror and Literature." Yet, the authors recognize that, post-Lovecraft,

    also recognizes that an encounter with Lovecraft sometimes resonates with readers sensitive to the sort of cosmic posthumanism articulated by contemporary philosophers of horror. So much of what has come to be valued in Lovecraft has been built posthumously by collaborators who have made his Mythos their own.

[5] For VanderMeer:

    New Weird is a type of urban, secondary-world fiction that subverts the romanticized ideas about place found in traditional fantasy, largely by choosing realistic, complex real-world models as the jumping off point for creation of settings that may combine elements of both science fiction and fantasy. New Weird has a visceral, in-the-moment quality that often uses elements of surreal or transgressive horror for its tone, style, and effects—in combination with the stimulus of influence from New Wave writers or their proxies (including also such forebears as Mervyn Peake and the French/English Decadents). New Weird fictions are acutely aware of the modern world, even if in disguise, but not always overtly political. As part of this awareness of the modern world, New Weird relies for its visionary power on a "surrender to the weird" that isn't, for example, hermetically sealed in a haunted house on the moors or in a cave in Antarctica. The "surrender" (or "belief") of the writer can take many forms, some of them even involving the use of postmodern techniques that do not undermine the surface reality of the text. (VanderMeer 2008, xvi)

[6] Its authors see the Old Weird emerge in a period between 1880 and 1940, with the term related to the flourishing of *Weird Tales* (1923–40). They view the New Weird emerge as a reworking of the material from the pulps in which writers like Thomas Ligotti avoided "the pastiche and repetition that had tended to dominate post-Lovecraftian weird fiction and formulated a new and desolate conception of a fundamentally chaotic universe" (Noys and Murphy 2016, 119).

"the most successful 'Lovecraftian' works are not the direct adaptations of his fiction but those that inhabit the 'Lovecraftian aura' of cosmic horror" (124). This aura is what has expanded Lovecraft's reach into popular culture, and TRPGs.

A focus on the emergence of a cosmic horror aura as the defining part of the Lovecraft event only tells half the story; the often-ignored part foregrounds the attempt to represent the monstrous metaphors of the cosmic horror elements in Weird fiction. These emerge, typically, as finely drawn pulp-inspired monsters or (on the opposite pole) as the suggestion of unrepresentable horror. The safe approach is to avoid representation; this avoids the worst excesses of Weird fiction and cinema, the same sins that inspired Edmund Wilson to denigrate Lovecraft as a writer of whistling octopi. However, the demonstrated sophistication in the drawing of such difficult elements has proven to be a major appeal of recent Weird fiction.

As late as 1989, Lovecraft scholar Peter Cannon wrote a Twayne series contribution in which he constructed his book with two readers in mind: skeptics of and believers in Lovecraft's worth. The former, mostly "nonfans—including most English professors" (1989, xi) were his primary audience because Lovecraft had spent the bulk of his time on the periphery of the professional academy. Times have changed. Lovecraft has been vindicated in both popular culture and the professional academy. What connects them are his views of cosmic horror, and the existence of his Mythos that fictionalizes his philosophy. What makes him important for this study is how he exemplifies the range and impact of imaginary realized worlds, especially in TRPGs, as well as his post-anthropocene posthumanism.

After years of independent scholarship by individuals such as S.T. Joshi, and articles in the periodicals *Lovecraft Studies* and *Crypt of Cthulhu*, the publication by the Library of America of *H.P. Lovecraft: Tales* (2005) and the more recent publication of the University of Minnesota Press's *Age of Lovecraft* (2016), professional literary studies now enjoy scholarly articles that demonstrates Lovecraft's importance in both the popular and professional academic spheres. The designation that this 'Age' should be labeled after Lovecraft is a singular expression which locates Lovecraft's importance within the purview of modern studies.[7]

---

[7] The editors even begin with a statement some literary studies thinkers might find surprising: "Somehow, against all odds, Howard Phillips Lovecraft has become a twenty-first-century star" (Sederholm and Weinstock 2016, 1). Most interestingly, they cover in detail how Lovecraft has emerged in literature, film, comic books, music, transmedia, philosophy, academia,

The *Age of Lovecraft* recognizes that something about Lovecraft represents contemporary thinking. Their comprehensive introduction even notes that Michael Saler in *As If* (2012) dedicates an entire chapter to Lovecraft's 'public spheres of the imagination.' These public spheres comprised his numerous correspondences, readership of his *Weird Tales*, fellow writers, amateur press colleagues, etc., all of which earned this wide-reading autodidact a reputation for his stellar imagination and, as well, unfortunately, a despicable racism. Sadly, the nihilism, stoicism, and cosmicism Lovecraft developed in his fiction and numerous correspondences never developed into a bulwark against prejudiced thinking.[8]

For many people who have encountered Lovecraft, though, his popular influence reaches much further than his literary. This is due to the impact, not of his fiction, but of the fantasy framework used for his fiction, used by others who add to Lovecraft, and used as inspiration for their own work, what is often called the Cthulhu Mythos. For Saler:

> whether meta-myth or anti-myth, his Cthulhu Mythos represented a distinctly modern form of enchantment. It conveyed the centrality of "as if" narratives to human existence, while at the same time capturing the sense of wonder betokened by contemporary science. Lovecraft's answer to modern disenchantment was to embrace the virtual realities of the imagination as a way to cope with the "virtual unreality" of modern life. (Saler 2012, 135)

Such an insight from outside the small cadre of Lovecraft scholars reflects Lovecraft's wider influence and importance. To understand *Dread Trident*'s use of Lovecraft's Cthulhu Mythos as a pervasive example of a

---

etc., their selections and introduction a helpful overview of Lovecraft's rise. However, except for an interview at the very end of the book with novelist China Miéville, gaming is left unaddressed (see Chapter 7).

[8] Roger Luckhurst also sees in Lovecraft a man driven by the pessimistic social thought of his time, much of it documented with clear historiographies leading back to Schopenhauer, Haeckel, Spengler, etc. (Luckhurst 2013, xxii). And while Lovecraft's critics often gleefully pounce on his bigotry, they typically follow with a damning account of his style. As Luckhurst notes, along with Graham Harman, this began in earnest with Wilson's infamous denigration of Lovecraft as a purveyor of bad art. Like Harman, Luckhurst defends Lovecraft by turning Wilson's own critique against him. "The power of the weird crawls out of these sentences [Lovecraft's] because of the awkward style" (xx). Professional scholars are now taking Lovecraft seriously. As *Age of Lovecraft* notes, Lovecraft's inclusion into the Library of America might have dumbstruck Wilson.

complex realized world that has influenced many fantasists across many genres and media, a quick look is in order into the debates and issues of the Mythos's impact. This will explain the difference between the direct and indirect use of the Mythos.[9]

How did such popular-culture diffusion occur? After Lovecraft's death, his work was championed by two young fans of *Weird Tales* who had corresponded with him. August Derleth and Donald Wandrei formed Arkham House to republish his work, as well as the work of others writing under the Lovecraftian umbrella. It began with collections of Lovecraft stories edited by Derleth and Wandrei, *The Outsider and Others* (1939) followed by *Beyond the Wall of Sleep* (1943). Anthologies like these disseminated his fiction to mid-century fans, who grew into shapers of popular culture. Many wrote directly within Lovecraft's Mythos, such as Fritz Leiber, Robert Bloch, R.E. Howard, and Ramsay Campbell, while others were indirectly influenced and have publicly recognized the debt, such as Stephen King, Neil Gaiman, Terry Pratchett, Alan Moore, and Guillermo Del Toro. Alongside this branch of creative individuals grew a budding amateur scholarly branch dedicated to recovering Lovecraft from those who either misused his work in the creation of their own or who misunderstood Lovecraft (thanks, according to critics, to Derleth's revisionism). The most important milestone was the publication by Arkham House of Lovecraft's *Selected Letters*.[10] This provided the material to shed decades of palimpsest-like layering of others' views of Lovecraft over the man himself.

Leading this recovery was Richard L. Tierney, Dirk W. Mosig, and George T. Wetzel, followed by independent scholar S.T. Joshi. Joshi,

---

[9] While the professional academic Lovecraftian sphere is growing, it pales in comparison to the amount of Lovecraft-inspired popular-culture elements that exist by the creative descendants of Lovecraft. A recent article from *The Atlantic* sums up his unexpected popularity as a stunning surprise:

Lovecraft ranks among the most *tchotchke*-fied writers in the world. Board Games. Coins. Corsets. Christmas wreaths. Dice. Dresses. Keychains. License-plate frames. Mugs. Phone cases. Plush toys. Posters. Ties. Enterprising fans have stamped the name "Cthulhu" (Lovecraft's most famous creation; a towering, malevolent, multi-tentacled deity) or other Lovecraftian gibberish on nearly every imaginable consumer product. And it's not just merchandise. It's apps and movies and podcasts. It's a bar in New York City called Lovecraft. It's a parody musical called "A Shoggoth on the Roof." It's a celebrity fan club that includes Guillermo Del Toro, Neil Gaiman, Junot Diaz, and Joyce Carol Oates. It's Lovecraft festivals in Stockholm, Sweden; Lyon, France; Portland, Oregon; and Providence. (Eil 2015, online).

[10] See Lovecraft 1965; 1976b; 1976a; 1971; 1968.

in particular, has argued that what is most important are Lovecraft's themes in his fiction, as well as the cosmicism of his thought. Joshi has published the most extensive biographies of Lovecraft, beginning with the abridged *HP Lovecraft: A Life* (1996), followed by a more complete, two-volume, *I Am Providence* (2013). He also published a more-accessible condensed version, *A Dreamer and Visionary: HP Lovecraft in his Time* (2001). These paint a picture of Lovecraft as a man defined by his correspondences and that to understand his fiction a scholar must seek these comprehensive epistolary texts. In doing so, one will encounter a bedrock of cosmic philosophy.[11]

As Joshi agues from forty years of parsing through Lovecraft's correspondences, to understand the literary man, you must look beyond his fiction and into his recorded life. A few key elements define him, according to Joshi, and now form part of the general description of Lovecraft. Antiquity gave Lovecraft life-long pleasure. He was also influenced by the Hellenic world of Greek and Roman culture and then by British culture. Science was also a major influence, especially geography, anthropology, and astronomy. He was an avid fan of dime novels and early Munsey magazines, such as *Black Cat*, *All-Story*, and *Argosy*. These were ancestors of the later pulp magazines, such as *Weird Tales*, that Lovecraft would help to define. Letter-writing and commentary on the Munsey magazines led to Lovecraft's amateur journalism. His fiction blessed and cursed him after returning to it in 1917, with the writing of "The Tomb" and "Dagon" (Joshi 2001, 106). From this the mature writer emerged, whose curious life was self-documented in his numerous correspondences.

Contrary to Joshi's critical agenda, Lovecraft's style, his social theory, his literary merit bear less importance than his broadest influence within popular culture. To see the span of this reach, we must look to the 'Cthulhu' Mythos as a major element of any appreciation of Lovecraft because of its use as a foundational element of fantastic realized worlds. The Cthulhu Mythos is a loose, shared, imaginary fantasy universe that utilizes elements of Lovecraft's pantheon of interstellar beings, his infernal sacred texts and the cults who champion their contents, his band of scholarly investigators who would unravel their mysteries, etc. It has grown far beyond the conception of those who helped Lovecraft form it, such as Clark Ashton Smith and R.E. Howard, Derleth, etc.,

---

[11] For Joshi, "it is this 'cosmic' stance that gives Lovecraft's own writing the intellectual and aesthetic substance to continue being of relevance nearly a century after it was written" (2011, 6). This cosmicism for Joshi leads to viewing Lovecraft as a pre-eminent writer of 'weird' fiction.

morphing through the addition of elements written by fellow writers, as well as those who followed after Lovecraft with their own tales. Some work can be situated directly within a tight use of the Mythos, such as Derleth's and Ramsey Campbell's fiction. Others operate indirectly.[12]

Joshi and purist Lovecraftian scholars, though, would refocus our attention on Lovecraft and the particulars of his thought and style, especially his philosophy of cosmicism and how this influenced his literary theory of the Weird.[13] Lovecraft, according to Joshi, feared the corruption of traditional Western 'civilization' in the form of machinic culture. Fantasy for Lovecraft formed a bulwark behind which he lived his life. From a literary position, this explains how his writing reflects his worldview. But the Mythos also represents a sustained, complex, and influential example of a realized world that has influenced subsequent creative artists.

Lovecraft, though, never popularized the term 'Cthulhu Mythos,' much less conceptualized a comprehensive system. In a letter to Frank Long, of February 27, 1931, Lovecraft wrote about 'Yog-Sothothery,' a phrase that appears to represent what would become the Cthulhu Mythos.[14] The extended pantheon, the great gulfs of space, cultists and their abyssal books, mad cults, scholars who hunt them, monsters from the depths, all figure into this tapestry. Joshi notes that Lovecraft juxtaposes this concept with another, broader cosmic concept he labeled the "sense of outsidedness [...] the provocative abyss of the unknown" (Lovecraft, qtd. in Joshi 2001, 299), referring here to the grandest scale of the unknowable in the universe. Joshi would argue that for individuals interested in directly using the Mythos, this cosmicism acts as an important frame that must be present in any work worthy of the title 'Lovecraftian.'

[12] See Derleth 1958; Campbell 2017 for early work written directly within the Mythos. See also Campbell 1997, a book edited by Campbell of his and Derleth's versions of the Mythos. To take just two of many recent indirect examples, Charles Stross wrote *The Atrocity Archives* (2004) and Frank Darabont directed the film *The Mist* (2007) based on the earlier novella written by Stephen King. Both detail Lovecraftian monstrosities breaking free into reality. With Stross, he posits a secret governmental organization designed to battle such intrusions, while King's novella and the later film and TV series use the intrusion as narrative background.

[13] Joshi argues that "if it [Cthulhu Mythos] can be said to be anything, is [*sic*] not the tales themselves nor even the philosophy behind the tales, but a series of plot devices utilized to convey that philosophy [cosmicism]" (2001, 244).

[14] See Lovecraft 1971, 293–4.

Lovecraft's 'Yog-Sothothery' should be thought of as the aliens/ deities of his famous pantheon; however, as symbols of his cosmicism, as Joshi would have it, they are better served by looking through his correspondences for his attempts to justify and clarify his worldview (rather than his use of the framework). One statement encapsulates his outlook:

> The time has come when the normal revolt against time, space, & matter must assume a form not overtly incompatible with what is known of reality—when it must be gratified by images forming supplements rather than contradictions of the visible & measurable universe. And what, if not a form of non-supernatural cosmic art, is to pacify this sense of revolt—as well as gratify the cognate sense of curiosity? (Lovecraft 1971, 295–6)[15]

Taken together, both the simplistic use of the Mythos framework as elements for fiction writers to populate their stories with monsters and aliens, as well as Lovecraft's explicit statements about cosmic indifference and humanity's horror at its revelation, have now emerged as reasons Lovecraft is seriously considered. The Cthulhu Mythos has become more than just a series of plot devices and, instead, has inspired representations in popular culture of complex SF and fantasy tropes. The catalyst has been the deep cosmicism (and its representatives monsters) acting as scaffolding for these tropes.

Lovecraftian scholars often point to a few portions of letters to clarify the critical cosmicism found in his thought. In a letter to Farnsworth Wright of July 5, 1927, Lovecraft writes:

> Now all my tales are based on the fundamental premise that common human laws and interests and emotions have no validity or significance in the vast cosmos-at-large. To me there is nothing but puerility in a tale in which the human form—and the local human passions and conditions and standards—are depicted as native to other worlds or other universes. To achieve the essence of real externality, whether of time or space or dimension, one must forget that such things as organic life, good and evil, love and hate, and all such local attributes of a negligible and temporary

---

[15] Joshi even claims that "this may be the most important utterance Lovecraft ever made" (1996, 151) and that the letter in which it is found to Frank Belknap Long should be considered alongside his best fiction "as one of his towering literary achievements" (241).

race called mankind, have any existence at all. Only the human scenes and characters must have human qualities. These must be handled with unsparing realism, (not catch-penny romanticism) but when we cross the line to the boundless and hideous unknown— the shadow-haunted Outside—we must remember to leave our humanity—and terrestrialism at the threshold. (Lovecraft, qtd. in Joshi and Schultz 2000, 209)

As Joshi notes, this idea of "the essence of [...] externality" and "boundless and hideous unknown—the shadow-haunted Outside" was written within the context of Lovecraft's views on Weird writing, in particular, how extraterrestrials should be represented as non-humanoid. What we see here is that Lovecraft's techniques of the Weird (as does his letter writing) reinforce his cosmicism. Contrary to how the Cthulhu Mythos was used as a background frame to allow his cosmicism to imbue his stories with mystery and horror, here, the very mundane aspect of discussing writing techniques becomes fodder for a philosophic posthuman/post-anthropocene cosmicism.[16]

Literary-minded thinkers, like Joshi and others who wish to craft literary respect for Lovecraft, typically find the bulk of imitative material that followed Lovecraft providing "almost uniformly poor results" (Joshi 2001, 392) and that only those writers who developed their own voices are worthy of comment. But this demand forces the material through a literary lens rather than looking at it within a more complex matrix of popular culture and, in particular, the modern fantastic. Broadening beyond the literary allows evaluative criteria to focus less on literary merit (as valuable as that may be) and more on the experiential possibilities the material fuels within the context of engaging a realized world in play. In this regard, even a poorly written story by a juvenile can suffice if it helps create an imaginative, playable experience.

Others have been more open to a liberal use of Lovecraft beyond the strictures of serious writing. An early attempt to understand the Mythos is Lin Carter's *Lovecraft: A Look Behind the Cthulhu Mythos* (1976). He associates Lovecraft with the genre of SF, rather than supernatural horror (1976, xvii), and, contrary to much Lovecraft scholarship that came later and that would situate Lovecraft within a respected literary frame, Carter argues that Lovecraft's most important influence, especially

---

[16] The question emerges: how can one draw or represent such outsidedness? This becomes a central task for Lovecraft-inspired writing and games (see Chapter 6 on Warhammer 40,000).

within popular culture, is the Mythos.[17] He is near the mark. Yet, the Mythos alone is not a complete explanation. Lovecraft's creation is a symbol of a complex realized world driven by the mixture of analog/digital elements and, most importantly, provides an aura of inspiration for gameplay experience. Carter's assessment is closer to understatement than to capturing the Mythos's true impact, especially now that fantasy realized worlds are becoming so prevalent.

A number of articles and books address the Mythos's importance beyond Carter's monograph, as well as beyond another important, early work, L. Sprague deCamp's *Lovecraft: A Biography* (1975). The debate over the Mythos's merit continues among Lovecraftians, with no final word. Joshi edited a recent examination of the Mythos's most important essays, *Dissecting Cthulhu* (2011), that follows the decades-long tradition of maligning August Derleth for his role in systematizing Lovecraft's creative framework beyond its original conception. Joshi foregrounds how Derleth deviated from a 'purist' view of Lovecraft as a writer whose cosmicism defined his work, rather than as a creator of a pantheon of monsters and forbidden books at war in a good vs. evil battle for the stars.

At stake here is Lovecraft's position as an important Weird writer of literature. Serious Lovecraftian scholars want readers to search within Lovecraft's fiction and letters for weighty themes, rather than mine them, for example, for references to the fictitious *Necronomicon*. Such an activity is important within literary studies, but it is too narrow to contain Lovecraft's most important cultural significance. It turns a blind eye to the phenomenon of Lovecraft's persistent reach. What Derleth has done, as well as anyone who has followed him, is add content. Regardless of the motivation or literary quality, such a process continues with TRPGs, both directly and indirectly, that provides a framework for play. It denies that Lovecraft's Mythos is merely background material for literary consideration, although these elements may function this way in Lovecraft's fiction and thought. Outside of it, the elements are much more.[18]

---

[17] He even claims that the Mythos "is as remarkable a literary phenomenon as this century has seen" (Carter 1976, xvii) and asks what power is in this Mythos that has such reach to influence so many writers, and why have other accomplished contemporary writers, such as Clark Ashton Smith or A. Merritt, or those who won greater fan support, such as E.R. Burroughs or R.E. Howard, failed to have achieved the international influence of Lovecraft. Carter seeks the answer in the Mythos.

[18] One of the more insightful essays is Steven J. Mariconda's "Toward a Reader Response Approach to the Lovecraft Mythos." He builds on Stanley Fish's literary theory of how readers define meaning in texts via interpretive

The importance of the Mythos does more than dominate the imagination of fantasy writers. Many of them who have been influenced by Lovecraft never directly reference his creations. The Mythos in its purest form as a shared universe is still a niche creative property, yet the Mythos represents how fantasy realized worlds function as hackable assemblages with a definitive 'aura.' As the editors of *Age of Lovecraft* note, journalist Jess Nevins claims Lovecraft created "the first open-sourced fictional universe" (Sederholm and Weinstock 2016, 10), an insight that this shared quality marks Lovecraft as prescient and relevant in today's world in which hacking and modding are the norm in digital gaming, a key activity also in TRPGs.

These major threads of Lovecraft's thinking also figure into two of the most dominant traditional TRPGs, Call of Cthulhu and D&D, and many of their descendants. Most Lovecraftian scholarship, though, has avoided detailing these connections.[19] Filling this empty space are the analog-and-digital game elements that comprise the modern fantastic's crystallization into fantasy realized worlds. The indirect influence of the Cthulhu Mythos proves to be a striking example of how such worlds function as complex Deleuzian assemblages far beyond the scope and control of any one creator. TRPGs demand such use because of their focus on distributing and consuming gametexts, inviting it, demanding it, in fact, by all involved.

What Joshi calls "a fulcrum in the history of supernatural fiction" (2011, 5), Lovecraft's Cthulhu Mythos, is more than that; it represents a complex popular-culture phenomenon wherein shared imaginary worlds become realized. Even more so, its influence on a game like D&D, and

communities, rather than finding pre-existing meaning within the texts themselves. Mariconda notes that *Weird Tales* magazine is a key element in the direct creation of the Mythos and that Lovecraft wrote with the magazine in mind, as well as acted as a ghost writer for many of its stories. Moreover, he notes that it is significant that Lovecraft corresponded with many other writers offering such material to the magazines. This encouraged inside jokes among writers becoming playful hoaxes for readers as a driving factor for Lovecraft. What should not be lost is how the analog tool of a printed magazine, as well as individual writers and readers and their letters, contributed to the Mythos. Mariconda argues that the interpretive community of *Weird Tales* writers and readers created an experience of encountering the Mythos, and that scholarship shouldn't be worried over terminology or classification. These are impossible to resolve.

[19] Joshi ends his condensed biography with a telling quote listing popular-culture media influenced by Lovecraft listed in this order: radio, film, comic books, role-playing games, computer games, "and the like" (2001, 391–92). His reference to "the like" reveals the lacuna my book fills.

other RPGs, is significant beyond the direct use of Mythos elements (which do exist in them) and, instead, rely on the ironic, playful, and later systematic development of such universes. Lovecraft's pantheons and new worlds, his forbidden books, and his intrepid but doomed investigators (i.e., adventurers) serve as an early example of what now fills the bulk of niche TRPGs and, more importantly, reflects the broader impulse of the exploration of fantasy spaces in digital RPGs and beyond. The 'game' of creating the Mythos for Lovecraft and his fellow writers now occurs in a much more complex and sophisticated manner, as can be seen in D&D, as well as the many analog/digital realized worlds influenced by Lovecraft.

Yet, among literary-minded Lovecraftians like Joshi, we risk too much in such a view. Even more recently, his revised *The Rise, Fall, and Rise of the Cthulhu Mythos* (2015) reiterates the refrain that we must not confuse Lovecraft the writer and thinker with the Mythos attached to his most popular creation. Joshi is quick to draw a distinction between the Lovecraft Mythos and the Cthulhu Mythos, the former being the direct creations of Lovecraft, the latter those direct and indirect creations of him and his successors. Such a distinction quarantines Lovecraft. I am less interested in terminology than in understanding his range and influence.[20]

Determining which stories should be part of the official Lovecraftian (Cthulhu) Mythos poses a difficult problem. A variety of lists have been suggested. For example, Carter provides a list in his monograph that helps:

---

[20] A quick note on what most experts consider to be critical in any distinction clarifies how far Lovecraft's reach exceeds beyond these direct uses. Joshi identifies five needed elements in any conceptualization of a proper 'Lovecraftian' Mythos (2008, 17–19). First, the use of a fictionalized New England locale dominates much of Lovecraft's fiction and acts as a point of departure for much Mythos writing outside of Joshi's acceptance. This also situates Lovecraft within the respected literary frame of serious writers who created fictional universes, such as Thomas Hardy and William Faulkner, both of whom Joshi notes. Second, Joshi identifies "a growing library of imaginary 'forbidden books'" (18) and, third, "a diverse array of extraterrestrial 'gods' or entities" (18). Fourth, Joshi demands a sense of cosmicism to any tale defining Lovecraft's true Mythos framework, while the fifth and last in the list is a "scholarly narrator or protagonist" (19). This type of strict categorization is uncontroversial among Lovecraftian purists, but determining which tales should be considered as part of the Mythos is much more contentious. I sidestep the debate because it swings the focus too far away from the goal of seeing how even a strict version of Lovecraft's Mythos exemplifies a broader process at work, especially in TRPG gametexts.

- The Nameless City
- The Hound
- The Festival
- The Call of Cthulhu
- The Dunwich Horror
- The Whisperer in the Darkness
- The Shadow Over Innsmouth
- At The Mountains of Madness
- The Dreams in the Witch House
- The Thing on the Doorstep
- The Shadow out of Time
- The Haunter of the Dark
- *History and Chronology of the Necronomicon*
- *Fungi from Yuggoth* (191)

However, in Joshi's *Complete Cthulhu Mythos Tales* (2013), he provides a longer list.[21] Chaosium's latest edition of the award-winning TRPG, Call

[21] See the Table of Contents for Joshi 2013:
    Dagon
    Nyarlathotep
    The Nameless City
    Azathoth
    The Hound
    The Festival
    The Call of Cthulhu
    The Colour out of Space
    History of the Necronomicon
    The Curse of Yig
    The Dunwich Horror
    The Whisperer in Darkness
    The Mound
    At The Mountains of Madness
    The Shadow over Innsmouth
    The Dreams in the Witch House
    The Man of Stone
    The Horror in the Museum
    The Thing on the Doorstep
    Out of the Aeons
    The Tree on the Hill

of Cthulhu, provides a list of reading material for novices who need introduction to Lovecraft's work.[22] Michel Houellebecq also provides a concise list of Lovecraft's "great texts" in *Against World the World, Against Life* (2005).[23]

While agreement on which tales to include remains contested, and whether Derleth be treated as a heretic or a loving admirer, Lovecraft's thought is becoming increasingly important for posthuman/post-anthropocene philosophy as a core philosophical posture within the modern fantastic.[24] I have shown that of most importance is his cosmicism, but his materialism is also as important (see below). As I have also tried to show with my analysis of Lovecraftian scholarship on the Mythos, elements that define a pure form of his Mythos act as a framework that carries weight beyond his fiction. They have provided decades of material for budding writers and artists, now making Cthulhu a popular-culture icon (enough so to have even appeared on *South Park*).[25] Joshi's critical stance demands we view Lovecraft as a cosmicist rather than a launching pad for popular-culture makers who would use and abuse

     The Shadow out of Time
     The Haunter of the Dark
[22] See Fricker and Mason 2016, 17:
     The Lurking Fear
     The Horror at Red Hook
     The Colour Out of Space
     The Dunwich Horror
     The Shadow Over Innsmouth
     The Dreams in the Witch-House
     The Haunter of the Dark
     The Shunned House
     The Call of Cthulhu
     The Case of Charles Dexter Ward
     The Whisperer in Darkness
     At the Mountains of Madness
     The Shadow Out of Time
[23] See Houellebecq 2005, 41:
     The Call of Cthulhu
     The Color Out of Space
     The Dunwhich Horror
     The Whisperer in Darkness
     At the Mountains of Madness
     The Dreams of the Witch House
     The Shadow Over Innsmouth
     The Shadow Out of Time
[24] See Thacker 2011; Harman 2012; Thacker 2015b; 2015a.
[25] *South Park*, season 14, episode 11.

him. Lovecraft's fiction, though, can be mined for material reflecting the classificatory impulse within the modern fantastic that drove early forms of TRPGs such as D&D. Lovecraft is a master of cosmic horror, and he is important as a precursor for the rise of the modern fantastic's realized worlds. But, ironically, his imaginary creations are just as much grounded in the meaty stuff of the material world, as they are the cosmic.

"Nerdy Categorizing"

British novelist of the Weird, China Miéville, reveals an overlooked quality of Lovecraft central to *Dread Trident* in an interview in which he challenges those who focus on Lovecraft's non-representationalism and untranslatability.[26] Miéville reminds us that Lovecraft's many-faced monsters are symbols of the universe as indifferent and that they are often spoken of as unrepresentable. If one were to ask, Lovecraft might demand a particular atmosphere of requisite dread during reading as the goal for a Weird story, rather than any attempt at giving form to the ultimate source of such dread. For many thinkers, this refusal of representation reflects the highest form of Lovecraft's literary value. His deities must not be faced. However, Miéville rightly notes:

> I think the approach to Lovecraft that only stresses the "beyond representation" sometimes misses the kind of nerdy categorizing— almost Pokémon-like—specificity of impossible physical form. (Joshi 2008, 232; qtd. in Weinstock 2016, 232)

I would swap D&D for Pokémon, although Miéville's example, like that of Magic the Gathering, demonstrates how a collectible card game defines the idea of 'specificity' and 'nerdy categorizing' today more so than do TRPGs.[27]

---

[26] Graham Harman's *Weird Realism: Lovecraft and Philosophy* (2012) uses Lovecraft to elucidate theories in object-oriented ontology, many of which focus on this untranslatable quality in Lovecraft's work. Harman looks to the weird elements in Lovecraft to imagine a world of things outside of human perception, while Eugene Thacker's use of horror in the three-volume *Horror of Philosophy* (2011–15) reinvigorates the genre beyond simply a mode of revulsion to acknowledging an often-terrifying Lovecraftian world beyond us.

[27] It should be noted that Wizards of the Coast are also the intellectual property owners of Magic the Gathering. And that this card game distills magic use and spell casting into a highly tactical game focused simply on these

I have chosen a few stories as examples of such categorizing of the material because they contain the creative mechanisms that have captivated the imaginations of Lovecraft's fans. But they do much more. In these stories we see an expected Lovecraftian posthuman/post-anthropocene cosmicism that reflects an interesting type of post-Gothic horror, but also the "nerdy categorizing [...] specificity of impossible physical form" referenced by Miéville and one that demonstrates an embodied scientific physicalism in Lovecraft's language. In the end, Lovecraft's physicalized fiction reveals how his instinct for materialized writing resists his literary theory that cosmic horror must be unrepresentable—a thesis refined to perfection by Thomas Ligotti, yet challenged by writers like Clive Barker, Miéville himself, and gameworlds like 40k. The most striking parts of Lovecraft, and those that demonstrate a marked style we now consider his own, emerges when we tease through his most textured embodied language of the monstrous to see how ideas of cosmic horror creep into material reality as elements from his Mythos.

"The Dunwich Horror" (1929) is a quintessential Lovecraftian example about an entity from the gulfs of space related to the alien-deity Yog-Sothoth. Its power incarnates in glaring detail when Lovecraft provides a classificatory description of a young Wilbur Whateley who has broken into the Miskatonic University Library to read the dreaded *Necronomicon* and has been mauled to death by a guard dog. The transformed Wilbur

> lay half-bent on its side in a foetid pool of greenish-yellow ichor and tarry stickiness was almost nine feet tall, and the dog had torn off all the clothing and some of the skin. [...] It was partly human, beyond a doubt, with very man-like hands and head, and the goatish, chinless face had the stamp of the Whateleys upon it. [...]
>
> Above the waist it was semi-anthropomorphic; though its chest, where the dog's rending paws still rested watchfully, had the leathery, reticulated hide of a crocodile or alligator. The back was piebald with yellow and black, and dimly suggested the squamous covering of certain snakes. Below the waist, though, it was the worst; for here all human resemblance left off and sheer phantasy began. The skin was thickly covered with coarse black fur, and from the abdomen a score of long greenish-grey tentacles with red sucking mouths protruded limply. [...] On each of the hips, deep set in a kind of pinkish, ciliated orbit, was what seemed to be a

mechanics, rather than on role-playing. In this sense, D&D is very much the progenitor of Magic the Gathering and all of its clones, like Pokémon.

rudimentary eye; whilst in lieu of a tail there depended a kind of trunk or feeler with purple annular markings, and with many evidences of being an undeveloped mouth or throat. The limbs, save for their black fur, roughly resembled the hind legs of prehistoric earth's giant saurians; and terminated in ridgy-veined pads that were neither hooves nor claws. (Lovecraft, "The Dunwich Horror," qtd. in Luckhurst 2013, 97–8)

We also learn that before doing so:

the thing itself [...] crowded out all other images at the time. It would be trite and not wholly accurate to say that no human pen could describe it, but one may properly say that it could not be vividly visualised by anyone whose ideas of aspect and contour are too closely bound up with the common life-forms of this planet and of the three known dimensions. ("The Dunwich Horror," qtd. in Luckhurst 2013, 97)

This rich description is in marked contrast to the narration of the final seen of the story in which Wilbur's twin brother emerges as a barn-sized monstrosity. Lovecraft retreats from detailed material description in the final scene and opts for distance, restraining the narrative focus to individuals looking through a telescope rather than alongside Dr. Henry Armitage and two others on top of a hill casting a spell to reveal and destroy the monster (a fine example of the sort of narrative choices TRPGs demand of player characters). Lovecraft's reliance on dialog provides him with a hint of representation, without requiring the sort of detailed, physical language that describes Wilbur Whateley's mutation. Curtis Whateley's claim that the thing is "Bigger'n a barn ... all made of squirmin' ropes [...] great bulgin' eyes all over it ... ten or twenty maouths" (qtd. in Luckhurst 2013, 116) lands a weaker punch than the earlier description. It must be believed because Lovecraft refuses to provide it with narrative credence by fully drawing the scene. Compared with the earlier description of Wilbur's transformation, this scene falls flat.[28]

At the Mountains of Madness (1936) demonstrates, though, how a mature Lovecraft captured the mystery of material organisms with highly

---

[28] Lovecraft's strength is in his handling of the material world's imagined oddities, the "invisible whistling octopus" (Wilson 1980, 48) that Wilson suggested was the absurd reason for Lovecraft's many adjectives. Here he refused.

textured language that delineates discrete material 'things' as objects. In describing how scientists in the Arctic discovered early life-forms during a sand-and-limestone drilling operation, we recognize the SF heart of this novel in its use of biological classification. The narrator learns of

> early shells, bones of ganoids and placoderms, remnants of labyrinthodonts and thecodonts, great mososaur skull fragments, dinosaur vertebrae and armour-plates, pterodactyl teeth and wing-bones, archaeopteryx debris, Miocene sharks' teeth, primitive bird-skulls, and skulls, vertebrae, and other bones of archaic mammals such as palaeotheres, xiphodons, dinoceras, eohippi, oreodons, and titanotheres. (*At the Mountains of Madness*, qtd. in Luckhurst 2013, 196–7)

The narrator provides classification of mundane biological lifeforms to juxtapose and foreground alien lifeforms.

In a detailed passage that describes an ancient, intelligent race that journeyed to the Earth and built prehistoric cities, Lovecraft's narrator writes in a journal seven continuous paragraphs that catalog the details of these 'Elder Things':

> Objects are eight feet long all over. Six-foot five-ridged barrel torso 3.5 feet central diameter, 1 foot end diameters. Dark grey, flexible, and infinitely tough. Seven-foot membranous wings of same colour, found folded, spread out of furrows between ridges. Wing framework tubular or glandular, of lighter grey, with orifices at wing tips. Spread wings have serrated edge. Around equator, one at central apex of each of the five vertical, stave-like ridges, are five systems of light grey flexible arms or tentacles found tightly folded to torso but expansible to maximum length of over 3 feet. Like arms of primitive crinoid. Single stalks 3 inches diameter branch after 6 inches into five sub-stalks, each of which branches after 8 inches into five small, tapering tentacles or tendrils, giving each stalk a total of 25 tentacles.
>
> At top of torso blunt bulbous neck of lighter grey with gill-like suggestions holds yellowish five-pointed starfish-shaped apparent head covered with three-inch wiry cilia of various prismatic colours.
>
> Head thick and puffy, about 2 feet point to point, with three-inch flexible yellowish tubes projecting from each point. Slit in exact centre of top probably breathing aperture. At end of each tube is spherical expansion where yellowish membrane rolls back on handling to reveal glassy, red-irised globe, evidently an eye.

Five slightly longer reddish tubes start from inner angles of starfish-shaped head and end in sac-like swellings of same colour which upon pressure open to bell-shaped orifices 2 inches maximum diameter and lined with sharp white tooth-like projections. Probable mouths. All these tubes, cilia, and points of starfish-head found folded tightly down; tubes and points clinging to bulbous neck and torso. Flexibility surprising despite vast toughness.

At bottom of torso rough but dissimilarly functioning counterparts of head arrangements exist. Bulbous light-grey pseudo-neck, without gill suggestions, holds greenish five-pointed starfish-arrangement.

Tough, muscular arms 4 feet long and tapering from 7 inches diameter at base to about 2.5 at point. To each point is attached small end of a greenish five-veined membranous triangle 8 inches long and 6 wide at farther end. This is the paddle, fin, or pseudo-foot which has made prints in rocks from a thousand million to fifty or sixty million years old.

From inner angles of starfish-arrangement project two-foot reddish tubes tapering from 3 inches diameter at base to 1 at tip. Orifices at tips. All these parts infinitely tough and leathery, but extremely flexible. Four-foot arms with paddles undoubtedly used for locomotion of some sort, marine or otherwise. When moved, display suggestions of exaggerated muscularity. As found, all these projections tightly folded over pseudo-neck and end of torso, corresponding to projections at other end. (*At the Mountains of Madness*, qtd. in Luckhurst 2013, 199–201)

This surgical description precedes a later clinical history that the Arctic explorers find detailed in sculptures of these "star-headed things" (Luckhurst 2013, 240), the Elder Things or Old Ones. This deft technique front loads SF-materialist language of overt classification and detailed field work of a biological and architectural find. Our narrator, Dr. William Dyer, learns of a variety of alien life forms we now consider canonical Mythos elements, such as Cthulhu Spawn and the Mi-Go. Mysterious winged Elder Things arrived from space, lived under the sea, built cities, and engaged in battles with other life forms. They are scientifically advanced. The narrator tells us they first created life on this planet, a perennial theme in SF and popular culture.[29] They also created a slave race of terrifying Shoggoths:

[29] See the mythology of the popular alien film such as *Prometheus* (2012) and *Covenant* (2017), the History Channel show *Ancient Aliens*, as well as any number of pseudo-scientific works in popular culture from Erich von

shapeless entities composed of a viscous jelly which looked like an agglutination of bubbles; and each averaged about fifteen feet in diameter when a sphere. They had, however, a constantly shifting shape and volume; throwing out temporary developments or forming apparent organs of sight, hearing, and speech in imitation of their masters, either spontaneously or according to suggestion. (*At the Mountains of Madness*, qtd. in Luckhurst 2013, 245)

And later:

Formless protoplasm able to mock and reflect all forms and organs and processes—viscous agglutinations of bubbling cells—rubbery fifteen-foot spheroids infinitely plastic and ductile—slaves of suggestion, builders of cities. (*At the Mountains of Madness*, qtd. in Luckhurst 2013, 273)

These monsters caused much trouble for the Elder Things, the increasing concern of the narrator over the demise of the Elder Things adding to the tension of discovering the truth of the matter.

Lovecraft also presents details for the "Cyclopean city of no architecture known to man or to human imagination" (*At the Mountains of Madness*, qtd. in Luckhurst 2013, 209) discovered in the icy mountains of the Arctic. He describes these inhuman architectures with their odd geometries, of cones and shafts, pyramids and star-shaped structures, immensely high bridges. They exist on a massive scale that suggested a mirage or illusion to the narrator, reinforcing that the mind cannot categorize such cosmic sublimity. This hints at an answer to what Danforth sees, the "final horror" (Lovecraft, qtd. in Luckhurst 2013, 282), as he and the narrator flee the Arctic mountains in an airplane. Lovecraft refuses to draw such a representation in the end, again, leaving it to the imagination because he believes the ultimate 'horrors,' rather than their proximate incarnations, must be beyond representation.

He uses his narrator to make an argument that the darkest of mysteries must be kept hidden and secret, "lest sleeping abnormalities wake to resurgent life, and blasphemously surviving nightmares squirm and splash out of their black lairs to newer and wider conquests" (*At the Mountains of Madness*, qtd. in Luckhurst 2013, 283). We are to believe from the ramblings of Danforth that what he saw was something other

Däniken's *Chariot of the Gods* (1968) to the more recent work by Graham Hancock that continues a tradition of working outside of respected scholarship in making bold claims.

than material architecture; quite probably a vision into the abyss within which the most cyclopean and horrific of Lovecraft's deities can be found. Lovecraft ends the novel with these ramblings:

> "The black pit", "the carven rim", "the proto-shoggoths", "the windowless solids with five dimensions", "the nameless cylinder", "the elder pharos", "Yog-Sothoth", "the primal white jelly", "the colour out of space", "the wings", "the eyes in darkness", "the moon-ladder", "the original, the eternal, the undying." (*At the Mountains of Madness*, qtd. in Luckhurst 2013, 283)

We are to make of this list an attempt to state plainly what these unnameable things are, bereft of description. Lovecraft's constant backing away at the last minute from confronting the nameless horror, like Dr. Armitage on the hilltop incanting spells to thwart the barn-sized Whateley transformed by Yog-Sothoth, suggests a lack of nerve when his prodigious talents at "nerdy categorizing" specificity could have provided a clinical description of such a creature or place.

Thomas Ligotti might disagree. But he is a fiction writer (see Chapter 7). Of note is the fact that Games Workshop's (GW) writers and designers of the 40k shared universe is comprised of the very sort of cosmic horrors that Lovecraft refused to represent. And they do so across a number of media (many visual), with success, even more so than D&D, which also has pantheons full of Lovecraftian horrors. GW's intention is other than capturing the literary dread of encountering such madness-inducing horror. Its creators want to sell products. They do so by providing artistic renditions that capture enough of the essence of these horrific creatures to work at a game table. In this way the weird, strange, terrific, and horrific find a place within an ironic understanding that buffers players and consumers from any true anxiety or tension. This may be a lessening of the effect Lovecraft would have for fiction. But it demonstrates empirically that systematization of cosmic horror is possible or, at least, a continued project of physicalizing the unimaginable.

Call of Cthulhu TRPG

Of critical interest for my study of Lovecraft is the Call of Cthulhu (CoC) TRPG. It systematizes the Lovecraftian-Cthulhu Mythos in such a way to crystallize the Mythos into something beyond the creation of a shared world into a playable realized world. Juxtaposing it with another version of the game, Monte Cook's interpretation of the CoC for D&D,

Call of Cthulhu: Roleplaying Game (2002) demonstrates that the Mythos is flexible enough to move beyond any purist insistence that it remain truly Lovecraftian. The incorporation of a variety of other elements transforms any strict reduction of a Lovecraftian Mythos, such as Joshi would prefer, into the truly polymorphous creative field that has always been the Cthulhu Mythos.

CoC has seen seven editions since Sandy Petersen and Chaosium published the original boxed set of *Call of Cthulhu* (1981). Variations have occurred, but a reliable consistency in content and mechanics exists from the first edition (1e) to the sixth edition's (6e) *Call of Cthulhu* (2005). The seventh edition (7e) maintains continuity but has changed the game in significant ways, so I will focus on 6e in this analysis. Historically, CoC is important because it challenged D&D-style gameplay of the typical dungeon delve to replace it with horror investigation. A section in the core rulebook, 'Avoid Gunfights,' even separates its gameplay from typical D&D combat. A gunfight may happen in CoC, but "the only use for a gun may be to shoot oneself if in danger of permanent madness" (Petersen and Willis 2005, 29). This change in gameplay is reflected in dramatic mechanic shifts away from those first established by D&D. As well as changing core attributes and providing a sophisticated skill system, the most dramatic change is its insanity mechanic. In CoC, as in Lovecraft's fiction, even glimpsing the dark horrors can cause madness. CoC tracts this because the game's ultimate goal is for players to see how much knowledge can be gained of the Mythos before his or her character suffers full insanity.

One of the most important skills is the 'Cthulhu Mythos' skill. Like being able to dodge or conceal oneself, to have skills in biology or chemistry, characters become skilled in the Mythos by encountering it. However, such encounters have corresponding and devastating effects: they lower sanity points. Each time the Mythos is encountered, a player must roll against this decreasing number, each roll becoming harder. A failed roll means a character experiences some form of insanity and a loss of overall sanity points. A glimpse of a body desecrated by a cult might be a low amount; glimpsing Cthulhu himself has the potential for a complete loss of sanity points. Like hidden knowledge, magic becomes a mechanism of danger.[30]

The core rulebook provides a chapter dedicated to 'The Cthulhu Mythos,' a concise example of gametext systematization of literary

---

[30] Likewise, this tension corresponds to the way magic is treated in Warhammer 40,000, with its magic users, called psykers, risking exposure to the denizens of the magic-infused Warp with each use (see Chapter 6).

material.[31] Instead of the potential confusion for newcomers engaging the Mythos indirectly via a short story, or with an anthology dedicated to it, the core rulebook functions as a condensed reference source-book. In today's world of free online resources, such material can be found with minimal work, but when the game was first developed such a resource didn't exist. The gametext was invaluable. Peterson provided the difficult labor of reading Lovecraft and his successors and distilling the material into a reliable and playable system.

Of central confusion for anyone teasing meaning from the Mythos's central elements, its pantheon, is its terminology. CoC's helpful distinctions begin with disentangling the deities, aliens, and monsters found in the Mythos. The 'Outer Gods' are those that represent cosmic principles, such as "Azathoth, the demon sultan and ruler of the cosmos, [who] writhes mindlessly to a demon flute at the center of the universe" (Petersen and Willis 2005, 107). Azathoth represents the principle of chaos, or entropy, death. Another favorite, Yog-Sothoth, is the cosmic deity who represents time, a duality that balances Azathoth. Nyarlathotep is mentioned as the messenger of these Outer Gods. CoC moves too quickly through the use of 'Elder Gods' as a designator for possible rivals to the Outer Gods and 'Other Gods' as a conflation of the two. It does so to foreground 'The Great Old Ones,' the alien beings who have a presence on Earth and who cults worship. These are the more accessible aliens/deities that may impact gameplay. Cthulhu, of course, is the most famous. This section also provides a brief list of alien races, lesser beings than the Great Old Ones, but still monstrous and alien. The Elder Things from *At the Mountains of Madness* (1936) and the Great Race of Yith from "The Shadow Out of Time" (1936) are two of the most famous.

More detail can be found outside the core rulebook in supplementary source-books such as the *Malleus Monstrorum* (2006).[32] This comprehensive 'monster manual' for CoC attempts to be an exhaustive compilation that moves beyond the standard *The Creature Companion* (1999).[33] Others extend entries in the pantheons and bestiaries, such as *Ye Booke of Monstres* (1994), admitting that no cohesive whole can ever be constructed, that the Mythos is too dynamic for such a reduction.[34] Most recently, Chaosium updated its *S. Petersen's Field Guide to Cthulhu Monsters* (1988) with a 7e version (2015) that follows its predecessor

---

[31] See Petersen and Willis 2005, 106–11.
[32] See Aniolowski 2006.
[33] See Aniolowski 1999.
[34] See the introduction in Aniolowski, Behrendt, and Carnahan 1994.

in providing stunning artwork and information as if written by a naturalist.[35]

One of the most helpful single gametexts that provides a structure for understanding the Mythos can be found in a source-book licensed to Wizards of the Coast to develop a CoC game for the (D20) system *Call of Cthulhu: Roleplaying Game* (2002). Of primary importance to this version is the need to distinguish its aims from the original, and from the tone of Lovecraft's fiction. In CoC:D20, it recognizes that in a purist game, "knowledge is not power. Knowledge is annihilation" (M. Cook and Tynes 2002, 203). Yet, because it is being played within a system designed for D&D, it admits that players have a chance to make a difference (even if the ultimate outcome is the same: the end of the world). It states that in this game, "you cannot win. Earth is doomed and so is everyone on it" (214).

Granted, the original game does allow its investigators to fight back. According to one particular game master (what CoC calls a Keeper), in many games, rather than characters risking everything for glimpses into forbidden knowledge, games ended with players tossing dynamite through doorways.[36] But CoC:D20 challenges players to be even braver heroes in the face of ultimate horror, encouraging more than mere glimpses or tossed explosives. It encourages brandishing weapons and staring the ultimate horror in its multiple faces. Lovecraft himself might have shown a brave face if given such a chance in such a game. Such a heroic approach may smack of hubris, from a Lovecraftian perspective, but within the context of the modern fantastic's insistence on irony, and from within a gameist mode, it reflects how TRPGs encourage a traditional humanist agency for players embedded within its posthumanist imaginings.

Lovecraft, not Tolkien

Resisting narrow conceptions of SF and fantasy drives this book in theorizing the modern fantastic, as well as how to approach Lovecraft. J.R.R. Tolkien is often viewed as critical in fashioning fantasy and in its popularization; yet modern fantasy didn't begin with Tolkien. *Dread Trident*'s framing of the modern fantastic as an umbrella concept avoids Tolkien's theories of sub-creation detailed in "On Faerie Stories" and the poem "Mythopoeia." Instead, *Dread Trident* sidesteps his thinking,

---

[35] See Petersen 1988.
[36] Personal communication with 'Keeper' Kevin Martin, 1 July 2017.

a common ground in most fantasy studies. He attempted to correct the demythologizing effects of modernity but did so without a key ingredient that defines the modern fantastic: *irony*. For Tolkien, the ultimate aim of his fantasy (and any good fantasy) is a type of divine consolation, one that runs square in the face of Lovecraft's cosmic indifference. Such lofty aims by Tolkien in offering a saving grace and Lovecraft in denying such salvation are admirable, but demand too much. We can understand both sides of this endeavor by looking at Tolkien's primary contribution to the theory of fantasy, the act of sub-creation, or using one's divine-like imagination to move from the primary world of material, mundane objects into a secondary world of myth. For Tolkien, this process defines what he considered to be proper fantasy, a method of writing that reflected a divine process of creation for humans who had lost direct connection with a mythological past. This reveals in Lovecraft a playfulness in his use of ironic Yog-Sothothery, while hinting at a deeper metaphysics grounded in a hostile universe.

With removal of the divine analogy, and adding a requisite ironic distance, the concepts related to sub-creation and secondary worlds work fine with the modern fantastic's fantasy realized worlds, as do Lovecraft's literary cosmicism; however, Tolkien's concept of secondary worlds relates to the concept of *secondary belief*, which makes huge demands on fantasy, ones beyond Lovecraft's views of Weird writing and its effects. For Tolkien, he challenged Coleridge's 'willing suspension of disbelief' as backwards. He wanted secondary worlds to function like powerful myth. He wanted a deeper experience of fantasy, similar to the conviction of religious experience. It is worth quoting a key passage in detail:

> Children are capable, of course, of *literary belief*, when the story-maker's art is good enough to produce it. That state of mind has been called "willing suspension of disbelief." But this does not seem to me a good description of what happens. What really happens is that the story-maker proves a successful "sub-creator." He makes a Secondary World which your mind can enter. Inside it, what he relates is "true": it accords with the laws of that world. You therefore believe it, while you are, as it were, inside. The moment disbelief arises, the spell is broken; the magic, or rather art, has failed. You are then out in the Primary World again, looking at the little abortive Secondary World from outside. If you are obliged, by kindliness or circumstance, to stay, then disbelief must be suspended (or stifled), otherwise listening and looking would become intolerable. But this suspension of disbelief is a substitute for the genuine thing, a subterfuge we use when condescending

to games or make-believe, or when trying (more or less willingly) to find what virtue we can in the work of an art that has for us failed. (Tolkien 1965, 36–7)

Tolkien's attempt to wrest fantasy from mere make-believe and into something valuable for human experience is laudable. But his approach denies the power of irony to allow for the experience of fantasy that provides an ironic enchantment, or magification, albeit one without the magnitude of his "Eucatastrophe" (Tolkien 1965, 68). He is after this final effect, a type of joy similar to that found in the Gospels with belief in Christ's resurrection and ascension.[37]

The problem in Tolkien's demand, though, is that as the modern fantastic's realized worlds have proliferated, the critical requirement of irony has created a much-needed zone of safety. To imagine and believe in the existence of Cthulhu is a running joke within popular culture. Facebook memes can be found of people praying to Cthulhu for mercy so that he doesn't consume their minds. One must always be aware, for example, that casting spells or raising the dead in CoC is contained within a make-believe game, the imaginative but harmless activities Tolkien (and many critics) associate with childhood. To maintain true 'secondary belief' in these instances is to demonstrate a marked misunderstanding of primary and secondary reality or their complex miscible natures. A challenge for digital realized worlds that aim for increased haptic, aural, visual immersion is to provide convincing simulation while never going so far that users truly believe, in the Tolkien sense. When we cross such verisimilitude borders, we will have new challenges in managing realized worlds.

Directly related to how *Dread Trident* theorizes an ironic modern fantastic is how Tolkien's worldview, so defined by a fantasy that functions like religious belief, compares with that of Lovecraft's cosmic philosophy of a cold, uncaring universe. The tension isn't over choosing: that of a universe with inherent meaning or one without. The idea is that the modern fantastic, and its realized worlds, require irony to provide safe distance from either choice. This may deny individuals consolation, but it also acts as a bulwark against the pressures of an uncaring universe. It also demonstrates the power of realized worlds to affect modernized life in a positive manner. A touch of magification seems to be enough, even if terrifying. This may not provide the joy that Tolkien demanded

---

[37] Note that for Lovecraft the ultimate effect Weird writing should have on a reader is a sense of dread. See his ideas in the correspondence that leads on from "Notes On Writing Weird Fiction."

(or the dread demanded by Lovecraft), but it is something. Our realized worlds function well without secondary belief, especially when those are experienced through embodied play

While the aura of Lovecraft has permeated popular culture and gaming beyond direct reference to his Mythos (i.e., to his pantheons, forbidden books, of fantastic places, etc.), the use of his pantheon of alien-deities informs the settings of D&D and 40k and many other TRPGs, while his posthuman cosmicism continues to inspire writers such as Thomas Ligotti. These gameist elements lead to a unique form of fantasy-driven posthumanism, a tone that emerges in 40k, as well as in Eclipse Phase and the post-anthropocene TRPG Numenera. Of critical importance for any use of Lovecraft and TRPGs is how his cosmic posthumanism and his instinct to resist representing the ultimate horror in literary form finds willingness in TRPGS of the modern fantastic.

This chapter has ignored the complex literary history of how these scholars and collaborators reworked the Mythos in favor of the unexplored examination of how Lovecraft functions as an influence on TRPGs, the modern fantastic, and realized worlds. It built on the previous chapter's examination of how the Gothic sensibility withered and renewed itself, alongside a more complex and interesting cosmic horror that Lovecraft championed and that now defines the most interesting form of posthumanism as post-anthropocene cosmic horror. It has argued for a sense that the reality of things outside of human perception may be the most terrifying concept for humans and resists literary Lovecraftian scholarship that would see him primarily as a Weird writer. Instead, it explained both why the Cthulhu Mythos is rejected by some literary thinkers as an important part of Lovecraft's heritage and why it is critical in *Dread Trident* that Lovecraft's own work acts as a supreme example within the modern fantastic of how these elements are systematized (we find a fitting example in the TRPG, Call of Cthulhu).[38]

---

[38] Ultimately, this chapter provided an explanation of how Lovecraft finds refinement in popular culture beyond his direct influence. For example, we see such reach in a contemporary horror writer, Thomas Ligotti, and how a variant of the 'Cthulhu' Mythos influenced without full acknowledgment or confidence the first season of the Weird-driven HBO series, *True Detective* (see Chapter 7).

Chapter 6

Warhammer 40,000
A Science Fantasy Narrative

Games Workshop's (GW) popular Warhammer 40,000 (40k) setting is designed to sell miniature wargame models. Based on the 1983 initial release of Warhammer Fantasy Battle, GW developed the first 40k product, *Rogue Trader* (1987). It was followed by periodic gametexts that added detail to the setting. Since then, an archive of gametexts has evolved out of model painting and wargaming into a coherent if complex picture of a universe at war. The wargaming elements are still the focus; however, GW expanded with the publication of fiction under the Black Library imprint and the release of its first TRPG Dark Heresy in 2008. Dan Abnett's *Horus Heresy* (2006) was the first novel in a series that grounds the setting in its definitive pre-history, reaching back 10,000 years (i.e., often referred to as the 30k variant of the setting) from the current time-line to a moment of betrayal that defines the setting. That a wargaming (rather than role-playing) shared universe has proven to be one of the largest yet most unified imaginary realized-world setting is quite a surprise.

This case study focuses on a few main story-lines, such as the Horus Heresy, because they demonstrate the literary complexities in consuming such a realized world. The Horus Heresy encapsulates how the epic and tragic literary themes within 40k drive the lore in an archetypal fashion that appeals to GW's customers' sense of high drama in an expansive and seemingly endless possibility of untold narratives. But this case study also examines the cohesive Beast Arises series as an example of a contained narrative with finely drawn characters; this series fills one of many gaps between the Heresy and the most recent narrative. While the Beast Arises is cohesive compared with the narrative complexity of the Horus Heresy, it still demonstrates how the wider narrative of the 40k universe is ever expanding, and endless. This chapter also examines the advancement of the 40k time-line with the Gathering Storm narrative and the release of 40k's latest 8th edition. Like the Beast Arises and the Horus Heresy, the Gathering Storm demonstrates how such a complex realized world continually grows through the addition of gametexts and tools.

In examining such a broad canvas, this case study thus foregrounds the 'lore' that details these game settings as functioning in a few critical ways consistent with how *Dread Trident* theorizes the modern fantastic: it utilizes themes from trans-and-posthumanism; reworks Lovecraftian cosmicism as an actual battle among the stars, while representing reworked versions of Lovecraft's pantheon as the ultimate enemy; uniquely acts as both a draconic and posthuman example of science fantasy by blending the Gothic with high tech; and incorporates elements from epic and tragic literature into a grand, galaxy-spanning story. A 'grimdark' aspect emerges in the 40k realized world as the universe is besieged by Lovecraft-like entities. But, alas, heroes emerge to challenge the chaos. This resistance reworks purist notions within the Lovecraftian Cthulhu Mythos that forbidden knowledge causes insanity from a mere glimpse, the 40k setting imagining how humanity combats such a malicious or indifferent universe, even if losing a war of attrition. In 40k, Lovecraft-like alien deities are represented as they are battled. Its sourcebooks are full of visual art and narrative detail for such unrepresentable things. The study of a 40k-inflected realized world demonstrates how such science-fantasy is central in any understanding of fantasy, SF, horror, modernity, posthumanism, transhumanism, and the modern fantastic.

Early Gametexts: Fall of the Emperor

The products sold by Games Workshop (GW) as part of the popular *Warhammer 40,000* (40k) tabletop miniatures game support a complex, shared, fantasy universe that is a combination of narrative and gaming reflecting the major themes covered in *Dread Trident*'s examination of the modern fantastic, from science-fantasy, to posthumanism, to cosmic horror. The clearest way to analyze such complexity is to recognize that GW sells products for a profit but also designs them within a narrative framework that organizes play: often called 'lore' or denigrated as 'fluff' by wargamers uninterested in story and more interested in 'crunch,' i.e., game mechanics. The use of such lore in the expanding fictional 40k universe increases the reach of GW's products to non-gamers interested in the art or fiction rather than playing the game.

While the narrative elements remain secondary to the sales of miniatures, this extraneous material adds flavor to the gameworld so that the products (i.e., the models meant to be painted and tabled at a game, as well as the gametexts that describe the backgrounds or how the rules function for these models) have a narrative framework that stokes the imagination. These gametexts and tools, like those found in TRPGs, allow players to engage the material when not actually playing the game at a table. At this point, gaming intersects with more traditional forms of cultural consumption. The literary and visual lore of GW's 40k realized world demands comment when we feature them as integral to this process, rather than simply as additive.

To understand 40k as an array of products, a shared universe, and a realized world, we should begin with the broadest perspective and view it within the context of its historical importance as a wargame, as well as an arena for its in-game narrative lore, first as a framing device in the wargaming magazine *White Dwarf* and then, later, as one of the most developed gaming realized fantasy worlds created. With *White Dwarf* #93 (September 1987), the magazine had been in print for a decade. Increasingly an arm of GW/Design Studio's need to market and sell their own products, the magazine's aim at covering the widest range of fantasy and SF analog gaming allowed room for non-GW material. However, its own product line based on Warhammer Fantasy Battles' world of standard D&D-style motifs broadened into SF when it presented an expansion of the Warhammer universe—this one into space, and the future.

The 40k universe utilized many fantasy elements already found in the Warhammer universe, such as Orks, for one; plus a pantheon of Chaos demons/gods; not to mention the initial use of abhumans, i.e., Squats (dwarves), Halflings, Ogryns (ogres); and space elves called Eldar. But this expansion functioned like a parallel universe that departed from any real sense of harmonization (unlike what we have seen with D&D's constant use of mechanisms that unify its different campaign worlds). When GW introduced 'space marines' into the mix, it entered a new path that would supersede its traditional fantasy framework. At first, both the products being sold under 40k and the framing narrative remained within full comprehension of someone who wanted a complete collection of the universe's gametexts. That would soon change.

A month prior to the publication of the first 40k gametext, *Rogue Trader* (October 1997), the *White Dwarf* article provided a snapshot of the core elements that still dominate the setting. The designers explained the science fantasy nature of this new setting.[1] Genre determined,

---

[1] They write, "Well for starters it isn't just a science fiction game although it is set in the far future: 40,000 years more or less ... you guessed! We call it a fantasy game set in the far future ... a sort of science fantasy!" (Games Workshop Team 1987, 34).

it also reinforced a grand temporal scale: "For more than a hundred centuries the Emperor has sat immobile on his Golden Throne of Earth" (Games Workshop Team 1987, 32). The frame of 10,000 years from the time of the Emperor's zenith to his fall and the subsequent decline of his empire drives the setting's overall tone of despair. We are told the Emperor "is a rotting carcass writhing invisibly with power from the Dark Age of Technology. He is the Carrion Lord of the Imperium to whom a thousand souls are sacrificed every day" (32). The game was, thus, predicated on the macabre image of a universe in which a dead emperor demands multitudes of human sacrifices. This is a cruel world, bloody, full of conflict, with little hope. The progressive dreams of the Enlightenment, with technology as a driving force, has failed.[2]

The setting provides a universe with billions upon billions of inhabitants, of a sprawling bureaucratic system of governance. "One aim is to create an almost medieval attitude among the human societies" (Games Workshop Team 1987, 35); this science-fantasy medievalism emerges as an aesthetic blending an overwrought Catholicism with a revamped SF-inflected Gothicism. Add to that a hyper-rationalized, nightmarish Weberian bureaucratism, and you have a gameworld ripe for Lovecraftian cosmic war on a scale far beyond that of Call of Cthulhu, the Worlds of Darkness, or even Eclipse Phase. This dominant Catholic mode of framing the game finds its heart in a core part of the sprawling system of governance for the Imperium, the Inquisition. The early *White Dwarf* article even provides an organizational chart, with the Emperor listed at the top and his various organizations listed below. The Inquisition is identified, but, mysteriously, with no detail.[3]

Lovecraft's central idea within his Mythos is that humans would go mad if faced with even a glimpse of the gods/alien-beings in the universe. We have no recourse for understanding or any way to protect ourselves. The 40k universe imagines what happens if we maintained our technological drive toward the stars for 20,000 years, expanding into the galaxy as conquerors, encountering hostile alien life forms, and proving victorious, yet stumbling into superstition in the end. This

[2] We are told, "there is no peace among the stars, only an eternity of carnage and slaughter and the laughter of thirsting gods" (Games Workshop Team 1987, 32).

[3] See Games Workshop Team 1987, 42. One of the very first Black Library novels was Ian Watson's *Inquisitor* (1990). While the Space Marines have always been the driving force of both gameplay and lore, the Inquisition has developed into one of the most intriguing parts of the setting. It was also given a central role in the TRPG *Dark Heresy* (2008), where players create characters who begin as an inquisitor's acolytes.

failure, the lore suggests, might have been avoided had the Emperor's plans succeeded for a rational universe, full of Enlightenment, to have been built. At the beginning of this narrative, we are only told that the Emperor now acts as a psychic beacon for space craft, as well acts as a protector for humankind in a universe brimming with these dangerous aliens and demons.[4]

A direct nod to Lovecraft emerges when examining how magic is utilized in the game. Right away in this very first description of the setting magic is represented as dangerous. This threat arrives in the form of 'psykers,' psychically gifted individuals who can access the energies of the Warp, an immaterial realm in which the supernatural exists. These fantasy elements act as the central lynchpin for the entire setting. It is what both allowed the Emperor to save the world from the Dark Age of Technology's inherent failures that relied on rationality and technical progress, as well as damned him to become a corpse god, imprisoned in his Golden Throne where he neither moves nor speaks but engages in endless psychic battles with the demons of the Warp. The role of magic is what makes the game highly fantastic, while also imbuing it with a sense of danger. Magic in 40k means more than glimpsing Lovecraft's horrific gods; it means seeing them in full relief, as well as having the power to challenge them. It is very much a mechanism of playing with fire or, better yet, with 'the Devil.'

In the first gametext released soon after the initial article, *Rogue Trader* (1987) also detailed the rules for playing in this new setting. This gametext is an example of an odd 40k gametext, compared to the other editions of core 40k rulebooks. *Rogue Trader* owes much more to the role-playing games of D&D than to the later wargaming focus that now drives the game. It is also now much less reverent toward the current setting, some of its content and even its art more comic than serious.[5]

With the publication of this foundational text, we learn more of how the Imperium developed out of the will of the Emperor, even learning a bit of his backstory. Yet, a glaring mystery is presented here at the beginning of the setting's creation, a mystery that will later prove to be one of the most popular elements in the fully developed narrative.

[4] "Only the constant vigilance of the Emperor shields humanity from the thousand perils that threaten its destruction" (Games Workshop Team 1987, 35).

[5] See Snipe and Wib 2017 for an example of a well-produced bit of amateur sleuthing into *Rogue Trader*'s oddities. For example, the very first inquisitor designed for the setting is named "Obiwan Sherlock Clousseau" (Priestley 1987, 144). *Rogue Trader* is now famous among fans, many of whom find pleasure in teasing out the oddities of this initial source-book.

Early players knew that the Emperor sits entombed in a throne, nothing but a carcass with an indomitable psychic will that acts as a beacon for interstellar spaceships, as well as a god-like guardian for the Imperium. Yet, they didn't know the details of how it happened. These answers into the foundations of 40k's most important events lead to hints of mysteries to be revealed but also into details of how the products function as complex literary and gameist elements within the modern fantastic.

The Horus Heresy

The mystery surrounding the entombment of the Emperor leads to the development of the most important storyline in the setting, the Horus Heresy. It began as a simple sidebar in another 40k gametext:

> The Horus Heresy is reckoned by many to rate as the greatest single disaster ever suffered by the Imperium. The specific details of the heresy are known only to the Emperor, but is [sic: its] broader history is the stuff of popular legend. According to one version of the tale, Horus was once the most trusted servant of the Emperor. But in his heart there dwelt a hidden evil, and he became seduced by this evil, and came to nurture demons and other forces of destruction. Horus marched upon Earth with a third part of the hosts of the Imperium which he had seduced to his purpose. For seven days and seven nights the hosts battled until the Emperor caught Horus by the heel and cast him to the Eye of Terror and with him the third part of the hosts of the Imperium. (Games Workshop Team 1988, 13)

This small bit of information was enough to open the floodgates. As key GW employee Alan Merrett notes in *The Horus Heresy: Collected Visions* (2007), the Heresy expanded in a miniatures-wargame product, *Adeptus Titanicus* (1988), as well as in a supplement, *Realm of Chaos: Slaves to Darkness* (1988). It would also later be featured in another wargame called *Space Marine: Epic Battles in the Age of Heresy* (1989). The first true fleshing out of the setting's disastrous origin occurs with these initial gametexts as they detail events 10,000 years prior to the setting's current date. As the setting became detailed, the vague, biblical exposition of seven days and seven nights, and the villain caught by the heel and being cast away changed into a process of iterative development in which details emerged from a variety of points-of-view to paint a canvas of epic proportions.

In *Adeptus Titanicus*, the setting's broad history is structured along a few key events now standard canon. In a description of the history of the Imperium, we learn that for 25,000 years humanity explored the stars in a time called the Dark Age of Technology. Curiously, the use of the 'dark age' is not explained, only hinted at—that "humanity's machines achieved incredible levels of sophistication. There seemed nothing that Man [humanity] could not do" (Johnson 1988, 4). This was the time when the psykers emerged. Their new abilities opened them to the influence of demons, which caused a furor in the form of witch hunts. Millions were executed. As civilization crumbled under the weight of such horror, an Age of Strife began that lasted 5,000 years. This was a time dominated by warfare that lasted until the Emperor united humankind. At this point he had guided what would become the Imperium for 10,000 years, but a rebellion occurred at the beginning of the Imperium, a rebellion that changed everything. It began with a betrayal by the Emperor's favored son, Horus.

Realm of Chaos: Slaves to Darkness (1988) provides a detailed description of the Horus Heresy that acted as a model for the level of detail that would later be developed.[6] It is a supplement that presents fiend-like entities living in the Warp (the magical realm of space), as well as explains the origins of the most despicable of the Imperium's enemies. These are traitorous legions of Space Marines who live in a region of space called the Eye of Terror. They have hidden there for 10,000 years, working to destroy the Imperium through a series of Black Crusades. The Horus Heresy not only explains their origins, but also the fall of the Emperor and the death of Horus. Now players at tables aren't just battling evil space marines and monsters. They have narratives to expand their experience at the tables so that dice rolls and tactics matter beyond the last battle.

In *Slaves to Darkness*, the bulk of the story is constructed at this early stage—early enough to begin answering the question to this great mystery. We are told how the Emperor elevated one of his genetically enhanced sons, Horus, to Warmaster. That Horus fell ill and was tainted by demons in his recovery. How he used secret coven-like war lodges to spread this new corruption among the Emperor's followers. He convinced five legions of the Emperor's bravest warriors, the Space Marines of the Legion Astartes, to join him. On the planet Isstvan III Horus made his true intention known. Loyalist Astartes resisted, fleeing to earth on the

[6] It was followed by another *Realm of Chaos* supplement. See Priestley and Ansell 1990. This was released as a source-book for Warhammer Fantasy Battles that details the demonic monsters of the setting. These overlap with the 40k setting, as well.

ship *Eisenstein* to tell the horrible news. The war for Terra began. We learn that Horus's fleet assaulted the Palace, that the Emperor teleported to Horus's bunker to face him, that Horus was killed and the Emperor wounded. The Emperor, barely alive, was taken by another son, Rogal Dorn, to his Golden Throne and ordered the surviving traitors be chased into the Eye of Terror.

A design technique repeatedly utilized can be seen in a description of the Horus Heresy: "Only the Emperor and the Cyber-libraries of the Ordo Malleus have an accurate recollection of the Heresy" (Ansell, Brunton, and Forrest 1988, 240). This evocative technique hints that missing information exists, a literary mystery, in essence. Such a discursive lacuna constructs an intriguing narrative space to be filled by future designers, writers, novelists, gamers, etc. For example, narrative inconsistencies exist over the events of the final battle between the Emperor and Horus, in particular where the encounter takes places and who actually accompanies the Emperor. In the early version, they teleport to Horus's "bunker" (243), while later versions have them arriving aboard his flagship. Also, the curious case of who helps the Emperor challenge Horus at the critical moment has changed through the versions from no intervention being mentioned, to a saint-like guardsman, to a massive terminator. This becomes a Custodian bodyguard in *Collected Visions* (2007), and simply a soldier in *Visions of Heresy* (2014).[7]

This quick summary of the narrative as detailed in *Slaves to Darkness* provides glimpses of events that become detailed in later gametexts, novels, graphic novels, analog games, digital games, etc. Most of the information has remained consistent, although some elements have become antiquated.[8] Overlapping narratives should be expected. In fact, during the process of making it 'realized,' players themselves are able to challenge my reading with their own through fan-fiction, description of narrative play at the table, artwork, etc. This recursive aspect adds to the lore rather than diminishes it.

---

[7] See Merrett 2007, 365 and 388.

[8] For example, when the loyalist Astartes on Isstvan III flee, we read, "The seizure of the Eisenstein [by the loyalists] is regarded as the start of the first Inter-Legionary War" (Ansell, Brunton, and Forrest 1988, 240). Yet, in later texts, we learn that Horus not only bombs Isstvan III in a show of power, but that he has sent loyalist Space Marines to its surface as victims in the attack (see *Collected Visions*, below). The Isstvan III bombing and the betrayal of the Space Marines by Horus is not detailed in *Slaves to Darkness* but can be argued as the actual first major moment in which Space Marines betray other Space Marines in an 'Inter-Legionary' war. Such a clarification is expected as the shared narrative grows.

A further important expansion of the narrative occurs in *White Dwarf* (#161) and in a rulebook for a miniatures game *Horus Heresy* (1993),[9] designed by Jervis Johnson, with a narrative history written by William King. It explores the attack on Terra. Here we see details that personalize what was referenced only in the broadest of strokes in the earlier gametexts. We learn that another of the Emperor's sons, the angelic-winged Primarch Sanguinius, stands by his side in defense of Terra, as do his other loyal Primarch sons, Rogal Dorn and Jaghatai Khan. We are told about the arrivals of the traitorous Primarchs, the rebellious sons who have been mutated by the evils within the Warp. Their names are Angron, Mortarion, Magnus, Fulgrim. We learn that even human members of the Imperial Army play a role in the breach of Terra, that some of these Chaos-corrupted soldiers turn on their brothers and sisters at a critical moment. Even worse, Chaos demons materialize during the assault, all manner of monsters descending from orbit.

An intimate moment is described in which Angron approaches the walls of Terra and demands that its occupants surrender. His stalwart brother Sanguinius stands atop the walls in defiance. We do not know how they communicated. "Who knows what they saw there? Perhaps they communicated telepathically, brother Primarch to brother Primarch. The truth will never be known" (Bill King 1993, 14). This interesting encounter between Primarchs is excised from the more detailed version that came later (see *Collected Visions* below). Angron turns aside and orders all to be killed within the walls. Sanguinius retreats beyond the Ultimate Gate into the Palace itself; there he is attacked by a Bloodthirster demon. These two powerful beings take to the air. Sanguinius is nearly spent from days of defending the wall. He is cast to the ground. But he rallies and breaks the beast's back upon his knee.

The most critical part of Horus's attack is revealed in this early account. Horus learns that two other loyalist Primarchs, Leman Russ and Lion El'Jonson, will arrive in hours. He knows he must kill the Emperor soon to succeed. He lowers the shields on his ship, providing an opportunity for the Emperor to teleport aboard. Sanguinius and Dorn accompany the Emperor. Sanguinius arrives in the throne room, while Dorn and the Emperor are teleported far from it. Sanguinius refuses Horus's offer to switch sides. Horus throttles the life out of his already weakened brother. Soon, the Emperor finds Horus. He is alone when he faces his wayward son and all the powers of the Warp. We are told that "what happened next is the stuff of legend" (Bill King 1993, 16), a

---

[9] This information was also printed in *White Dwarf*, issue 161 (May 1993).

hint that this key moment in the narrative will receive multiple rounds
of clarification:

> The two mightiest beings in the history of mankind clashed. They
> met blade to blade, power to power, mind to mind and tested sinew
> and psychic power to the ultimate. Behind Horus was the massed
> power of the Chaos Gods. The Emperor stood alone and still he
> triumphed, although he was terribly wounded in the process. (Bill
> King 1993, 16)

From the omniscient point of view that dominates the narration of
these events, we learn that the Emperor was victorious, although gravely
wounded; however, another section in the *Horus Heresy* (1993) rulebook
details the teleportation event with a more subjective narrative focus.[10]
We see the events through the eyes of the Emperor, with actual dialog
between Horus and the Emperor. The mystery is illuminated, the battle
described. We learn that Horus lashes out and cuts the Emperor's throat,
as well as severs tendons in his wrist. Horus lifts the Emperor over his
head and slams him upon his knee, breaking his back (a favored *coup
de grâce* among 40k writers). Horus even rips an arm from its socket. At
this point, a "solitary Terminator" (Bill King 1993, 19) charges Horus in
an act of foolish bravery. Horus melts the flesh from this loyal warrior's
bones, alerting the Emperor to Horus's final, incorrigible state. The
Emperor has been restraining himself, hoping beyond hope that his
favored son can be saved. When he realizes this cannot happen, the
Emperor strikes with all his psychic power, blasting his son's heart.
We are told that as Horus dies he is freed from corruption, that he
realizes his mistake, that even tears of remorse form. The result causes
a psychic shockwave through the traitors on Terra, all of whom retreat.
Rogal Dorn finds the Emperor and hears a whisper from his father to
take him to the Golden Throne in the Palace. The key moment of the
Emperor's fall has formed.[11]

The story of the Heresy can also be gleaned from careful reading
through four *Index Astartes* gametexts (2002–05) that assembled articles
from *White Dwarf* about Space Marines. An exhaustive look at how
these add to the lore of the Horus Heresy is far beyond the scope of
this chapter, but it is worth noting that these 'indexes' are predicated
on understanding that 40k Space Marine 'chapters' (particular groups)

---

[10] This would later be republished in *Collective Visions*. See also the Ollanius Pius
retcon in Lexicanum: https://wh40k.lexicanum.com/wiki/Ollanius_Pius.

[11] The novel version of this event has not been written yet.

and 40k Chaos Space Marines are the result of what happened in the Horus Heresy. The Foreword to the first *Index Astartes* gametext, written by Andy Chambers, states that "the very forces that freed Mankind went on to plunge the newborn Imperium into the terrifying civil war of the Horus Heresy" (Games Workshop Team 2002, 1).

These indices are helpful because they focus on the specific Space Marine Primarchs, their legions, and successor chapters. And each one has a section exploring involvement in the Heresy. They reveal interesting details, such as when the disloyal Primarch Fulgrim and his Emperor's Children attacked Terra they murdered civilians over forty times their number to satiate their addiction for violent pleasure (Games Workshop Team 2002, 29). At this point, though, the first *Index* gives no mention of the infamous 'Drop Site Massacre' on Isstvan V and Fulgrim's battle with his brother Ferrus Manus in which Fulgrim kills Manus. In the second volume, a detailed account of Lehman Russ's Space Wolves' attack on Magnus's home world of Prospero mentions the 13th Wulfen Company—Space Wolves who turn into werewolves and spearhead the attack to hunt down their enemies. These details add to the number of mysteries that will be illuminated in later texts—or not.[12]

Collected Visions

With the success of the Horus Heresy, a variety of new gametexts emerged. Forge World, a subsidiary of GW that focuses on the production and sales of high-quality models, began a series of Horus Heresy campaign gametexts that do more than simply function as a type of codex-like reference for the armies during that era. Along with extensive game mechanics, the Forge World books also provide extensive lore for what is now known as the 30k period of the setting—in particular, delving into the details of the precursor events and battles primarily from an omniscient, mythic frame, rather than the fictive frame of the Black Library novels. The lore, in this case, is in the direct service of playing through the events of the Horus Heresy at the table, each of the seven volumes so far published detailing the events with enough granular information for an extended campaign to be played at the table.[13]

---

[12] See McNeill 2014b for the death of Manus and Abnett 2014b; McNeill 2014a for Russ's attack on Prospero.

[13] An examination of these for descriptions of current lore is valuable but far beyond the scope of this chapter. As of the writing of this chapter, the Forge World series number seven published books: see *Betrayal* (2012); *Massacre*

The sparks that ignited massive interest in the 30k period, the time of the Horus Heresy, led to the first cohesive description in *Horus Heresy: Collected Visions* (2007), a supplement for the collectible card game *Horus Heresy* (2003), by Sabertooth Games. It is a book of art from the card game, primarily the sketches of GW Art Director John Blanche, and so reflects another important aspect of the 40k universe: visual art's role as a marketing tool and a gaming tool (see below).

Originally published as individual books, beginning with *Horus Heresy: Vol 1, Visions of War* (2004), *Collected Visions* combines all four volumes and tells the story from the beginning of Horus's rise as Warmaster to his death at the hand of the Emperor. It was updated as the single art book *Horus Heresy: Visions of Heresy* (2014). While this chapter is less interested in defining lore as canon, the most recent 'canonical' lore can be found in *Visions of Heresy*, the Forge World books, and the unfinished novel series, which currently number forty-one at the time of writing this chapter, each one expanding the narrative event-by-event in a non-chronological narrative (see below).

Visions of Heresy updates the lore with details from the novels, such as the description of the "anathame" (Merrett 2014, 98), a Chaos weapon used to corrupt Horus and described in the second Horus Heresy novel, Graham McNeil's *False Gods* (2006). It also describes events from the initial novels in the series, such as raging Angron and his World Eaters deployment on Isstvan III to finish off the loyalist Space Marines and how they were thwarted by Emperor's Children Captain, Saul Tarvitz.[14] Since *Collected Visions* provided the first attempt at comprehensive and detailed snapshots from key events in one book, I will use it in my analysis of how the Horus Heresy defines the setting.[15]

As a first attempt at a comprehensive portrait of the Horus Heresy, *Collected Visions* is an excellent gametext to mine for an understanding of this setting. It charts the main events and players in this drama but does so with more detail than those earlier attempts. A brief account helps understand how the texture and scale of the narrative blossomed through rounds of iterative additions. The key events begin with a War

---

(2013); *Extermination* (2014); *Conquest* (2014); *Tempest* (2015); *Retribution* (2016); *Inferno* (2017); *Angelus* (forthcoming).

[14] See Merrett 2014, 130–1.

[15] I have also chosen the earlier *Collected Visions* to analyze, because, while *Visions of Heresy* does update the lore to its most recent events, the Horus Heresy as detailed in the novels and Forge World books is incomplete. I fully expect a completed version of *Visions of Heresy* at some point in the future. When this gametext arrives, it will be the definitive description of the Heresy.

Council, which occurs while the Emperor wages his Great Crusade
to end the Age of Strife and unite the disparate worlds of humanity.
Deciding that the time is right to return to Earth for some mysterious
undertaking, the Emperor grants his favorite son, Horus, the title of
Warmaster. The War Council is now superseded in importance by the
Council of Terra designed to spread Imperial law. The Emperor retreats to
underground laboratories beneath his Palace to construct "great psychic-
engines" (Merrett 2007, 49) that prove to be such a mystery to the
disaffected Primarchs. Turmoil begins as some Primarchs feel confused
and neglected by their father. Most seriously, Horus takes offense that his
father has abandoned the Great Crusade. The true fall of Horus, though,
occurs on the moon of Davin, where he is struck by an assassin's blade.
A Davinite sect corrupted by Chaos treats (and infects) him, but also
saves him. He makes a pact with the daemons of Chaos to deliver the
Emperor to his enemies and be rewarded with the galaxy.

The tale of Horus's corrupting the traitor Primarchs focuses on the
initial betrayal by Angron of the World Eaters Legion, Mortarion of the
Death Guard, and Fulgrim of the Emperor's Children. As Warmaster,
Horus sends those whom he knows will remain loyal to the Emperor far
from Terra, i.e., Roboute Guilliman of the Ultramarines, Sanguinius of
the Blood Angels, and Lion El'Jonson of the Dark Angels. The bulk of
the remaining Primarchs and their legions are either too dispersed on
missions in the galaxy or already on Terra. The only other Primarchs
who might be easily swayed are Magnus the Red and his Thousand
Sons, Perturbo and the Iron Warriors, and Lehman Russ and the Space
Wolves. After Davin, the next critical event occurs when the disloyal
Primarchs convene in the Isstvan system. Here they have supposedly
met to quell a 'non-compliant' system, one that has not accepted the
Emperor's will. When it becomes clear that the disloyal legions still have
some loyal warriors, Horus decides on an act of ultimate betrayal of the
Legiones Astartes Space Marines. The warriors believed to remain loyal
are sent to the surface of the planet Isstvan III, ostensibly to make the
it compliant with Imperial law. Horus bombards the planet with virus
bombs. "Horus the Warmaster had at last declared his hand and openly
defied the Emperor" (Merrett 2007, 81).

This clarification of what happens on Isstvan III acts as an example
of how such shared universes expand recursively. An earlier statement in
Realm of Chaos: Slaves to Darkness (1988) that seizure of the Eisenstein was
the first major act in the "Inter-Legionary War" (Ansell, Brunton, and
Forrest 1988, 240) is rewritten here when we see the betrayal explained,
which occurred earlier. In fact, we learn that enraged Angron makes
planetfall and personally attacks those Astartes who survived the virus

bomb, a key event detailed in the novel *Galaxy in Flames* (2006). After the publication of the novel, *Visions of Heresy* summarized the events of a loyalist Emperor's Children Space Marine, Saul Tarvitz, and his struggle as he and his companions are betrayed. Yet, in the earlier, pre-novel version, *Collected Visions* provided an example of the broad, omniscient point of view that dominates the description of these gametexts and act as lacunae demanding to be filled at a later time.[16]

The next critical element concerns another Primarch, Magnus the Red, a sorcerer. Magnus's use of magic is a curious example of how the game designers provide radical differences in the Primarchs and their legions, enough to pique the interests of players who want a broad spectrum of warrior types from which to choose. Konrad Curze and the Night Lords are psychotic killers. Lehman Russ and the Space Wolves are archetypes of pure savagery, loyalty, and war. Roboute Guilliman and the Ultramarines represent secular reason, progress, and hope, and the perfection of Space Marine bio-engineering and ideology. And Magnus and his Thousand Sons? A sorcerer-king with warrior sons dedicated to arcane mysteries. This Primarch's fall from grace is a human one rooted in the biblical Fall, as well as the seminal Faustian idea that knowledge is seductive and dangerous, and enhancing.

A brief comment on the lore of the Space Marines and the Primarchs provides an understanding of Magnus's importance as the Primarch who sought knowledge and was damned. Before even the creation of the Primarchs, the Emperor created indispensable warriors, the Thunder Warriors, to help him pacify Earth. These warriors filled his legions and helped end the Age of Strife. They were also the precursors to the Space Marines, genetically enhanced posthumans with altered biology who would help the Emperor conquer the galaxy. As a way to unite

---

[16] It tells us that "the conflict on Isstvan III was the first battle in the history Imperium when Space Marines of the same Legion fought on opposite sides of former comrades and brothers-in-arms became bitter foes" (Merrett 2007, 82). A curious statement by Lehman Russ in the novel *Prospero Burns* (2014) seems to contradict this. The protagonist of the novel, a human academic named Kasper Hawser, asks the Wolf King if the Astartes fighting Astartes is unprecedented. Russ says, "That's not unprecedented" (Kindle version, Abnett 2014b, 8828 of 8927). Since this is said in dialog form, it must be taken less seriously than omniscient statements. And, the vagueness of Astartes fighting Astartes means Russ is referring to the Space Wolves' role as the Emperor's executioners. Or it could mean that Space Marines of the same legion had fought each other before. In *Betrayer* (2013), we know that the legions of Angron and Lehman Russ fought a bloody battle during the Crusade.

humanity during his Great Crusade, he created twenty Primarchs, posthuman generals who would conquer and recover the lost human worlds. Just as the Thunder Warriors were superior to normal human warriors, and the Space Marines superior to Thunder Warriors, the Primarchs were created to be superior to the Space Marines, exceeded only by the Emperor himself. A critical part of the 40k-Primarch lore is mentioned in *Collected Visions*.

> The Emperor's ambitions for the Primarchs appeared to be ruined by a cataclysmic event. A strange warp vortex snatched the still foetal Primarchs from the Emperor's laboratories and cast them across the galaxy. Each Primarch was cast onto separate worlds where they matured. As the years passed they came to dominate their worlds and became powerful warriors and leaders. (Merrett 2007, 24)

During the Great Crusade, the Emperor visited each of these worlds and reunited himself with his 'sons,' offering them legions who adopted their Primarch's homeworlds as their own. The curious bit of lore concerns the mysterious cataclysmic event of their dispersals. A series of questions follow that ask if this 'scattering' was possibly designed by the Emperor or, more ominously, by the Dark Gods themselves.[17] The mystery is maintained in both the updated *Visions of Heresy* as well as a recent Forge World gametext, *The Horus Heresy Book 1: Betrayal* (2012).[18] Yet, earlier lore detailed the event, a clear case that mysteries are often more fruitful for players than sharp detail.

> The Chaos Gods struck while the foetal super-humans grew in their incubation chambers. The Emperor had placed a psychic shield around the chambers, but the Chaos Gods managed to break it down and pluck the infant super-humans from Earth, casting them adrift into warp space. (Priestley and Chambers 1993, 20)

The Primarchs are cast to vastly different individual worlds where they rise to power as representatives of these worlds. They and their warriors are archetypes of basic human emotion or behavior. For example, Russ of the Space Wolves grew up on the savage ice-world of

[17] We learn "the truth will likely never be known" (Merrett 2007, 27).
[18] "The Emperor's ambitions for the Primarchs appeared to be thwarted by a cataclysmic event, the true nature and scope of which has never been revealed" (Bligh 2012, 18).

Fenris, a world whose top predator is the Fenrisian wolf; the Wolf King and his Space Marines exemplify such savagery in their personalities and war making. In stark opposition, Roboute Guilliman was found by nobles on the planet of Macragge and raised as an intellectual and martial prodigy. No wonder Guilliman and the Ultramarines are represented as the quintessential Space Marines driven by perfection.

Magnus landed on Prospero, a world of human psykers, a place where his natural psychic abilities could flourish. Magnus embraced the sorcery that the Emperor was trying to contain. He was responsible for the creation and recruitment of Space Marine Librarians, psychically gifted warriors instrumental in helping the Crusade succeed. However, some of the Primarchs considered the Librarians to be dangerous. Russ thought them to be warlocks, and Mortarion accused Magnus of being a Chaos sorcerer. To that end, the Emperor called his War Council to meet on the planet Nikaea, one of many obvious uses of Catholic history.[19] Within the 40k universe, they met to solve the Librarian crisis and to try Magnus. The Emperor ruled that the Librarians be disbanded and that Magnus stop using his psychic powers or that his "Legion's name will be struck from the Imperial record for all time" (Merrett 2007, 94).

This threat of erasure hints at another persistent mystery within 40k lore, that of the expunged two original Primarchs and their legions, numbers II and XI. Much fan theory has been generated based on cryptic readings in gametexts concerning the possibilities surrounding these two legions, chief of which is the idea that problems with the legion's genetics (called gene seed) caused their destruction. Evidence does exist for this, such as the conversation between Horus and Sanguinius in a pre-Heresy event in which they defeated alien giants called Nephilim. Sanguinius shares with his brother the truth of the Blood Angels' genetic flaw, "this crimson fury, this red thirst" (Kindle version, Swallow 2012, 424 of 7020). Like the loving brother that he was at the time, Horus asks why Sanguinius refuses to seek help from the Emperor. Sanguinius replies, "I will not be responsible for the erasure of the Blood Angels from the Imperial history. I will not have a third empty plinth beneath the roof the Hegemony as my Legion's only memorial" (Kindle version, Swallow 2012, 510 of 7020). Without delving into the variety of fan theories, the fear of Chaos taint by Sanguinius and the suggestion by the Emperor that sorcery-use is worthy of one being expunged hints more than proves what happened to the two expunged Primarchs and

[19] This alludes to the Council of Nicaea that met in c.e. 325 to determine the fate of Arianism.

legions. Even more, it demonstrates how GW designers structure their universe so that narrative mysteries remain to generate interest or act as lacunae to be filled later.[20]

A key event in the Horus Heresy history concerns Magnus's refusal to accept the Emperor's ruling at Nikaea. On his home world of Prospero, he continues to practice sorcery, further corrupting his Librarians and legion, the Thousand Sons. Because of his ability to see into the Warp, Magnus learns in "a terrible vision" (Merrett 2007, 98) that Horus has made a pact with Chaos. He also can see into the future, enough to know of the turmoil about to be unleashed as Horus betrays the Emperor. Curiously, Magnus decides to warn the Emperor, but does so by penetrating the Imperial Palace with a psychic assault that causes much damage to the Emperor's secret project.[21] He delivers his message. The Emperor, though, responds in rage and orders Russ of the Space Wolves, the Emperor's executioner legion, to show no mercy. They head for Magnus's home world and unleash their full fury upon the world, destroying it.

At the same time, the Primarch of the Word Bearers, Lorgar, had taken umbrage because the Emperor had chastised him for worshiping the Emperor as a god. The Emperor's most devout and pious legion had gone too far, its zealotry a hindrance during the Great Crusade. He told Lorgar "to look to Roboute Guilliman of the Ultramarines. He has faith in excess. He has faith in our mission, not I" (Merrett 2007, 126). This demand that the Emperor's empire be secular rather than religious demonstrates how 40k incorporates the corruption of religious and secular values into its setting. Lorgar's insistence on worshiping the Emperor as a god causes a crisis of faith in him, enough so that in his turmoil he looks to the Chaos gods as a replacement. He soon believes that the true gods of his homeward, Colchis, had not prophesied the Emperor's coming, but that of the Chaos gods. Horus knew of the Emperor's chastisement of Lorgar and of elevating Guilliman as a model. Under commands from Horus, Lorgar and the bulk of his legion hurry to Ultramar, the home world of Guilliman and his Ultramarines, and attack the Calth System while Guilliman is away following Horus's orders. More betrayal occurs when Horus

[20] Another interesting account concerns visions that Word Bearers are shown of the infant Primarchs. One claims: "The eleventh primarch sleeps within this pod—still innocent, still pure" (Kindle version, Dembski-Bowden 2010, 5472 of 9376). Dialog is never as reliable as an account from omniscient point of view. The suggestion that impurity is the issue broadens the possibilities rather than narrows them.

[21] See Merrett 2007, 324.

sends the Primarch Sanguinius of the Blood Angels, and his legion, to the Chaos-infested world at Signus.[22]

Perhaps the greatest betrayal, beyond that of Horus to the Emperor, occurs after word reached Terra that Isstvan was the site of Horus's attack on fellow Space Marines. With the Emperor busy in his laboratories developing his secret project to consolidate the Warp Gate beneath the Palace, the task to organize the defense of Terra fell to Malcador the Sigillite and the Primarch Rogal Dorn of the Imperial Fists. It was decided that a massive contingent of seven Primarchs and their legions would travel to the Isstvan system to confront Horus. Leading them would be Ferrus Manus of the Iron Hands; he would also be the first to arrive, fueled to speed by his anger at his brother Fulgrim for siding with Horus and betraying the Emperor.

With only half the Primarchs sent to defeat Horus having arrived, Ferrus prematurely begins the attack, expecting the late Primarchs to follow him in battle. Along with Primarch Corax of the Raven Guard and Vulcan of the Salamanders, they land on the fifth planet of Isstvan where Horus has made his headquarters. What Ferrus Manus doesn't know is that when Horus's force appears to retreat from battle, a trap is being laid. Ferrus takes the bait and pushes forward, hoping to meet Fulgrim on the battlefield, unaware that the supposedly loyalist Primarchs who will soon arrive to follow him into battle will do so at his back, and in favor of Horus. Soon, the duplicitous legions arrive, those of the Iron Warriors, the Night Lords, the Alpha Legion, and the Word Bearers. The 'Drop Site Massacre' occurs with the loyalists Iron Hands, Raven Guard, and Salamanders being nearly destroyed by their traitorous brethren.

At this point in the narrative, we learn that Fulgrim defeats Ferrus on the battlefield, that Corax and Vulcan are missing and presumed dead. Later, when the survivors reach Terra, a wounded Corax is placed in a stasis vat. But no sign of Vulcan can be found. Magnus's hand is forced against the Emperor after losing Prospero to Russ and the Space Wolves. He vows common allegiance with Horus and awaits the order to attack Terra. Horus gives his traitorous Primarchs specific tasks to aid in the final victory, his own tactic to be a lightning strike on Terra. The Emperor has been trying to seal the wards and gates that Magnus's psychic message destroyed. Beneath the Palace of Terra, the Web Way has been overrun by the hordes of Chaos demons. The Emperor has commanded his own Custodian Guard, the elite of his genetically enhanced warriors, as well

---

[22] See Abnett 2012 for attack by the Word Bearers on the Ultramarines, and Swallow 2012 for the revelation of the Blood Angel's flaw.

as the Sisters of Silence, women who can nullify the magic of the Warp, to defend the passages. He, himself, joins them in this critical moment, barely managing to seal the final gate to the Imperial Palace before the demonic denizens of the Warp storm the Palace.[23]

One of the most important events in 40k lore is the Siege of Terra, the battle in which Horus's traitorous legions attack Terra, breaching its walls, and nearly overrunning the Palace. Angron, Fulgrim, Mortarion, Lorgar, along with Magnus, all send their warriors forward, and soon surround the Palace, victory seemingly assured. Atop the Ultimate Gate, which leads directly into the Palace, we know from previous lore that Sanguinius stands guard. This key moment from the narrative's early construction finds depth in *Collected Visions* when Sanguinius spots a monstrous form among the enemies, the demon Ka'Bandha, whom he fought on Signus. In an epic aerial battle detailed in earlier accounts that evokes biblical demons and angels in a contest over the fate of Heaven, Sanguinius breaks the demon's back upon his knee. Seeing the inexorable resolve of the Emperor's forces, and with news that the Space Wolves and Ultramarines would be arriving soon at Terra, Horus decides to lower the shields on his ship to lure the Emperor aboard via teleportation.

More of the mystery of the Emperor's fall is detailed in this later account. After the defeat of Horus and the wounding of the Emperor, Rogal Dorn follows the Emperor's orders to confine him to the Golden Throne. Malcador, the Emperor's chosen regent, had sat upon the Throne while the Emperor challenged Horus. Malcador became "tortured and wasted" (Merrett 2007, 367) from the Warp energies he contained to keep the Webway portal closed. After Dorn returned the Emperor to the Palace, the Emperor gains enough strength to tell his followers that his psychic strength will return, but his body is beyond repair, that he will remain forever entombed in the Golden Throne. "I am now bound to the machine for all time" (367). He tells Dorn and Kahn that they must cleanse the galaxy of Chaos, his final words, "Be vigilant!" (367). The time that follows, the Scouring, sees them chasing all of the traitorous legions into the Eye of Terror, a swath of Chaos-infected space. Most cruelly, though, is the continued sacrifice of 1,000 human psykers a day to keep the Emperor's spirit from failing, which, itself, fuels the Astronomican, a great beacon of light guiding space vessels through the Warp and allowing faster-than-light travel. At this time, the organization of Terra changes, as do the legions, the current 40k game setting clarified with more detailing of its most important historical events in the 30k period.

---

[23] See Dembski-Bowden 2017.

Horus Heresy Fiction

The Horus Heresy novels, novellas, and anthologies of short stories add details non-chronologically, and with varied focus. While they provide close, subjective point of views of the Primarchs, they also often foreground secondary characters' perspectives of the events, jumping back and forth in time. This provides flexibility for the writers and designers of such a complex shared universe, while presenting newcomers to the narrative with challenges, the most difficult of which is managing the material so that the most important events emerge in relief while secondary events recede into the background. A quick look at a few important novels and their events reveals the difficulties in determining this placement.

The first novel in the series, *Horus Rising* (2006), explores the nuances of individual stories like that of Luna Wolves Captain Garviel Loken who became an adviser to Horus at this pivotal early time in the Heresy when the Emperor made Horus Warmaster. The other two that follow, *False Gods* (2006) and *Galaxy in Flames* (2006) fictionalize the initial descent of Horus into Chaos and his betrayal of his Space Marine brothers on Isstvan III. Key stories such as Fulgrim's corruption by the Chosen of Slaanesh, the Chaos god of decadent pleasure, can be found in *Fulgrim* (2007). The damning results of Magnus's presumptuous warning to the Emperor and all that follows is fictionalized in *A Thousand Sons* (2010).[24]

Other key moments, such as Lorgar's embarrassing censure and the Word Bearers' descent into Chaos, can be found in *The First Heretic* (2010) and the destruction of Magnus's homeworld Prospero by Lehman Russ and the Space Wolves in *Prospero Burns* (2010). *The Outcast Dead* (2011) provides narration of Magnus's intrusion into the Palace when he delivers his warning, as well as a cryptic vision an astropath, Kai Tulane, has with the Emperor. In it, the Emperor explains why certain horrible events must happen and that "sometimes the only victory possible is to keep your opponent from winning" (Kindle version, McNeil 2011, 6352 of 6536). The Emperor then claims he knows he must die, an admission that it must happen for Horus to be defeated and the Imperium to continue. This also acts as a hint toward resolving another mystery, that of how such a powerful individual like the Emperor could so bungle his empire.[25]

The novels vary in scope and direct relevance, but each paints a portion of the larger canvas, with some more important than others.

---

[24] See McNeill 2014b; 2014a; Abnett 2014a; McNeill 2014c; Counter 2014.
[25] See McNeil 2011; Dembski-Bowden 2010; Abnett 2014b.

Stories are told of Guilliman's belief Terra has fallen and the creation of a second empire, the Imperium Secundus, in *Unremembered Empire* (2013); of Sanguinius and the Blood Angels' genetic flaw that would eventually see them rampaging after he is wounded on Signus Prime by the Greater Daemon of Khorne Ka'Bandha, in *Fear to Tread* (2012); of the myriad battles fought across the galaxy as Primarchs fought Primarchs, and Horus's move on Terra. At the time of this chapter's writing, the most recent novel is *Master of Mankind* (2016).[26] It fictionalizes the critical events that occurred beneath the Imperial Palace, as Custodian Guards and Sister of Silence keep Chaos from claiming the Webway.[27]

One of the strongest examples of 40k fiction comes from 40k-favorite, Dan Abnett. He has published many of the most popular novels within the setting, from the *Eisenhorn* (2001–02) and *Ravenor* trilogies (2004–07), to the Gaunt's Ghosts series (1999–2019).[28] We see the 40k grimdark ethos emerge as a refrain throughout his Heresy novel *Know No Fear* (2012), with tension between the Emperor's secularism and how it is exemplified in the quintessential Space Marines, the Ultramarines, and the degradation of a rational worldview for one corrupted by superstition and the dominance of Chaos. "The Emperor's truth was the secular Imperial truth. He tolerated more pious attitudes amongst his sons, but only so far" (Kindle version, Abnett 2012, 553 of 4382).

Such omniscient exposition works because it reinforces the overall frame upon which must hang so much of the lore. Most books written in the setting, not just those of the Horus Heresy, utilize such a technique because of lore requirements. Abnett demonstrates a ratcheting up in sophistication of style requisite for effective fantasy fiction. In particular, he is adept at alternating various point-of-view distances, from a close-subjective outward to the omniscient to the purely objective. For example, the requisite omniscient is ever-present when we learn that a tertiary character, "Hellock [who] screams out a curse, draws his auto pistol and fires. He makes the first active loyalist kill of the Battle of Calth" (Kindle Version, Abnett 2012, 2023 of 5382). Hellock, though, is drawn with a closer subjective point of view when we hear his personal thoughts about why the Ultramarines are mustering. He believes it is to thwart an Ork incursion. How should Space Marines respond, according

[26] See Dembski-Bowden 2017.
[27] Once the Horus Heresy novels reach the Siege of Terra and describe the events that led the Imperium to pursue the remaining rebels called the Scouring, they will be a ripe archive for literary analysis that will reveal the complexity involved in understanding a realized world like 40K.
[28] See Abnett 2005; 2009; 2017; 2018.

to Hellock? "You take [...] two full Legions of the Emperor's finest, and you pile-drive it through the septic green heart and rancid green brain and green frigging spinal cord of the Ghaslakh xenohold, and you end them" (Kindle version, Abnett 2012, 234 of 4382). The voice here is very much that of an Imperial Army sergeant with fear and hatred for Orks.

Abnett utilizes the best of pulp science-fantasy as a myth-making form of fiction coupled with a Lovecraft-like use of embodied, physicalized language (see Chapter 5). Where he shines as a stylist is in pulpy language used for description that reflects the same sort of nerdy material categorizing of the science-fantasy monstrous as seen in Lovecraft, Sterling, Miéville, Barker, etc. Abnett writes:

> The thing is growing, still growing. Lorgar's empty skin sloughs off like a snake's. It is a horror from the most lightless voids.
> It is glistening black flesh and tangled veins, it is frogspawn mucus and beads of blinking eyes, it is teeth and bat-wings. It is an anatomical atrocity. It is teratology, the shaping of monsters.
> Filthy light veils it and invests it like velvet robes. It is a shadow and it is smoke. Its crest is the horns of an aurochs, four metres high, ribbed and brown. It snorts. There is a rumble of intestines and gas, of a predator's growl. A smell of blood. A whiff of acid. A tang of venom. (Kindle version, Abnett 2012, 2616–5382)

The use of such 'purple' diction harkens back at least to the best of pulp writers, yet in Abnett's use with a sense that a Lovecraftian clinical focus has been retained. It drives the effect, while foregrounding a material reality that must be represented.

The Beast Arises

Abnett was also chosen to pen the first novel in The Beast Arises series, *I am Slaughter* (2015).[29] Juxtaposing the twelve novels in the series with the complex Heresy series reveals key differences in approach. They number far fewer and their story resolves, whereas The Horus Heresy, while containing major events formed within a known frame, is a series with an indefinite number of stories to be told. The Beast Arises demonstrates how flexible the 40k universe is and how open its lore is, while (like the

[29] For the complete series, see Haley 2016a; Thorpe 2016a; Sanders 2016a; Annandale 2016a; Guymer 2016b; 2016a; Thorpe 2016b; Abnett 2016; Sanders 2016b; Annandale 2016c; 2016b.

preceding Heresy) it is also subsumed within an overarching narrative of the Imperium's fall into superstition and eternal war.

The Beast Arises details events over 1,000 years after Horus's defeat and the Emperor's retreat to his tomb throne. It succeeds in a multi-authored grand history of the period because it focuses on seminal characters who provide continuity between the novels, as well as provide details into the histories behind certain foundational legends. It switches the focus from the 'Ruinous Powers' of Chaos demons to rampaging Orks who have recovered since the Emperor defeated them at Ullanor during the Great Crusade. The Beast Arises highlights a tension that exists within the broader narrative, as well as among players, concerning the worst villain in the 40k universe. Most will say the demonic creatures of the Warp, or maybe the unstoppable Tyranid swarms, but xenos Ork hordes in the form of psychic and technically sophisticated natural monster-aliens prove just as formidable, if not more. After defeating the indomitable Imperial Fists, as well as ravaging many worlds in the Imperium, they manage to teleport a space-port moon directly above Terra and send Ork diplomats to the Palace itself. Such an intrusion (and insult) has never happened since Horus's betrayal. What this series demonstrates is that a key event in the setting can be contained within a few momentous novels. This proves to be much less of a challenge for readers and fans.

Where The Beast Arises explores the threat of an Ork empire dominating the universe and does so through a wide canvas composed of many individuals and institutions, the lore proves flexible enough to also foreground sharply drawn literary characters. Abnett's initial novel introduces the strongest protagonist in the series, an Imperial Fist named Koorland. His 'wall name' (battle name) is Slaughter. He survives an encounter with a gravity weapon of the Orks, who forced insect-like aliens to overrun a planet the Imperial Fists expected to easily cleanse of the threat. Instead of victory, Slaughter's entire chapter is destroyed, leaving him as the last of the vaunted Imperial Fists, the descendants of the Primarch Rogal Dorn's legion who led the defense of Terra during the Heresy War.

Koorland becomes the focus through the bulk of the series, becoming Lord Commander of Terra's forces. He leads the recovery of the lost Primarch Vulkan, as well as witnesses Vulkan's supposed death at the hands of the Ork warlord called the Beast.[30] Koorland also organizes a

---

[30] The final confrontation is narrated ambiguously, no doubt to allow Vulcan to return. No body is recovered, even though everyone assumes Vulcan dies. This follows the trajectory of lore that surrounds Vulcan as immortal.

new Space Marine chapter, the Deathwatch, kill-team specialists selected from other chapters who paint their armor black as mourning for their fallen comrades at Ullanor. They are charged by Koorland with leading a do-or-die assault on the Beast, aided by recovered Sisters of Silence and kidnapped Ork psykers they plan to unleash. Koorland manages to battle a massive Ork warboss he believes is the Beast, killing the warboss but then dying at the hands of the real Beast. His death occurs in *The Last Son of Dorn* (2016), two novels before the end of the series. This bold narrative choice of killing Koorland is unexpected; it demonstrates that these novels function to tell a full story of 40k's lore, rather than explore individual characters. Yet, complex characters do emerge.

One pivotal character provides continuity between the Horus Heresy and the current period. Inquisitor Veritus is an aging veteran kept alive by ancient technologies and a power suit. He appears to resist, almost naively, the threat of the Ork invasion, arguing that the real dangers to the Imperium come from Chaos. He survives until the final book in the series, *The Beheading* (2016), where we learn that he is, in fact, 1,500 years old, that he knew Horus during the Heresy, and that his name is Kyril Sindermann, an iterator (poet/orator) during the Crusade.[31] On his death bed, he urges his fellow Lady Inquisitor Marguerethe Wienand to support the creation of a "bicameral" (Kindle version, Haley 2016b, 1242–3193) institutional Inquisition along lines dedicated to hunting aliens (Ordo Xenos) and hunting demons (Ordo Malleus). This use of a character who reaches back to the Heresy shows the importance of such literary techniques in revealing key elements of lore that explain the history of products. He also provides Wienand access to a secret fortress on Titan where the mysterious Grey Knights exist, psychic Space Marines dedicated to fighting Chaos. He charges her to use them as the military force of the new Ordo Malleus, while Koorland's recently formed Deathwatch will serve the same purpose of the Ordo Xenos.

The backstory of the Deathwatch and its connection to the Inquisition also demonstrates how lore is 'retconned' (i.e., edited through retroactive continuity) when one text supersedes another. The TRPG *Deathwatch: Core Rulebook* (2010) allows players to choose Space Marines as their characters because the Deathwatch is organized with small groups of Space Marine elites experienced in fighting aliens.[32] This specialization

---

See *Vulkan Lives* (Kyme 2014), in which he is killed repeatedly, and always returns. Yet, in *Deathfire* (Kyme 2016), his body is recovered, and he eventually lives again.

[31] See Abnett 2014a.

[32] Thus 40k's TRPG expanded with supplements and other rules that would

focus allows for gameplay that encourages scenarios comprised of squad-specific missions. In this core TRPG rulebook, though, we learn that the "origins of this practice are lost to history [...] The Chapter's origins are even more shrouded in secrecy" (Fantasy Flight Games Team 2010).

The TRPG does provide general information about a conclave of Inquisitors who make a pact with the Adeptus Astartes (the organization of the Space Marines) to send their best alien hunters. It also suggests that the Orks may have been the cause of the Deathwatch's creation:

> It is entirely possible that it was the Ork race that the founders of the Deathwatch had in mind when they prophesied the end at the hands of Humanity's alien foes. According to the most learned of Ordo Xenos Inquisitors, the Orks believe that one day, a great leader will rise up and unleash the greatest of all battles, which will draw to it every Ork in the galaxy. That leader, it appears, has yet to come, but the Deathwatch is ever vigilant for signs of an especially powerful Ork Warlord uniting the fractious race. (Fantasy Flight Games Team 2010)

Such a version of the Deathwatch's history is rewritten (or clarified) in The Beast Arises series with Koorland as the originator of the Deathwatch. Like the reworking of the Emperor's fall, such a 'retcon' should not be considered a failure or weakness in the setting. It is an expected outcome of creating a shared universe, even if it poses problems to individuals first encountering the setting. To fans or independent scholars, though, it offers a welcome bit of expanding lore.

Along with the destruction and recreation of the Imperial Fists and the detailing of the Deathwatch's creation, The Beast Arises also succeeds in explaining the return of the Sisters of Silence. In particular, *Shadow of Ullanor* (2016) explains how the Sisters were ostracized in the millennium after the Heresy War. The Emperor had used them to great effect because as "pariahs" they negate the powers of the Warp, their very presence a mechanism that creates a nullified pocket of anti-psychic space in which the Warp fails to function. They are returned to service as unflinching guardians of the Emperor, their

allow for a variety of play. Rogue Trader (2009); Deathwatch (2011); Black Crusade (2012); and Only War (2013) allow players to choose roles beyond those of the Inquisition. One can play as a space-jaunting rogue trader, as a Space Marine on the lookout for xenos dangers, as one of the traitorous Space Marines mutated by the Warp, or as part of the Imperial Guard. For the core rulebooks, see Fantasy Flight Games Team 2014; 2009; 2010; 2012; 2013.

leader Lady Brassanas sacrificing herself in the final battle between Koorland's successor, Maximus Thane, and the Beast. In this pivotal narrative scene, she grips a chain binding an Ork psyker, her nullifying effects mollifying it. With the aim of releasing its latent power as a way to destroy all the Orks in its vicinity, she sees the Beast defeating Thane and her allies. Realizing she can't withdraw tactically, she kills herself and unleashes the Ork's psychic power. This causes the Beast's head to explode with psychic energy, along with every other Ork on the planet—grand world saving in the best of pulp-SF tradition. As Brassanas's role demonstrates, 40k is more than Space Marines in their Heinlein-inspired power armor.

The End of the 41st Millennium

The 40k universe as a realized world within the modern fantastic, though, is also more than its beginning with the Horus Heresy and the numberless events of the intermediate millennia. History in this setting has a purpose. These earlier moments clarify the current game period, what has now turned from the 41st millennium to the beginning of its successor. The 'Time of Endings,' those final centuries of the 41st millennium, has been advanced in the official storyline with the release of the Gathering Storm material and with the release of the 8th edition of the game.

The importance of this timeline advance for the lore is one of grand harmonization, unlike what we see in D&D, which utilizes various mechanisms to allow easy (but loosely connected) movement from one campaign world to another yet offers no true overarching narrative, only a working cosmology. The Gathering Storm, 40k's recent lore, connects to the Heresy in the form of Horus's Captain Abaddon the Despoiler, who survived the time of the Primarchs. It finds grounding in events that happened in the long stretches of time after Horus's defeat, i.e., the various Black Crusades Abaddon championed, as well as the wounding of Guilliman, the Primarch of the Ultramarines, and offers a touch of hope that the Emperor's original vision of a rational, secular galaxy might still be possible. The hope arrives in the resurrection of a Primarch, Guilliman himself, the Emperor's most eager, representative son, and his promise to create a new crusade. The recent novel *Dark Imperium* (2018) shows Guilliman beginning his new Crusade, with the ultimate goal of returning to Terra and possibly replacing the Emperor himself.[33]

[33] See Haley 2018.

This advancement can be found, primarily, in three gametexts of the *Gathering Storm* trilogy: *Fall of Cadia* (2017), *Fracture of Biel-Tan* (2017), and *Rise of the Primarch* (2017).[34] These books are representative for their addition of lore, but also in how they utilize various narrative techniques to create a frame for gameplay. Of critical importance is the 13th Black Crusade that Abaddon waged against the world of Cadia and its pylons restraining Warp energies from flooding out of the Eye of Terror. *Fall of Cadia* details the heroic efforts in combating this tragedy. In each of the books, key characters are introduced that can be bought as models and played at the table—in this instance, Saint Celestine and her Geminae Superia, Genevieve and Eleanor; Inquisitor Katarinya Greyfax; and the barely human cyborg Archmagos Belisarius Cawl. Others are offered, as well—all of them providing a cast that can be bought, painted, and outfitted in a game.

A look at the major elements in the conflict demonstrates the complexity of this narrative, and the demand placed on players in absorbing it. *The Fall of Cadia*'s title details the main event in which, valiant as the defenders may be, they fail in holding the world from the onslaught of demonic Chaos hordes. We learn of Ursarkar E. Creed, the human commander determined to defend Cadia, no matter the cost, while Belisarius Cawl labors on Cadia to uncover its mysteries in the hopes of thwarting Abaddon. Saint Celestine and her Geminae Superia are a trio of holy warriors who act in the Emperor's name and whose pure faith radiates goodness in the face of evil. Inquisitor Greyfax was once a prisoner, held for centuries by the Necron Overlord Trazyn the Infinite in a psychic prison called a Tesseract Vault. She now finds herself released and forced to join forces with the likes of pious Saint Celestine. Cawl, Celestine, and Greyfax form a triad, each one an expensive model that centers the narrative and any campaign that would be played around it. *Fracture of Biel-Tan* has an actual 'Triumvirate' of the Elder god Ynnead: Yvraine, its emissary; The Visarch, the Sword; and The Yncarne, the Avatar. *Rise of the Primarch*, as well, is centered around three critical characters/models: i.e., Roboute Guilliman, the resurrected Primarch of the Ultramarines; Grand Master Voldus of the Grey Knights; and Cypher, the Lord of the Fallen. Each of these books offers a number of other models and important characters, like that of Eldrad Ulthran in *Fracture of Biel-Tan*, or Creed in *Fall of Cadia*.

In each of these gametexts, the major conflict foregrounds purchasable models detailed in a variety of forms that also tells the overarching story. Narrative distance moves through three stages, at its most distant is the

[34] See Games Workshop Team 2017c; 2017b; 2017a.

expected mythic tone seen in many of the 40k gametexts. Interspersed between the bulk of this content are short vignettes of fiction, each utilizing dialog, and a closer subjective point of view. In between are sidebar reports, usually written from an objective point of view about the events. Most interestingly, though, is how each of these stages must be interpreted to understand the narrative, as well as how the striking imagery functions as visual clues for the major characters and events in the drama. A type of intellectual game occurs between the readers and the gametext itself in which the readers must read closely to understand what is being narrated so that he or she can identify the principal characters in the images. In *Collected Visions*, for example, the use of titles for the images means no such challenge exists. Yet, in these most recent gametexts, readers/players must work toward a full understanding. This is a type of discursive reward, just as is winning at the table.

In each of the three *Gathering Storm* books, the most important character-models are displayed in full-page photographs directly following their table of contents. The models are on display in battle formations, as if readied for gameplay. Each gametext's primary characters stand ready, surrounded by their armies. Without reading the gametexts, even practiced players solid in lore will have no idea how to identify the bulk of these individuals. Some will be known, like Guilliman, in his blue power armor with gold filigree, or the mysterious Cypher, but Saint Celestine and Inquisitor Greyfax will require a refresher even for those who may have encountered them before. The game of interpreting the identities of the principals begins by diving into the narrative. Then all becomes clear as the images act as visual representations of story elements. Such a challenge can be demonstrated when a newcomer to 40k happens to see any of these images, taken out of context. They are confronted with one mystery after the next.

This literary requirement is part of GW's creative mission that works because it is coupled with its visual art. These gametexts tell stories for the 40k setting through their use of exposition, but also through their series of images. In a book of 40k art, GW visual designer John Blanche explains how images work: "Like all my pictures, the character has an implied story. I leave it to others to work it out" (qtd. in Ralphs and Gascoigne 2006, 100). The process of 'working it out' allows players to analyze images and parse them into the larger narrative. Such images must do more than provide ornamentation. "We did not want these pictures to be just of people shooting guns and shouting. They are character studies" (Karl Kopinski, qtd. in Ralphs and Gascoigne 2006, 106). Novelist Gav Thorpe writes about an inquisitor Grundvald illustrated by David Gallagher: "This picture paints a thousand words. The detail on and around the character gives away who he is" (Thorpe, qtd. in Ralphs and Gascoigne 2006, 101). Yet, players must parse these images with narrative information for them to make sense within the context of 40k lore.

This interpretive pattern can also be seen in most of GW's gametexts. One of the most iconic images from 40k lore is found in *Collected Visions*. Encountered on its own, without the frame titles, a newcomer would be challenged to understand Sam Wood's "Blades of the Traitor" image (Merrett 2007, 262–7). It depicts Horus on the bridge of his ship, the Vengeful Spirit. With him stand his traitorous allies. Without being well-versed in lore, someone would be unable to identify Horus, Abaddon, Fulgrim, or the other lieutenants and allies. *Collected Visions* helpfully details these in cut-out images with titles. Viewed without direction, though, Blades of the Traitor requires major analytical work from any student of 40k.

Such deep reading is a key aspect of consuming the modern fantastic's 40k universe; it becomes realized as it draws players into its orbit, encouraging comment. A quick search through various types of material on *Youtube.com*, for example, reveals a wide range of player-generated content. Not only visual art, but fan films are increasing, as well as fan-generated amateur scholarship that theorizes much of the lore's unwritten backstory.[35] Such playful theorizing characterizes players' level of commitment with the setting and demonstrates how shared universes within the modern fantastic become realized.[36]

---

[35] One channel, *40k Theories*, speculates on unsolved mysteries related to lore. One recent question asks whether Sigmar, from the Warhammer universe, is one of the expunged Primarchs. See "Sigmar: The Mad Primarch," at https://www.youtube.com/watch?v=ApmVcV0a2wI for an example.

[36] The complexity in charting all of the elements in the disparate but connected gametexts I have mentioned for any comprehensive understanding of 40k lore is immense, and far beyond the scope of this book. Just to parse the new lore added to the Horus Heresy novels would be a massive undertaking in critical, textual analysis, not to mention all the fiction within the shared universe. To work through the additional lore of the TRPG gametexts also requires its own project. A more manageable endeavor would be to select specific events or characters and chart their progression from initial conception or emergence to a fully fleshed-out piece of lore. For example, the accretion of information surrounding the confrontation between Horus and the Emperor serves as a critical example because it was represented with much detail in the early texts.

Chapter 7

Beyond Borders with Miéville, Borges, Wolfe, Ligotti, and Numenera

This case study views the TRPG Numenera through the lens of a setting that imagines a post-post-anthropocene world. Both the novelists China Miéville and Gene Wolfe help here because they provide literary examples of how to approach such a textured game, the former indirectly, the latter directly. They have also both constructed masterful settings populated with fabulous characters, monsters, landscapes, etc., as has Numenera. Each works outside generic constraints, while utilizing enough recognizable scaffolding to provide continuity while altering expectations.[1] With Miéville, *Dread Trident* examines a literary example of how fiction finds parallels within the gameist mode. Miéville's Bas Lag novels fit within a scheme that attempts to represent the unrepresentable, offering a challenge to Lovecraft's call for a Weird fiction that resists such attempts. With Gene Wolf, the trajectory veers obliquely in an embrace of magic within a SF context, one that valorizes the fantastic impulse. The will to represent the embrace of the magical find sure footing in Numenera, a TRPG that refuses genre distinctions.

This chapter ends with a brief examination of horror writer Thomas Ligotti, and how he amplifies Lovecraft's philosophy of cosmic horror. While Numenera posits a return of human-like persons after the erasure of humanity, it does so without the horror of erasure. Ligotti's thoughts on the Weird, his indirect use of the Mythos, and his refraction of Lovecraftian horror reflect a literary need to resist representation, rather than embrace it. While he does utilize elements from Lovecraft's Mythos, these are minimal compared to his many stories of bleak horror, in which physical space itself becomes a doorway to the unthinkable.

---

[1] While Miéville's trilogy of Bas Lag is an imaginary world of fiction ripe for game-setting translation, Wolfe's Solar Cycle novels are a literary work of demanding complexity that directly influenced the creation of Numenera.

His influence on the Mythos, though, demonstrates how realized worlds work within the modern fantastic.

Dread Trident concludes this case study by arguing that Ligotti is an heir of Lovecraft's most sophisticated literary achievements, while also now (without his doing) an inspiration for the continued expansion of the Mythos and its accompanying philosophy. We see this inadvertent influence in HBO's *True Detective* (2014–present), an example of the Weird's reach into a complex, TV series drama. The first season of *True Detective* works within the pulp-inspired aura of a Lovecraftian-like Mythos as it channels elements from Robert Chamber's *The King and Yellow* (1895) through the sieve of the Lovecraft-inspired supreme nihilism of Ligotti's version of cosmic horror. Yet, in the end it failed to embrace its fantasy with confidence, an unfortunate fact that diminishes rather than enhances the series' first season.

Miéville and Numinous Swillage

Ann VanderMeer and Jeff VanderMeer's introduction to an anthology of short fiction and popular-sphere articles dedicated to the resurgence of the Weird tale, *The New Weird* (2008),[2] details how the concept of a 'new weird' genre originated from conversations started by John M. Harrison in 2003 over the nature of the term. The catalyst for a new definition, according to the authors, was the popularity of British writer of urban horror China Miéville's *Perdido Street Station* (2000) and a sense that something original had emerged out of the (old) weird writing of the pulps beyond the experiments of New Wave writers like John M. Harrison himself, or Michael Moorcock, and later the blood/body focus of Clive Barker.[3]

Miéville sees in Weird fiction a type of resistance in its complex representations.[4] He backs away from representation at a certain point,

---

[2] The VanderMeers' introduction first appeared as the article, "The New Weird: 'It's Alive,'" in *The New York Review of Science Fiction* (May 2008).

[3] Barker is another writer who has attempted to draw the unrepresentable. His Books of Blood (1988), as well as the pivotal *Damnation Game* (1985), utilized a granular focus on the physical. His Cenobites, in particular, attempt the sort of representation of the untranslatable that TRPGs exemplify.

[4] He writes, "If considered at all, Weird Fiction is usually, roughly, conceived of as a rather breathless and generically slippery macabre fiction, a dark fantasy 'horror' plus 'fantasy' often featuring nontraditional alien monsters thus plus 'science fiction' [...] Indeed, Weird Fiction may serve as the

though. This refusal occurs when switching focus from the unrepresentable sublime, so ingrained in the Lovecraftian conceptualization of
the Weird, to an aesthetic response to the socio-economic failures of
progressive liberal democracy in the twentieth century, what Miéville calls
"capitalist modernity" (Miéville 2009, 513). A socially concerned Weird
writer such as Miéville expands a numinous, non-traditional teratology
beyond Lovecraft's cosmic forces to argue that the Weird does have a
radical element, this one best left undrawn. In the face of the modern
crisis's worst examples, the great modernist complaints find echoes in the
Weird's insistence that the unutterable is the final record in the face of
actual horror. We are reminded of Adorno's insistence of poetry's demise
after Auschwitz. This version of the "Weird does not so much articulate
the crisis as that the crisis cannot be articulated" (Miéville 2009, 514). In
this sense, only the scream of silence offers a proper response.

Yet, outside such actualized horror from the worst excesses of modern
history, Miéville works within a tradition of 'nerdy categorizing' that
he acknowledges in Lovecraft (see Chapter 5). *Dread Trident* situates him
in a continuum inaugurated with Lovecraft's writings on the Weird, a
tradition Miéville reinterprets with his own tone of galvanized wonder,
a sort of 'swillage,' what he calls the "numinosity under the everyday"
(Miéville 2009, 510). In expected fashion from a stylist of the Weird,
Miéville writes:

> The Weird, though, punctuates the supposed membrane separating
> off the sublime, and allows swillage of that awe and horror from
> "beyond" back into the everyday—into angles, brushes, the touch
> of strange limbs, noises, etc. The Weird is a radicalized sublime
> backwash. (Miéville 2009, 511)

This idea of the Weird's numinous swillage of awe and horror resists the
mundane and hints at an enchanting process inherent in the modern

---

bad conscience of the Gernsback/Campbell paradigm" (Miéville 2009,
510). Resistance, though, for Miéville is political, as well as aesthetic. The
Weird carries such weight for writers like Miéville because of its direct
application for social theory. While a common approach to Miéville is to
view his fiction through the lens of the left-oriented politics he champions
or to see him breaking new ground in fantasy, Sherryl Vint argues for
his importance because "Miéville is blazing the trail for a new model of
fantasy literature that eschews the consolatory mode perfected by Tolkien
and made superfluous by his herds of imitators" (2009, 197). I would also
add that outside of minimizing the importance of politics he eschews a
fear of representation.

fantastic and, especially, in its TRPGs, because such swillage demands brave representation instead of refusal.[5]

Miéville's most applicable work began with the publication of the innovative *Perdido Street Station*, a novel that upends genre expectations in both high fantasy and standard SF and channels Lovecraft and D&D as inspiration. Unfortunately, to limit my brief discussion to elements from this novel and the two that follow in constructing Bas Lag inadvertently denies the range of Miéville as a SF and fantasy novelist. My focus reinforces the importance of his trilogy as expanding the world-building ethos of Lovecraft and D&D, rather than negates the importance of his other work.[6] My commentary on Miéville in relation to the Weird and TRPGs reveals how a SF-and-fantasy novelist resists generic constraints to innervate his fiction with well-drawn tropes, all the while exhibiting a tone any TRPG player will recognize. A look at this aspect of his work demonstrates his importance as a writer working within a gameist mode of fiction. *Perdido Street Station* is ultimately a gamer's novel, written by a former gamer.[7] In it, we see a love of the elements found in traditional TRPGs in a similar fashion to those found in other game-focused media.

For example, a Weird-inflected gameist mode has seen traction recently in the first season of *Stranger Things* (2016–present); a D&D monster, Demogorgon, features in a D&D game played by the characters, as well as foreshadows the Lovecraft-like, faceless monster in the series. Other nods to D&D can be found in the simplistic *Ready Player One* (2012), a novel that features a virtual world, the Oasis, that expands on the ideas of a Gibsonian matrix of digitally constructed 3D environments

---

[5] For a broad range of criticism, see the special issue of *Extrapolation* 50(2) (2009) dedicated to Miéville: https://online.liverpooluniversitypress.co.uk/toc/extr/50/2.

[6] *Kraken* (2010), for example, presents obvious parallel elements, one of several urban fantasy-driven reimaginings of London, this one centered on a cult worshiping a mighty tentacled squid. Lovecraft would approve.

[7] According to *Dragon Magazine* 352, an issue dedicated to Miéville's imaginary world, upon reading *Perdido Street Station*, the editor, Erik Mona, discovered Miéville's gaming roots:

> New Crobuzon, the metropolis at the heart of Perdido Street Station, was as vibrant a character as any in the book, conveying a sense of place more strongly than perhaps anything I had ever read. Absent the plot, the novel seemed almost like an RPG source-book at times, with details included that only a game master might think up to add a sense of immersive realism to his locale. And here, where the action kicked into overdrive, was a team of adventurers that might have stepped right out of the Tomb of Horrors. (Mona 2007, 8)

and features an adventure story in which the main character must accept a quest to solve a series of riddles by the founder of the Oasis. It pays homage to the decade of the 1980s, as well as to the fact that the digital worlds of M.M.O.R.P.G.s owe much of their cultural history to TRPGs like D&D. It even names one of its worlds 'Gygax' and sends its protagonist to a virtual Tomb of Horrors. In this sense, *Ready Player One* continues the articulation and representation of virtual worlds and avatars.[8] *Perdido Street Station*, though, more concretely draws its worlds, characters, and monsters with the care and world-building sophistication seen in the decades of gametexts since D&D inaugurated this form.

In particular, the Bas Lag novels are fitting literary examples of Weird gamespace favored by TRPGs. Miéville's primary city, New Crobuzon, finds literary continuity with the expansive city-state of Harrison's Viriconium and Mervyn Peake's convoluted castle Gormenghast.[9] Miéville channels the 'weird' of New Crobuzon into a Victorian landscape of mercantile districts and disjointed structures dominating a city-scape of ill planning and ill repute, where ghettos and slums abound, yet where wealth is flaunted by noble families in luxurious houses. Crime and corruption are rampant. The area from which the novel takes its name is a hub that connects the city's rails and trams. With titles like Bonetown, Kelltree, Griss Twist, the Ribs, Ludmean, the Crow, Sheck, these districts comprise a canvas in which characters of all types struggle for survival. Such a quick overview ignores many of the other world-building elements, such as the governmental structures, the history of the city, the wars that shaped the world, the wider continent Rohagi, and even the impact of earlier civilizations.[10]

What is evident though is that Miéville demonstrates confidence that representing the fantastic, and the monstrous, is possible. As I have shown in the chapter on Lovecraft, a conundrum is translating the untranslatable. In this specific sense, the philosopher has a lesser challenge than the novelist or visual artist. Spread across the narratives of the three novels, we see a cast of weird creatures that could easily fit into a D&D monster manual. A *Dragon* article even categorizes some of them with stats, making them playable in a D&D campaign as unique 'races.'[11]

[8] See Cline 2012.
[9] See Harrison's Fantasy Masterworks collection, *Viriconium* (1988) and Peake's *The Gormenghast Novels* (1995).
[10] For more detail, see the article in *Dragon Magazine* 352.
[11] For example, the Cactacae have "powerful vegetable muscles and thick fibrous skin in varying shades of green studded with spines extending from tiny to finger long" (Baur 2007, 42).

Miéville's creatures such as these follow Lovecraft in resisting standard Gothic-inspired conventions. The Khepri are female humanoids with beetle heads and a penchant for crime. With a nod to D&D's use of Lovecraft and piscine characteristics emerging from the influence of sea-gods like Dagon and Cthulhu, that of D&D's frog-faced humanoids called Bullywugs and fish-like creatures driven to worship their watery masters, the Kuo-toa, Miéville transforms them into the Vodyanoi who "resemble fishy frogs with large human faces and huge hands" (Baur 2007, 48). More direct influence from Lovecraft can be seen in the Slake Moth, a descendant of the Night-Gaunt, both of which concern the deadly quality of dreams.

Also, when Miéville writes in language such as "things lunged at her as she walked past and she shuddered with the glass. Something swirled oleaginously through a huge vat of liquid mud: she saw toothy tentacles slapping at her and scouring the tank" (2000, 127), he not only channels Lovecraft but the style of writing Gygax used in his source-books. This hints at the material actuality of weird objects, as both discursive and physical things. At the end of the novel, when its protagonists, led by crisis-energy professor and scientist Isaac Dan der Grimnebulin, face a Lovecraftian-like Slake Moth, Miéville describes this encounter in a direct manner focused on the material realm.

> It tried to shriek as its wings and chitin roared and split and crisped, but the whip prevented it. A great gob of acid sprayed the twisting moth square in the face. It denatured the proteins and compounds of its hide in seconds, melting the moth's exoskeleton. (Miéville 2000, 819)

Descriptions of such immediate, physical objects function other than as gratuitous shock elements; they demonstrate a will toward representation, as well as hint that the literary mode itself must contend with other modes. While the cinematic may come to mind, I suggest a gameist mode unconcerned with such playful language. Such embodied monstrous objects reflect the need for material, analog interaction so necessary in an experience of a TRPG. One is tempted to imagine, as does the *Dragon* article, what it might be like to encounter a world such as New Crobuzon, or its Slake Moths. A novel can only go so far though, as should a game.

Literary Fantasist: Borges

The expansion of the modern fantastic via gametexts becomes clearer when we look at the fantasism of a canonical twentieth-century writer Jorge Luis Borges, a favorite of literary theorists, rather than SF and fantasy fans, but one who speaks across the divide into the popular-culture work of writers such as China Miéville and Gene Wolfe, as well as many others who explore the weird and nebulous. He also encouraged the sort of complex representation of the fantastic now found in a game like Numenera.

Borges is a literary fantasist whose snapshots of imaginary worlds rival the originality of anything found in popular culture and TRPGs, yet he works through the medium of language to prefigure many of the complex posthuman concerns we now face in our digitized world. A brief comment into his type of wild imaginings demonstrates they prefigure a trend in TRPGs, as well as the modern fantastic, toward today's genre-resisting fictions of the draconic-posthuman. This chapter focuses on elements of weird fiction, as well as posthuman cosmicism as recent, highly imaginative forms of the modern fantastic. Borges thinking is a bridge between the imaginative within the literary world, and the posthumanizing process within the modern fantastic's realized gaming worlds.

Borges wrote through the bulk of the twentieth century. His themes often echoed the absurdity of life favored by existentialists; yet for him literature was a form of philosophizing through symbols, reminding us of the Deleuzian notion of affects and intensities we encounter with the multiplicities and flows of life: all of this flux a contradiction of order and chaos that is the universe. Borges used a variety of literary devices to dream worlds into being and to explore the unknowable mystery lying behind it all. Imagined analog tools, such as libraries, mirrors, maps, labyrinths, etc., impose order, yet with futility, because language itself is suspect. These facets of his work remind us of the creative Deleuzian-like faculty that makes philosophy a process of identifying problems and creating conceptual solutions.

The themes of Borges as a literary thinker go beyond my brief description, but of importance is how his cartographies of complex spaces remind us of a central aspect of the modern fantastic: how unreal the real world is, how constructed it is with fictions and, likewise, how fictions carry the weight of reality in their importance. We are surrounded by examples of fantastic spaces in his thought and fiction: territories, maps, terrains, environments, etc., sometimes interesting in themselves, sometimes as places for subjects to emerge.[12] We see this process for Borges when he peers within the deepest mysteries of the universe, and one that began for him as a child with a peculiar biscuit can that displayed a Japanese scene but also, in the corner of the tin, displayed the tin and the scene again.[13] Such recursive mechanisms in fiction in which novels feature in novels, such as in *Don Quixote* (1615), or plays in plays, such as in *Hamlet* (1603), disturb us with the fantastic because "these inversions suggest that if the characters of a fictional work can be read as spectators, we, its readers or spectators, can be fictitious" (Borges 1964, 187).[14]

Working through Borges's fiction of mirrors, labyrinths, books, libraries requires its own extensive study, but one story illuminates how analog objects become tools to access fantasy realized worlds, a process that echoes the creation of TRPGs. In "Tlön, Uqbar, Orbis Tertius," a mystery emerges over the insertion of pages in the 1917 Anglo-American

---

[12] One example is to see Borges's short story, "On Exactitude in Science" (in which a map is drawn in such a manner that it covers its entire territory) as a comment on how empire in the twentieth century functioned (Barlow et al. 2005). More broadly, such a map is also a trope of spatial recursion that demonstrates Borges's "fascination with infinitude" (Stabb 1970, 85).

[13] See Borges 2000, 160.

[14] By attempting to map the most difficult of these (i.e., a human's place in the universe), Borges acts as a precursor to the posthuman narratives of both popular SF and the critical theory of Haraway, Hayles, and other later important posthumanism theorists. For example, poststructural critical theorists Stefan Herbrechter and Ivan Callus strip away posthumanism's technological dressing to see what is left with a non-technological posthumanism. They find in Borges an answer. They argue in an anthology dedicated to this subject that "what Borges contributes to posthumanism is a memory of cyborgs and of the challenges they pose to experience and thought—but one that contrives to proceed before the invention of cybernetics" (2009, 17). They see him as a philosophical literary writer whose fiction thinks through problems of the human, his fiction a type of early posthuman thought experiment. They note that even Hayles recognizes his thinking as a precursor for the reflexivity found in cybernetics, but they are after how his writing problematizes itself via spiritual rather than technological metaphors, paving the way for so many theorists (e.g., Haraway) who would challenge the stable categories of humanism. Here, they tie Borges, literally, with the title of their anthology (*Cy-Borges: Memories of the Posthuman in the Work of Jorge Luis Borges*), to the notion of the cyborg, a trope many consider dominant in both posthumanism theory and SF. However, the cyborg's exhaustion has been detailed, as has the threat of screens, enough to suggest the need for new tropes, or, even more possibly, completely new ways of discussing the subject.

version of the *Encyclopedia Britannica* (1902) about an assumed nation called Uqbar, its pages not found in other copies. The mysterious Volume XLVI contains 921 pages instead of the standard 917. The new material provides information on Uqbar. The narrator mentions that

> The section on Language and Literature was brief: Only one trait is worthy of recollection: it notes that the literature of Uqbar was one of fantasy and that its epics and legends never referred to reality but to two imaginary regions of Mlejnas and Tlön. (Borges 1964, 5)

Later, the narrator finds a book in which he "experienced an astonished and airy feeling of vertigo" (Borges 1964, 6). This is an encyclopedia of Tlön, a physical document corroborating the original mysterious article.

Viewing this within the frame of how TRPGs are constructed, we see that this encyclopedia of Tlön is analogous to source-books used to describe gameworlds. Borges provides such a document in his story for the world of Tlön, and even makes his narrator ask, "Who are the inventors of Tlön" (Borges 1964, 7), posing a central question that must be answered in the plural for both the narrative and for anyone engaging a realized fantasy world. Borges's story reflects the creative process of how realized worlds are formed through the combination of digital and analog elements, between game designers and players and the complex assemblages of elements that construct such worlds.

The narrative continues this process of world building by detailing the strange elements of a place (setting) comprised of a cosmos with its own laws. This is a space of pure idealism in which its language refuses to acknowledge the existence of objects. It lacks nouns. Instead, it uses verbs and adjectives as descriptors of things, none of which are believed to exist in a material sense. This monism represents a supreme example of Borgesian world creation. In such a world as Tlön, "poetic objects" (Borges 1964, 9) magically appear as *hrönir*, "accidental products of distraction and forgetfulness" (13). Such artifacts come into being through pure thought, enough so that an excavation that at first produced nothing, eventually produced the prize of any D&D campaign: "a gold mask, an archaic sword, two or three clay urns and the moldy and mutilated torso of a king whose chest bore an inscription which it has not yet been possible to decipher" (15).

The narrator soon learns of a secret society, possibly in London, from the 17th century, and with Bishop Berkeley himself as a member, who devised a plan "to invent a country" (7), which eventually became a planet. The idea was to write an encyclopedia of this imaginary place. It would ultimately form a work written in the language of Tlön, the

Orbis Tertius. Such a massive undertaking would be assumed, in the end, to be a hoax. However, the narrator notes two troubling intrusions of the fantastic into mundane reality. First, he finds a compass decorated with the letters of Tlön's alphabet. It vibrated, as if searching for a missing magnetic north. The second intrusion occurred when the narrator endured a sleepless night in which a drunkard raved. They find him dead, with coins and "a cone of bright metal, the size of a die" (16). A grown man can barely lift it from the ground due to its weight. The narrator knows such cones represent the divine in Tlön. The imagined has become real, impossible boundaries crossed, stable categories demolished.

Borges's story can be read as an example of the mysterious emerging in reality, or as an insightful look at how realized worlds are created. Such a metaphysics is to be taken seriously in the world of his narrator, although we read it from the vantage of the modern fantastic's irony. The baroque worlds created by Borges, with his insistent fantasism, are ones of infinite creativity. In such spaces, conundrums emerge in which the divine opens through endless mysticism, but also ones of cyclical time in which the eternal return sees Caesar murdered again as a gaucho recognizing his own Brutus in an adopted son.[15]

Such complex and subtle literary examples exemplify the power of fiction to explore concepts far beyond the range of TRPGs, whose players are after experience rather than literary depth. Yet, those worlds echo Borges in complexity and depth. And, like the fantastic objects of Tlön that enter reality, the actual objects of literary gametexts provide the creative ground upon which realized objects emerge. Fantastic fiction functions mytho-poetically, then, even if reinforced with irony. Borges leads us to Weird fiction, the challenge of cosmic horror in the face of such unreality, and the inherent relationship we have with texts, both analog and digital, as tools in shaping the modern fantastic.

Gene Wolfe: Magic and Mystery

In encountering even the most physicalist of Weird fiction, we are reminded that literary and gameist modes share affinities, such as the primary use of texts, but that they demonstrate marked differences as well. The detailed historiography of literary studies and critical theory has charted the complexities of how texts function—in particular, reading's inherent ludic quality. The scholarly games James Joyce

---

[15] See Borges's ultra-short story "The Plot."

created with *Ulysses* (1922) and later with *Finnegans Wake* (1939) has been repeated many times in both modernist and postmodernist fiction.

Yet, until recently, this historiography has de-emphasized the experience of imagined play beyond the frame of textual encounter. Gene Wolfe's most complex series of science-fantasy novels inspires a middle ground. Often identified as the Solar Cycle, *The Book of the New Sun* (1980–83), *The Book of the Long Sun* (1993–96), and *The Book of the Short Sun* (1999–2001) act as fitting examples of how literary texts make discursive demands of readers that gametexts do not; yet they also detail a complex, imaginary world that has inspired a direct-descendant TRPG, Numenera.

Wolfe's Solar Cycle novels demand close, critical reading. His settings within the Solar Cycle demonstrate how SF and fantasy can be situated within a fantastic frame that foregrounds the odd, uncanny, weird, strange, etc. *Dread Trident* posits the Weird, in this instance, as the most interesting form of fantastic fiction that blends SF and fantasy in such a way that the modern fantastic emerges as the disturbing or odd within imaginary realized worlds full of hybrid elements, chimerical constructions, monsters and madmen, etc. These new forms in Wolfe's work have recognizable re-skinned elements, as they do in Miéville and Numenera. Moreover, while the Weird within later games like Numenera highlight the cosmic horror of a post-anthropocene posthumanism (see below), they emerge most clearly in Wolfe when we upset stable generic divisions with border-crossing hybridization.

Wolfe's most lauded work is the first four books of the Solar Cycle, *The Book of the New Sun*, what SF theorist John Clute encourages us to consider as a single novel broken up into four separate parts, plus a final novel, making the tetralogy a pentalogy: *The Shadow of the Torturer* (1980), *The Claw of the Conciliator* (1981), *The Sword of the Lictor* (1982), and *The Citadel of the Autarch* (1983); and, later, *The Urth of the New Sun* (1987).[16] How are readers to approach such a complex multi-part and multi-published 'novel'? First, we must acknowledge the difficulties of encountering such convoluted literary depth within a science-fantasy text. Critics often approach them as exercises in serious reading.[17] For readers unconcerned with determining greatness in a writer but

---

[16] See Clute 1983.

[17] Thomas M. Disch calls Wolfe's work "odd," with the final book, *Citadel of the Autarch* (1983), the oddest (2005, 123), while Clute echoes the existence of this challenging effect concerning the "essential strangeness of the great writer" (2003, 69). The 'greatness' Clute refers to here in relation to Wolfe must contend with why he is not considered one of the great writers of SF or even of primary influence of science fantasy as a genre.

willing to work through a difficult text like Wolfe's Solar Cycle, the final reward is a finely wrought setting full of interesting characters. Such care with reading demonstrates marked differences in complexity with a TRPG like Numenera, whose setting is modeled on Wolfe's but whose gameplay makes much less literary demands. Wolfe scholarship typically foregrounds a conversation over his merit, and his opaqueness. It remains limited, though, most focusing on Wolfe as a baroque stylist, his use of religious elements, or his role in expanding the dying-earth genre popularized by D&D favorite, Jack Vance.[18]

In the original tetralogy of the *Book of the New Sun*, religious/mythic themes emerge as the most salient.[19] One of the most helpful, concise readings of Wolfe follows Clute in providing a religious frame for understanding. Adam Roberts's *History of Science Fiction* (2006) provides this reading to construct a lineage for SF, associating it with ancient Greek travel adventures and later '*voyages extraordinaires.*' What is most interesting in understanding the importance of Wolfe for my study is how Roberts situates Wolfe within a dialectic between magical thinking (Catholic) and materialist thinking (Protestant). Roberts sees the Protestant imagination responding to the world in a non-ecclesiastical/Catholic/magical manner, and this constructed a world picture that was materialist and empirical rather than one based on magical

---

[18] Clute and John Grant identify Wolfe "as one of the central figures of twentieth-century sf and an important author of fantasy" (1997, 1028), while Frederic Jameson situates Wolfe in *Archaeologies of the Future* (2005) within the generic conversation about the distinctions or harmonies of SF and fantasy (2005, 68). Wolfe's "hybridization" (see G.K. Wolfe 2011, 45) functions beyond the strictures of science fantasy romances; instead, they allow a needed distancing so that "connections to our own [world] are nearly unrecognizable" (G.K. Wolfe 2011, 45). Such a quality in Wolfe has been a key part of his output since he began writing for *Orbit* magazine when its editor Damon Knight allowed him the flexibility to write without constraint because his stories crossed generic boundaries (Ashley 2007, 129).

[19] Literary theorist John Clute sees influences as wide as Borges and Nabokov in the "dark Catholic sensibility" (1983, online) of a novel that defies genre to represent its complex self. Clute also argues that Wolfe "must be taken as attempting something analogous to Dante's supreme effort [The Divine Comedy]" (1983, online). Clute reads the Solar Cycle within a Christianized frame, seeing in its protagonist, Severian, a Christological figure, a messiah, in a world of the miraculous, replete with priests and nuns, with artifacts like the Claw of the Conciliator, with themes as grand as revelation through hermeneutics. Wolfe's greatness in this context is constructing such a challenging novel that resists the collapse of interpretation, even as it provides clues.

revelation.[20] This dialectic, shift, or replacement helps as another inflection of how the modern fantastic has emerged. Roberts is astute in seeing SF as fantastic romance; in fact, while the technological focus (rather than magical) is a helpful yet non-exhaustive method in separating the major differences between SF and fantasy, I see the fantastic imbuing both.

Roberts's frame for SF locates Wolfe in a domain driven by Clarke's famous dictum: that of technology as magic. Roberts asks us to view the fantastic as non-realist, as a magically imbued Catholic sensibility.[21] Such clear generic lines of demarcation allow Roberts to work from the broadest view possible in understanding the primary motivations of the fantastic and that, for him, this dialectic between materialist and supernatural (i.e., magical) cultural trends drives different literary forms. Along with the example of Walter M. Miller's *A Canticle for Leibowitz* (1959), Roberts argues that "Wolfe cannot abandon magic" (2006, xii). Regardless of the underlying naturalism/materialism, an inexplicable supernatural impulse reasserts the fantastic in Wolfe's novels to the point they define them.

Peter Wright's *Attending Daedalus: Gene Wolfe, Artifice and the Reader* (2003) attempts a critical analysis of Wolfe's work that had hitherto been lacking in professional scholarship. Wright argues that Wolfe "remains one of the most neglected and misunderstood writers of contemporary science fiction and fantasy" (2003, 3). His project runs counter to Roberts's insistence that magic is fundamental to Wolfe's Catholicism and his hybridized novels.

Wright argues that the rhetorical games Wolfe plays with readers in presenting his often-cryptic novels must be viewed within the context of a literary game of puzzles and ambiguities that demands active interpretation by his readers. He works from an understanding of the

---

[20] He calls this the "scientific imagination" (Roberts 2006, x), one rooted for him in the Protestant imagination, and one that has become increasingly materialist. Opposed to this, he sees the "magical-fantastic" imagination as tied to a traditional Catholic worldview that leads directly to the rise of fantasy. For Roberts, "SF as that form of fantastic romance in which magic has been replaced by the materialist discourses of science" (xi) defines the core of what became modern SF.

[21] But a separation begins here in the broad stream of 'fantastic' or 'non-realist' fiction. 'Catholic' imaginations countenance magic and produce traditional romance, magical-Gothic, horror, Tolkienian fantasy, and Marquezian magical realism. Protestant imaginations increasingly replace the instrumental function of magic with technological devices, and produce science fiction (Roberts 2006, xi).

fundamental story (what happens in the narrative) to one of interpretation. If we are to take Wright seriously (and, with him, Wolfe), the novels of the original tetralogy, plus the final novel, form a literary construct that comprises a challenge to literary studies on a par with anything Pynchon wrote, or even master prankster Joyce. For Wright, the literary game ultimately reveals a work of rational SF with a materialist metaphysics.

Wright notes that the initial Solar Cycle novels of Urth—what Wright calls "the most complex work in Wolfe's oeuvre" (2003, 49)—concerns a torturer's apprentice named Severian, who becomes a supreme ruler of a far-future Urth (earth) called an Autarch, and, later, a divine being himself. The literary challenge in parsing Wolfe's difficult novels is his use of both neologisms and archaic language that allows him to mix SF and fantasy tropes to the point of obscurity in telling this grand tale of ascension. Yet, these surface effects suggest a deeper game in play, one that requires a deciphering of codes that Wright argues works through the narrative to suggest, ultimately, a rational world situated within SF, whose far-future, magic-like elements are misunderstood both by the peoples of Urth and by readers. Following Clute, Wright seeks a grounding of these novels in SF rather than in fantasy, an expected response from thinkers who see seriousness in the former and childishness in the latter. Accepting Clark's dictum at work here, and highlighting the novels' rational base, Wright provides an interpretation that untangles the text, but also denudes it of its mythological power. Disenchantment is rarely fun.

Even though a SF bias emerges in Wright, he works against any criticism that would shoehorn these novels into rigid genres. He lauds their hybridism and "intergenericism" (2003, 57), reveling in this ambiguous tapestry as the ultimate puzzle—what Wright calls Wolfe's "interpretive game with the reader" (2003, 103). Wright argues that the novels demand a hesitation in parsing these generic difficulties. This allows us to view Wolfe's Urth Cycle from outside a standard literary frame as a complex example of the dying-earth genre. It does this, and much more.

For Wright, these novels demonstrate how a complex representation of a hybridized science-fantasy world encourages the sort of creative reading in our most demanding literary examples, as well as hints at the 'gameplay' inherent in such world creation. For example, while Wolfe owes a debt to other dying-earth writers, such as Vance, as well as a debt to his own Roman Catholicism, both these influences are subverted by the sort of interpretation demanded by Wright in which the myth-making and the use of Catholic tropes appear to be mere "paraphernalia" (2003, 202). If they are more, what then are they? They are examples of literary depth jettisoned in TRPGs for the sake of gameplay experience.

Both Roberts's and Wright's approaches reveal that genre discussions are problematic. *Dread Trident* asks for a different viewing angle: one that sees in such a complex literary work inspiration for a complex *TRPG*, Numenera. The complexities are different, the former representative of the literary, the latter one within a gameist frame.

Numenera and the Post-Anthropocene

In 2013, iXile Entertainment crowd-funded a project on *Kickstarter.com* for a new game, *Torment: Tides of Numenera* (which appeared in 2017). It far surpassed its initial goals, reaching promises totaling $1 million more quickly than any other game, and eventually generating over $4 million in funding. At the time, it was the highest-funded video game campaign on Kickstarter.[22] This was a successor to *Planescape: Torment* (1999), a popular D&D video game based on the complex, non-standard TRPG setting of Planescape. Game designer Monte Cook worked on supplements for the Planescape setting and later designed the TRPG Numenera. The choice to follow the original D&D-based game with one set in Numenera demonstrates a kindred spirit in the textures and tones of both complex settings.

Dread Trident ends its examination of fantasy gametexts with a comment on this particular TRPG—Monte Cook's Numenera—that provides Miéville-and-Wolfe-like "impossible landscapes" (M. Cook 2013b, 132) for gameplay and does so by foregrounding Weird genre elements hybridized from SF and fantasy. Numenera works within the dying-earth genre popularized by Jack Vance and later utilized with literary distinction by Wolfe. The influence is noted by Cook when he explains in the core rulebook that he found much of his inspiration from "the French artist Moebius and the writer Gene Wolfe" (2013b, 5). This chapter builds on the analysis of how Numenera reflects Wolfe's aesthetic as a game rather than a demanding literary text; in particular, it sees the game's complex cartographies and Weird elements as representing a posthuman/post-anthropocene world. Yet, one impossibly repopulated with humanoids.[23]

---

[22] See https://www.polygon.com/2013/4/5/4188366/torment-tides-of-numenera-kickstarter-top-funded-game.

[23] Before *Numenera*, an attempt was made to turn Wolfe's setting into a TRPG

This far-future setting imagines the reemergence of sentient humanoid life "approximately a billion years in the future" (M. Cook 2013b, 14).[24] Such diachronic disruption provides an interesting perspective for the discourse of SF-inflected posthumanism; it reinserts aspects of the human into a space that looks backward to an unknowable past rather than imagines how technological change affects the present and future with pure erasure. In fact, the game setting of Numenera's Ninth World posits eight prior worlds, each of which was built upon the last, the remnants and traces of these civilizations called 'numenera,' "a term that refers to anything that seems supernatural and that comes from the prior ages of the Earth" (M. Cook 2013b, 1276).

Cook is an accomplished game designer who spent years working on D&D as well as a number of other games. His most recent contribution has been the creation of his Cypher System, a narrative-focused game engine with simplistic yet flexible rules.[25] Along with Numenera, the Cypher System powers The Strange, a game that allows players to travel to 'recursions,' dimensions in the forms of different genre narratives. In The Strange, players move with ease between high-magic or high-tech settings. Such broad, genre-experiencing possibilities, though, provide micro-settings with particular genre flavors for play rather than truly hybridized settings, as does Numenera. Cook's experience with the complex D&D campaign setting of Planescape provided him with the

---

for the GURPs system. *GURPS: New Sun* (1999). This is a highly detailed depiction of Wolfe's setting by Michael Andre-Driussi, who also authored the *Lexicon Urthus* (1994).

[24] This has parallels in literary SF, of course. At the ending of H.G. Wells's *Time Machine* (1895), a far-future sun has turned red, the moon has disappeared, "the sky no longer blue" (Wells 2009, 64); crab-like monsters live on desolate, salt-caked shores. Humanity is long gone. Even further in the future, silence meets our time traveler: "All the sounds of man, the bleating of sheep, the cries of birds, the hum of insects, the stir that makes the background of our lives—all that was over" (66). This denouement is followed by a horrific dimming as the sun is eclipsed, bringing darkness and cold suggestive of the final moments of a dying world. Before leaving, the narrator glimpses a monster with tentacles hopping on the beach and feels overcome by a "terrible dread" (Wells 2009, 67). From such a canonical SF novel, we see a core element inherent in much complex fantastic SF: imagining the horror of a universe bereft of humanity.

[25] See http://cypher-system.com/. Cook's mechanics are interesting, but outside my focus. It is worth noting he reduces a character to a simple line that is easy to remember. "I am an adjective noun who verbs" (Monte Cook Games Team 2015, 18). The player then fills out the information with descriptors and foci.

credentials needed to create the Ninth World, a setting that solves a long-time problem in explaining why D&D-like adventurers risk life and limb to brave the wilds for a few gold pieces or chance magic items. The cross-genre Weird elements that pepper the Ninth World in the form of numenera act as the 'treasure' that adventurers seek. Ultratech as magic provides this motivation. Numenera takes Clarke's dictum in which magic and science are conflated as its guiding ethos to the point where the game merges both. These numenera reveal knowledge of a hidden past, the ultimate currency in the game.

The persons of this setting have been affected by the passing of immense time and by interaction with different modes of intelligence to the point that technology and magic are indistinguishable. With the detritus from eight prior civilizations, players contend with archaeological sediment deep enough to allow the use of any genre conventions in SF and fantasy. The core rulebook explains that the prior worlds were comprised of civilizations that had conquered space travel and planet-scale engineering. Others could break the laws of physics or manipulate matter at the molecular level. One civilization had access to parallel universes. Of course, "at least some of these civilizations were not human" (M. Cook 2013b, 130). The great mystery at the heart of the game concerns the nature of these civilizations: how human-like sentient creatures still even exist.[26]

Numenera's most interesting aspect is how it reverses the scope of post-anthropocene concerns of a posthuman world in which humanity has suffered the ultimate horror of its own erasure. At some point in the Ninth World's past, the planet had already been denuded of human life, repopulated with successor species, again and again. The Ninth World passed beyond this extinction and, with the requisite humanism of a game played by human beings, reinserts humanoids into a world ignorant of its past. The game's mechanics encourages the exploration of playing in such a remade world, and it recognizes a need for simplification.

Unlike the many choices in Eclipse Phase, players in Numenera have fewer options.[27] This is a world where the animals of the past are extinct,

[26] "Perhaps an even better question is: After a billion years, why does the earth still have humans at all, in shapes and forms that we—the people of the 21st century—can recognize? This might seem particularly curious once you consider the fact that many of the prior worlds were distinctly nonhuman. Ninth Worlders don't have that specific perspective, but they do wonder where they came from. They have a sense that Earth was once theirs, and then it wasn't, and now it is again. How can this be? Perhaps one day they'll find the answer" (M. Cook 2013b, 131).

[27] 'Glaives' are warriors; 'Jacks' are multi-skilled rogues; 'Nanos' are

but basic biological types can be identified. Even more so, its monsters reveal its inherent hybridized fantasy located in the Weird:

> mutant beasts, engineered creatures (or their descendants), automatons, biomechanical blends of organism and machine, extraterrestrial and ultraterrestrial beings, creatures of energy, and stranger entities roam the planet. (M. Cook 2013b, 133)

Along with such beings, the landscape defamiliarizes the present into a unique imaginary world:

> Islands of crystal float in the sky. Inverted mountains rise above plains of broken glass. Abandoned structures the size of kingdoms stretch across great distances, so enormous that they affect the weather. Massive machines, some still active, churn and hum. (M. Cook 2013b, 134)

Such creatures and landscapes demand attention to the game's genre flexibility but also to its inherent weirdness. While Numenera can be played as a science-fantasy game set in a dying-earth genre, the designers have provided supplements that allow gamemasters and players to heighten both Weird and Lovecraftian elements.

The source-book *Injecting the Weird* (2014) begins by stating that "Numenera is all about the weird" (M. Cook 2004, 2), explaining its use of the Weird as something uncommon from the everyday, as something even beyond standard SF and fantasy. This is the attribute of wonder in modern SF, laced with a tinge of the unsettling, or uncanny. To 'inject' this quality into the game, the designers suggest an inaccessible past for the characters. "The point is to reinforce that the inhabitants of the prior worlds were incomprehensibly advanced and alien" (M. Cook 2004, 3). The supplement provides tables full of examples of the Weird, from an ancient structure you can only enter while unconscious to one whose atmosphere inhibits all sound. Flora and fauna are also subject to weirdness, such as mist that forms tendrils and follows characters, or a pool of water that reflects the thoughts of anyone peering into it.[28]

---

tech-sensitive mages. This clear balance of three basic character types finds its roots in the early years of TRPGs: i.e., D&D's fighters, thieves/rogues, and wizards.

[28] Characters may even encounter "horselike mammals that are only a few inches tall" (M. Cook 2004, 10) or a "single reptilian eye that can phase in and out of reality" (M. Cook 2004, 11).

Injecting the Weird into a game with subtle disruptions of the everyday or common leads to a more intense version of such fissures and ruptures. In *Strange Aeons: Lovecraftian Numenera* (2013), Cook presents a source-book that infuses the setting with cosmic horror in which humanity must face a universe beyond its understanding and one in which humanity has no place.[29] Doing so allows players to experience the Weird with a Lovecraftian version of cosmic horror. This supplement also fits into the sophisticated view of Lovecraft as a precursor writer of the post-anthropocene and posthuman. Numenera is a game about such a Weird and horrific world, although one that looks backward to a time when humanity once existed rather than looks forward to its coming demise.[30]

In this heightened version of Numenera, the setting comprises three important layers: science fantasy, the Weird, and cosmic horror. Yet, at the character-creation level, the requirement of representation asserts itself in player options. The game suggests ways to reskin (adapt) characters for the Lovecraftian version.[31] In such an extreme version of Numenera, characters may gain new attributes that might make them insane or doomed, a nod to Lovecraft that the ultimate horror of witnessing such truths are too much for frail human-like minds. Player characters, though, are encouraged not to look away.

Ligotti and Cosmic Despair

Foregrounding the problem of representation returns us to Lovecraft and his descendants. While much scholarship into Weird-inflected fantasy notes Lovecraft's "Supernatural Horror in Literature" as seminal in the shift away from Gothic-themed fantasy, Lovecraft's thoughts in the essay "Notes on Writing Weird Fiction" elicited further elaboration from him in

---

[29] "In Numenera, GMs are encouraged to make things weird. In Lovecraftian Numenera, if anything, it should be weirder" (M. Cook 2013a, 4).

[30] "Humans of the Ninth World who begin to think about the billion or so years behind them, and the immense civilizations that have come and gone in that time—each so much greater than the Ninth World that humans can't even comprehend them—can easily begin to feel the grip of cosmic horror" (M. Cook 2013a, 3).

[31] They may be Non-Euclidian, which means they don't exist in normal reality, making them blurry; or Squamous, a direct nod to Lovecraft's fascination with and fear of sea creatures; or Tentacular, meaning they have the martial benefit of many appendages; or Unnamable, a character quality that marks them as unnatural.

a letter written in 1935 to Alvin Early Perry.[32] His workmanlike method, though, found its inspiration in "dreams, reading daily occurrences, odd visual glimpses, or origins so remote I cannot place them" (Lovecraft, qtd. in Joshi and Schultz 2000, 262). This located the Weird, for Lovecraft, in the odd turn, a genealogy that finds its early articulation and practice with Lovecraft but emerges full force with a contemporary writer, Thomas Ligotti.

The Weird in Ligotti transforms far beyond the scope of Lovecraft's cosmicism and his Cthulhu Mythos to encompass a sophisticated response to SF-inflected posthumanism, as well as to demonstrate a complex and creative form of the literary modern fantastic. Yet, Ligotti is a direct heir of Lovecraft, both of whom produced, and produce, stories that posit a universe of supreme despair and whose language reflects the weight of such knowledge. Ligotti, though, refuses to stop at the edge of the abyss. He would look inside; and does. With Ligotti, the most frightening facts that the universe offer are seductive beacons rather than warnings Lovecraft would suggest we heed. This leads to the worst sort of knowledge: what Ligotti calls "the icy bleakness of things" (From the "Bungalow House," in Ligotti 2008, 221).

In many of Ligotti's stories of the Weird, uncanny architectural space is critical and heralds an important discussion about representation in horror. In such stories we see his preoccupation with physical rooms, windows, doors, passes, ladders, stairways, streets, towers, roofs, etc. Dreaming in such spaces reveals a more mysterious realm within these spaces.[33] Like his characters, Ligotti wants readers "transfixed in the order of the unreal" (Ligotti 1990, 262). His penchant for stories that indirectly represent follow his preoccupation with the real world as a pale and disenchanted place, a gauzy phantom of the unreal world. And many of his narrators reflect that such knowledge is horrible.

---

[32] He detailed his writing process in clear steps, from conceptualizing "a rough approximation" (Lovecraft qtd. in Joshi and Schultz 2000, 263) of the story, to following it with a detailed synopsis in the order of the actual events, rather than that of the narrative. He suggested a second synopsis that reflects how the story is to be told. Writing and revisions follow. The original essay can be found in Lovecraft 1995, 113–16. The elaboration can be found in Joshi and Schultz 2000, 262–6.

[33] The narrator of "The Sect of the Idiot" dreams he is in "a high room whose windows look out on a maze of streets which unraveled beneath an abyss of stars" (Ligotti 1990, 227), while in "Vastarian" we see such dream-like spaces function as the primary narrative focus, one in which can be seen Ligotti's choice for the difficult terrain of a fugue-like state, rather than clinically real representations of the monstrous.

Ligotti rethinks Lovecraftian cosmic horror as supreme nihilism, while his use of the Weird still finds roots in Lovecraft enough to burgeon into a scaffolding for his philosophical revision.[34] Ligotti seeks to describe a sense of the unsettling ineffable: "There remains at the heart of the tale a kind of abyss from which the weird emerges and into which it cannot be pursued for purposes of analysis and resolution" (From the Foreword, Ligotti 1994, xii). Ligotti's intermixture of the cosmic with the odd reflects *Dread Trident*'s use of interesting science fantasy as a combination of the Weird, with degrees of cosmic horror.[35]

Ligotti is often considered a horror writer, although he was anthologized in VanderMeer's *New Weird* (2008) and, for my study, represents a rethinking of Lovecraftian cosmicism. He follows Lovecraft, as well as later philosophers such as Harman and Thacker, in seeing in Weird fiction a powerful attempt at hinting at what lies beyond the knowable, translatable, representable. Literature works as an effective medium for Ligotti, as it did for Lovecraft because of its function to trigger the imagination through words. In Ligotti's case, language suggests rather than denotes, forgoing a mimetic exactitude and, thereby, avoiding the same problem Lovecraft faced, describing the indescribable, and one that a gameist mode, and some writers like Barker or Miéville, solve with finely drawn representation. This problem in representation continues in Ligotti, which gaming sidesteps because gametexts work on a different level from the literary. They are not interested in such deep psychological effects as an objective description of Azathoth or an encounter with a Shoggoth. TRPG gametexts function without demanding proper emotional reflection of such an experience, as would a literary story. Gametexts avoid such poetry for the creation and experience of realized worlds, safe behind a protective barrier of irony.

What, though, is lost in a gametext that can be found in a powerful literary account of the Weird, cosmic horror, or ultimate erasure? A work of independent scholarship, *The Thomas Ligotti Reader* (2003), attempts a serious investigation into the power of Ligotti's thought, seeing in a

---

[34] For example, his collection of short fiction in *Noctuary* 1994 begins with an essay that states, "No one needs to be told about what is weird" (from the Foreword to 1994, vii); his argument follows that the experience of weirdness prepares us for an appreciation of Weird literature, what Ligotti calls "macabre unreality" (xi).

[35] These blend within gaming-realized worlds that utilize familiar frameworks from SF and fantasy, yet rework most of the tropes so that they have fresh facades atop stable and reliable frames. Numenera, in particular, allows one to experience the reading of Wolfe's Solar Cycle series in a setting inspired by it, while also channeling many precursor elements.

few critical stories a continuation of Lovecraft's project.[36] For example, it recognizes that key stories such as "The Last Feast of the Harlequin," dedicated to the memory of Lovecraft, allow fans of both writers to read Ligotti as following Lovecraft by continuing what he started, "a distillation and expression in contemporary terms of what was best in Lovecraft" (Cardin 2003, 16). This emerges in Ligotti as an extension of cosmic horror, rather than as Lovecraft's Mythos. Unlike Barker or Miéville, Ligotti proves less adept in the finely drawn monster as he is in presenting unsettling nuanced details that suggest the horrific. Ligotti's thinking develops from Lovecraftian cosmic horror because he highlights above all else humanity's insignificance. While this is a core element in Lovecraft, the Mythos that emerged in a playful manner holds equal (if not more) weight in considering Lovecraft, while Ligotti's work fails to present such scaffolding. Instead, Ligotti offers us a literature of "terrible enlightenment [... and] infernal wisdom" (From "The Sect of the Idiot," in Ligotti 1990, 229–30).

Such a narrower, nuanced perspective views Ligotti as a technical stylist with a bleak vision of the world that gives power to his writing, one the editor of the *Reader* suggests works from Ligotti's own personal views that underlie all of his writing and may affect sensitive readers already attuned to such insights. Direct references, though, tie Ligotti to the Mythos he has chosen mostly to ignore.[37] For example, "The Sect of the Idiot," begins with a quote from Lovecraft's imaginary *Necronomicon* about Azathoth, while in "Tsalal" this unseeable deity provides the reader with a bare glimpse of such cosmic darkness, a hint that peering through reality to another reality triggers actual Lovecraftian-like entities. "The Sect of the Idiot" ends with the narrator realizing his hands have been replaced by tentacles, another direct nod to Lovecraft. These "drooping tentacles" (From "The Sect of the Idiot," in Ligotti 1990, 229) are barely described when the narrator views the entities who have been whispering to him in his dreams. Yet, Ligotti keeps such mysteries at a distance.

The connection to Lovecraft's Mythos continues with the use of recognized motifs, such as ancient cults worshiping unknowable deities and the use of mysterious texts. This also connects Ligotti to Borges, who

[36] The *Ligotti Reader* presents three dominant Lovecraftian themes that emerge in Ligotti's writing: (1) the meaninglessness or evil within the universe; (2) the instability of the material world that fronts this universe; and (3) the living nightmare of individuals in this universe. Despair "is foundational to Ligotti's fictional universe: there is simply no solace to be found anywhere in this or any other world" (Cardin 2003, 20).

[37] See Cardin 2003, 21.

shared a love of mysterious libraries and inscrutable texts.[38] While in such literature the imaginary is made real to be revealed as unreal, the realized worlds within the modern fantastic suffer no such confusion or possible Ligottian terror. They are cushioned by irony, yet, still effective, except for anyone in need of a true experience, like those in Ligotti's stories.

Regarding Ligotti's ultimate hesitation in attempting to represent the unreal in a material fashion, his story "The Medusa" symbolizes this refusal when it could have embraced the monstrous as a supreme example of 'nerdy categorizing.' In it, a philosopher, Lucian Dregler, investigates any lead or hint that the mythical Medusa actually existed. But, as everyone knows, to behold the Medusa is to be turned to stone:

> And the Medusa will see to it that we are protected, sealing our eyelids closed with the gluey spittle of her snakes, while their bodies elongate and slitter past our lips to devour us *from the inside*. This is what we must never witness, except in the imagination, where it is a charming sight. (From "The Medusa," in Ligotti 1994, 22)

With an ironic Medusa, who would never seal our eyes shut, we are protected, a fine example of how realized worlds function. Yet, in a world where monsters exist, we are faced with the unreal made real, or the virtual made actual. "On the other side is the unthinkable, the unheard-of, that-which-should-not-be: hence, the Real" (From "The Medusa," in Ligotti 1994, 23).

Ligotti's story posits this process of the horrific-unreal-made-real. Dregler learns of a Brownstone with a small space under the ground-floor stairs. He sees typical objects in the storeroom and, curiously, "bandaged hoses that drooped like dead pythons from hooks on the walls" (From "The Medusa," in Ligotti 1994, 20). He sees nothing else of note but does encounter a variety of odors, the combination of which Ligotti describes as an image, as if the senses have switched: "its complete image was dark as shadows in a cave and writhing in a dozen directions over curving walls" (From "The Medusa," in Ligotti 1994, 20). At this point, our narrator may be unreliable, his possible encounter with the unreal-made-real distorting his understanding.

We are told he was unsure how long he stayed in the room before leaving. He had seen an image of himself in a cracked mirror and had

---

[38] In "Vastarian" we see Ligotti's ideas about hallucinated worlds emerging from books as an example of the romanticized imagination with a dark-fantasy tint, what Ligotti derives from the Weird as "macabre unreality" (from the Foreword to 1994, xi).

rushed out in a panic, feeling himself being sucked back into the room to the point he lost his breath. When he realizes the tugging was only a loose thread from his overcoat attached to the door, he recovers from his dread and flees. We are led to believe he survived that encounter with the room, with full belief the Medusa was there. When Dregler returns to the Brownstone, he risks disenchanting his hope in her existence with proof she doesn't exist. He even finds the thread still attached to the door. He sees the cracked mirror, but also a man, like a manikin, frozen in horror. This image returns to him a horrible knowledge that he is seeing a description of his soul he once described in metaphor. "But it was no longer the charming image of the imagination" (From "The Medusa," in Ligotti 1994, 24). The story ends with Dregler reuniting with his stony form, suggesting he was given time after the initial encounter or it was all a hallucination after he was turned to stone. Yet, Ligotti refuses to draw Medusa for us, other than the suggestion of the pythons hanging from the wall.

His refusal to represent such horror beyond suggestion or a slight hint foregrounds his instincts for an atmosphere of the Weird dominated by cosmic despair. His characters typically find an existential problem as if straight from the pen of Nietzsche about starting into the abyss that exemplifies true horror. With Lovecraft, cosmic insignificance is an empirical fact of nature. For Ligotti's it is a refrain of Wagnerian scope:

> I was no more than an irrelevant parcel of living tissue caught in a place I should not be, threatened with being snared in some great dredging net of doom, an incidental shred of flesh pulled out of its element of light and into icy blackness. (From "The Sect of the Idiot," in Ligotti 1990, 227)

Such bleakness can be found in numerous points of Ligotti's fiction. In fact, it is the thematic inspiration for a recent Mythos element to emerge in TV from an aura popularized by Lovecraft and continued by Ligotti.

True Detective and the Modern Fantastic

Ligotti's influence extends from Lovecraftian cosmicism to contemporary popular culture through the success of HBO's first season of *True Detective* (2014–present) and Matthew McConaughey's character Rust Cohle.[39] The

---

[39] Of obvious similarity is Cohle's nihilistic philosophy with Ligotti's *The Conspiracy Against the Human Race* (2011).

reach of Lovecraft is far and wide, merging with other parallel mythoi, such as the Carcosa Mythos, named after fantastic elements created by Ambrose Bierce and later fictionalized by Robert W. Chambers in *The King in Yellow* (1895). Lovecraft read Chambers and was a fan of his Weird writing, enough to incorporate elements into his own Mythos.[40] In this way, the Carcosa Mythos precedes the more popular Cthulhu Mythos, yet with nowhere near the influence, or aura, in popular culture.

The recent success, though, of *True Detective*'s first season owes as much to Lovecraft's influence as it does to Chambers. With *True Detective*'s fantasy elements mined from Chambers's *Yellow King* and the philosophy of Ligotti, Weird fiction's Lovecraftian Mythos and cosmic horror has moved beyond the expected media of horror fiction, film-making, analog and digital video games to have influenced a popular-culture HBO series. The first season presented a serious fantasy drama that demanded we accept its strong mimesis and hinted with conviction that a latent fantastic framework might reveal itself. Sadly, it did not.

Season one of *True Detective* has been called a soulless rival to Scorsese, full of style but with a hollow center to a series that locates its existential horror not in Lovecraftian monsters but in the countryside.[41] It tells the story of two detectives who encounter a murder mystery full of occult references—the King in Yellow, and Carcosa, two of its dominate literary elements. We are encouraged to consider seriously the possibility of the supernatural within a mimetic frame. In fact, this tenor works through the entire show, promising a denouement with a material represen-tation of the monstrous. Yet, in the end, a lack of resolve in the face of these mysteries that the show painstakingly constructed but refused to embrace demonstrates a clear example of balking at the modern fantastic's acceptance as a serious impulse of fiction. This misstep occurs in the final confrontation between Detective Cohle and Errol William Childress (played by Glenn Fleshler). Cohle sees the ceiling of a chamber crack open to a vista of the cosmos. We are led to believe the great mystery will be revealed. The King in Yellow might appear, or a vision of Carcosa. Instead, in the end, the supernatural-made-real is denied. This refusal undermines the entire season.

The two core impulses of the fantastic and mimetic, as Kathryn Hume argues,[42] define the broadest approaches to literature and help us see the primary tension in the show between opposing tendencies: its

---

[40] See Lovecraft's comments on Chambers in "Supernatural Horror in Literature" and "The Whisperer in Darkness," where he mentions Hastur.
[41] See Nussbaum 2014a; 2014b and Collins 2014.
[42] See Hume 1985.

overt need to adhere to a 'respectable' literary realism, while utilizing the fantastic as a way to create dramatic tension only to undermine it in the end. After adamant admissions by creator and writer Nic Pizzolatto that the supernatural should not be expected to emerge in the finale,[43] he has our nihilistic hero hallucinate (we are led to believe) when he stares up at the cosmos rather than peer through a window into the dark gulfs so feared by Weird writers like Lovecraft and Ligotti. Later, in a coma, Cohle claims to have experienced a mystical reunion with his dead daughter and emerges as a redeemed fantasy hero, believing the light is winning its cosmic battle with the dark. Sadly, Carcosa remains only a puzzle-like ornament at best—at worst, a disingenuous attempt at trickery.

Season one of *True Detective* is a definitive screened text within the discourse of the modern fantastic, but one that retreats from the acceptance of the fantastic as a dominant impulse of contemporary fiction—even though this impulse drives the dramatic tension within the season. The fantastic supernatural/cosmic horror here is key in understanding how such a gritty police procedural is rethought from a fantasy-studies perspective. In fact, season one gained much currency by utilizing pulp fantasy, without full acknowledgment. Reframing the show's latent Weird elements as Lovecraftian/Cthulhu/Carcosa mythoi mechanisms foregrounds their roles in a larger canvas of realized worlds. One could certainly see *True Detective* inspire a campaign scenario in the TRPGs, Call of Cthulhu, or Chronicles of Darkness.

Instead of a proud example of the reach of Weird writers like Lovecraft and Ligotti, Pizzolatto's refusal demonstrates that the often-derided pulp writers such as Lovecraft, Chambers, R.E. Howard, and a host of modern fantasists still have much ground to cover to be considered serious material for fiction. I imagine George R.R. Martin might suggest the refusal was a mistake and that all manner of fantasy can be taken seriously today. Neil Gaiman would probably agree, as would Clive Barker, Ursula Le Guin, Margaret Atwood, and a host of others. Most recently, fantasist Kazuo Ishiguro has won the Noble Prize (2017) for Literature. The genres of fantastic popular-culture fiction, as HBO's *Game of Thrones* (2011–19) demonstrates, have never been more relevant. *True Detective* stood on the cusp of representing this influential yet derided inflection of the modern fantastic without shame but refused. Still, it functions within the modern fantastic's broader realized worlds

---

[43] For one admission, see Steele 2014. Pizzolatto made similar comments in a number of other interviews around the same time, all meant to demonstrate a marked non-fantastic approach to the series.

influenced by the aura of Lovecraft, as have so many other popular-culture texts.

*   *   *

Dread Trident's final case study has examined a TRPG, Numenera, as an example of postanthropocene/posthuman science fantasy. Within both the game and its literary influences reside the echo of D&D and Lovecraft, two precursors that also contain elements of the Weird and that resisted genre stability in fantastic fiction. Within such a context, this chapter examined fantasy novelist China Miéville as a definitive example of a modern-fantastic writer courageous enough to draw the Weird with full embodied representation. He follows the same instinct for the 'nerdy categorizing specificity' with which he describes Lovecraft, especially in the three novels presenting the world of Bas Lag and its exemplary fantasy city, New Crobuzon.

It continued its examination with a quick look at the thinking of Jorge Luis Borges as an example of a complex, mythic fantasist who is also quintessentially modern. He works within unconventional fantasy and SF to imagine modern subjectivity as fantastic, a true writer beyond genre, whose story, "Tlön, Uqbar, Orbis Tertius," exemplifies the analog/digital and material/discursive dynamics at play in the modern fantastic. Numenera, likewise, acts as a fitting example of how a fantastic-realized-world setting utilizes both the Borgesian baroque Weird-era motifs and Lovecraftian elements to create a unique setting. Yet, unlike the demand by writers of cosmic horror that a palpable sense of dread must arise from effective Weird fiction, this game presents its version of post-anthropocene space as playable. Safe behind a comforting irony, players can enjoy the injection of the Weird or of Lovecraftian elements into Numenera without existential or emotional tension.

Novelist Gene Wolfe, however, exemplifies a different use of the Weird, one with less an emphasis on the problems of representation than on the use of mystical elements in a language game with the reader. This chapter read the difficulties in parsing the differences between magic and technology as a reflection of the complexities in such a literary work absent in the play-focused experience of TRPGs. Wolfe's influence on a TRPG like Numenera happens in parallel with the emergence of Weird elements in fiction and TRPGs.

It has ended with a return to the literary in its argument that Thomas Ligotti continues Lovecraft's project of articulating a metaphysics of cosmicism. Yet, Ligotti also, albeit obliquely, adds to Lovecraft's Mythos.

Both writers find common ground in refusing the challenge to represent the ultimate horrors. While such a refusal is understandable from a literary perspective, whose rhetoric and poetry often benefits from intimation rather than delineation, this chapter sees in the brilliant first season of *True Detective* a continuation of Lovecraft's influence in cobbling together pulp elements of the Weird from a variety of writers, himself included. It also sees a major flaw in the season's ultimate refusal to embrace its own fantastic core.

Chapter 8

Conclusion

Dread Trident has argued that theorizing the modern fantastic within the context of TRPG texts is important for understanding SF and fantasy as academic disciplines, as well as for understanding the rise of realized worlds. It has worked through case studies of representative TRPGs to provide a variety of examples of this phenomenon, utilizing core concepts such as SF as modern myth-making, the Singularity as a fantasy trope, hyper-embodied language, enchantment-as-magification, fantasy's challenge to the mundane, gametext harmonization in imaginary worlds, the draconic-posthuman trope, the 'spectral return' of the gothic, cosmic horror, cosmic despair, realized-fantasy space, ironic distance, untranslatable and unimaginable representation, 'nerdy' categorization of the material, complexity of lore in fantasy gametexts, post-anthropocene posthumanization, etc. In the modern fantastic's realized worlds of TRPGs we have a wealth of unexamined gametexts that function like engineering tools along with discursive literary objects. They are both. And they are designed for material, embodied gameplay. They form a megatext of shared-world-setting creation far beyond those of any one author. The fantasy they offer provides a way of managing existence within modern, technologized life.

In this crucial sense, *Dread Trident* has argued for the importance of discursive techniques found in gametexts, but also for the engineering techniques of problem solving through tool creation that these game elements facilitate. Material artifacts in the form of gametexts and tools require continued attention because they are the mechanisms that allow for the construction of realized spaces. Of importance is how the terms 'gametexts' and 'gametools' equate to both analog and digital printed material. The latter, though, is less recognizable as popular-culture artifacts, but much more variable, from multi-sided dice to iconic pewter or resin-based figurines. These can also be analog and digital gaming aids, from encounter or party-management apps to monster cards or spell cards.

Dread Trident also examined how fantasy studies and SF studies must look to these key gametexts and tools for any full understanding of the modern fantastic, or the prevalence of its ironic-fantasy as a growing part of contemporary, technologized life. The modern fantastic, then, is this sense that we are now increasingly border crossing the shared (realized) universes of Marvel, Star Wars, Hogwarts, and a host of others, and that we enter them with a wink, experiencing a small portion of their enchanting power, while maintaining enough ironic distance to remember they are imaginary.

The digital is a key mechanism for such a phenomenon. While the digital acts as a primary substrate for knowledge and culture in the twenty-first century, traditional methods and objects of study like analog books (even in their digital forms) require our continued consideration. They demonstrate a stubborn insistence on materiality and embodiment in our often disembodied, technologized world. TRPGs provide archives of analog gametexts that allow the continued use of material objects in a world now dominated by the cultural mode of digital gaming. The analog, though, must continue to acknowledge its dominant and precocious younger sibling, the digital. What we see with this digital upstart is increasing demand that we enter virtual spaces from social networking sites to entertainment media platforms, many of them comprising an inherently fantastic landscape. Yet, the analog remains a persistent field of experience. The persistence of analog imaginary worlds, then, reflects the larger process of embodiment within the modern fantastic resisting its dissolution into vistas of data and screens.

TRPGs have one foot in the pre-digital world of imaginary fiction and one in the digital world of rendered space. The realized worlds of TRPGs differentiate themselves from short stories, novels, poems, film, theater, etc., as born of gametexts and tools providing an experiential arena that rationalizes fantasy/magic/super-tech with the excitement of play. Such rationalized fantasy elements also provide the best way to understand TRPGs as contemporary literary/ludic/gameist constructions resulting from the rise of science, technology, and engineering in the modern world. Due to their realized aspects, such experiences operate differently from the literary process of reading a novel, short story, poem, etc. Shared gameplay experience is foregrounded. Narrative elements prove to be less sophisticated than those found in complex novels.

In theorizing the modern fantastic, *Dread Trident* has relied on modern studies as a foundational discipline. Modern studies informs this book because the field also encompasses humanism, posthumanism, science fiction (SF), technology, fantasy studies, analog-and-digital game studies, etc. More ink has been spilled discussing the rise of the modern, the nature of modernity, the differences with modernism, the move into the postmodern, etc., than any of the other similar subjects outside of humanism itself. The modern fantastic is a topic one can't discuss outside twinning it with the rise of modernity.

Dread Trident finds its historical footing in a pivotal moment in intellectual as well as cultural history that occurred during the Age of Technology, beginning in the 1880s. According to critics of modernity, such as Max Weber and others, at that time a confluence of techno-logical, cultural, economic, and political changes exacerbated the modern crisis, a time which diminished the power of traditional myth. However, this process of mythic disenchantment has been rethought by recent thinkers, many of whom resist a 'disenchanted' West and see a modernity with degrees of enchantment-like experience. *Dread Trident* recognizes the rise of what historian Roger Luckhurst calls 'mechanism': engineering tools for solving problems, but tools often misunderstood as part of a dehumanizing disenchantment. Within the context of this book's theorizing the modern fantastic, they are just as much tools for challenging the modern crisis as they are culpable in its construction. They do so without replicating the full effect of traditional myth; instead, they provide a requisite irony within a magification mode of gameplay that cushions players from the weight of a purposeless universe, as well as from its horrors.

The concept of the modern fantastic that informs *Dread Trident* begins with the crises of representation, liberalism, and reason seen in literary, artistic, socio-political, philosophic, and scientific disciplines, and continues with Foucault's galvanizing declaration of the modern defined by consistent critique, especially in the area of critical popular culture. It is predicated on the Foucauldian notion of an enlightened modernity as ongoing critique. Foucault's response to Kant's question *Was ist Aufklärung?* helps beyond many other definitions because of its elegance and simplicity. It provides a flexible and invigorating approach to contemporary, technologized culture's rapid change. Foucault argued for a perennial notion of a renewed Enlightenment, the key impulse of modernity, one that frees us from the strictures of limiting (and now antiquated) literary or cultural modernisms, as well as frees us from exclusive forms of humanism.

Dread Trident departs from modern studies for literary studies, game studies, and cultural studies in its focus on the use of fantastic spaces in an understanding of the technologized modern subject. However, understanding the gameist logic of our current moment also requires new ways to conceptualize key developments in modern studies. The study of the modern fantastic in a global world challenged with continued social and economic problems may seem blinkered or, worse, irresponsible. The modern fantastic, though, is a defining mode for a wide range of persons in modern culture comprised of many similar subcultures. This demographic is an ironic 'revenge of the nerds,' a geek revolution. Events similar to 'Gamergate' in which females in the gaming industry were targeted in social media via reprehensible harassment campaigns reveal key injustices that still must be addressed for any hint of egalitarian gaming, much less an egalitarian society, or societies.[1] Analog/digital games refract these problems rather than solve them. Even in the rush toward digital life, with all of its obvious social problems, positive forms of the human are emerging that will be inclusive yet retain necessary borders, will be flexible yet stable, and will have a strong sense of social justice without jettisoning recognizable metrics of behavior.

This book's use of the modern fantastic has worked within the discourse of critical posthumanism by admitting that humanism, like the modern, is another key concept, one with an even broader range of comment than modernity. Critical posthumanism maintains Cartesian subjectivity as its primary target, i.e., the rational and normative human subject too narrowly modeled on educated white, European males. We must look to the critique of such humanisms if we wish to understand the modern subject, its crisis, its erasure, and its return as myriad subjectivities within realized fantasy spaces.

Dread Trident has intervened in the discourses of trans-and-posthumanism to explain how realized worlds proliferate via posthumanization. It argued that a shift from focusing on the body under technological pressure to the spaces created by technology defines the most interesting (and ignored) part of posthumanism and posthumanization. It also shifted the focus from the subject to spaces in which subjectivity arises. This reorients us. Space becomes as important as bodies. This does not diminish work done describing how discourses write bodies. Instead, it highlights a process in which the analog and digital prove miscible. This use of posthumanization derives from N. Katherine Hayles's insights that the disembodied posthumanism by those who wish for fantasy-SF scenarios such as mind uploading ignores the importance of embodied living and material experience at the crossroads between the digital and the analog. It follows Hayles in avoiding the nightmare scenario she excoriated, one defined by a disembodied posthumanism.

Of key importance here is Hayles's call for a positive form of technological embodiment, one *Dread Trident* sees reinforced by analog game space. Such spaces can be seen in the proliferation of fantastic

---

[1] For a first-hand account, see Quinn 2017.

spaces, *realized worlds*, a concept of the 'real' derived from Deleuze that complicates the common-sense notions of the real vs. unreal. Deleuze argued that the real emerges in a virtual sense out of the actual world, that the flows of energies that infuse reality must solidify in some way, a liminal place between what we consider the real and the imaginary. Instead of such a binary, this book offered the mundane vs. the fantastic, as well as ironic magification, as ways to rethink the discourse of dis-enchantment vs. re-enchantment. All of this theorizing is in the service of seeing how the new embodied subjectivities afforded by posthumanization require sophisticated conceptual frameworks.

This rational procedure of infusing the mundane world with a touch of the magical emerges in the sorts of fantastic spaces examined in *Dread Trident*'s case studies, a book that refuses the lament of disenchantment so prevalent in the modern crisis. This book, though, recognizes that a focus on space erases a stable, unchanging subject in a foreshadowing of a variety of possible literal extinctions. The discourses of trans-and-posthumanism contend with both the philosophical extinction of the subject and the potential actual extinction of material beings on this planet. Such weighty matters as post-anthropocene subjectivity suggest one possible response, that of Lovecraftian horror, as requisite in the face of humanity's own erasure: a major intellectual posture both in the horror genre and in TRPGs foregrounded in this study.

Dread Trident's analysis of TRPGs and the modern fantastic worked through a continuum of traditional genre elements, with SF and fantasy at the poles and horror vacillating between the two. In the hard-SF TRPG Eclipse Phase (EP) it saw elements from Bruce Sterling's Schismatrix stories given game form. Both the literary and gameist modes provide platforms for posthuman subjectivities within its realized world, each with a focus on hyper-material embodiment. In many ways, these imaginings are the stuff of fantastic SF, even as contemporary Singularitarians argue for such inevitabilities. Yet, *Dread Trident* sees these configurations as representative of the fantastic impulse in technologized culture, configurations which require a degree of irony.

In contrast to the SF focus of EP, the TRPG Dungeons and Dragons (D&D) provides a case study that demonstrated how a fantastic realized world is constructed over a period of forty years. This TRPG is an unmined treasure trove of discursive material, its gametexts primed for literary analysis driven by an engineering ethos coupled with the fantastic. This process emerges when examining the complex representation of its multiverse, a grand harmonizing concept that links all of its campaign settings from its first articulation in *The Dragon* magazine to its 5th edition sourcebooks. In particular, the focus on the Forgotten Realms and its use of a 'godswar' exemplifies how such harmonizing elements are instituted so that players have a way to engage such complex lore without being overwhelmed by super-powerful deities. Such mechanisms of realized world creation abound in the many official and unofficial published materials, even more so now that the actual game sessions can be streamed live via the Internet, a new form of entertainment that bridges a gap between the consumption of discursive gametexts and the performative presentation of enacted gameplay.

Dread Trident articulated the modern fantastic emerging as a common thread through SF and fantasy, while the Gothic and cosmic horror motifs in the Worlds of Darkness and Call of Cthulhu case studies demonstrated the centrality of horror as a middle-ground inflection. This foregrounded Lovecraft as a central figure, especially within the context of the Gothic's exhaustion and transformation as a 'spectral return' in a variety of forms from rethought vampires and werewolves to the inscrutable, mechanistic God Machine. With a focus on horror's monsters as key elements within most modern fantastic TRPGs, we see how these elements shift between standard tropes of devils, ghosts, vampires, witches, etc., to the universe itself as a monstrous entity from which emerges avatars of horror. When TRPGs utilize dark fantasy, SF, or horror elements, we not only see the tension between traditional Gothic vs. cosmic theme but see two major tropes of the fantastic, the *draconic* and *posthuman* (or *draconic-posthuman*).

A consistent challenge of stable representation emerged as a dominant theme in *Dread Trident*'s analysis, another major point foregrounded through the analysis of Lovecraft. It argued that a primary aim of TRPGs is to represent the untranslatable or unrepresentable. Such thinking stems from Lovecraft's resistance to such attempts, even as he developed into a writer who mastered a physicalist literary style. The purist line of Weird thinking that even a glimpse of cosmic-horror brings madness works well because of the limitations of the written word due to its inherent discursive tendency for abstraction over direct visual representation. The result when systematized within gameplay in a TRPG like the Call of Cthulhu provides a reason for players to keep their characters safe by never needing to glimpse such horror—thus reinforcing the insistence on literary distance because of the difficulties in describing such entities. At a game table, though, this suspension ignores the need for proper description and, even more so, ignores the need for game stats so that players might engage such entities. *Dread Trident* sees in Lovecraft a hesitation, where TRPGs embrace such impossibilities.

Realized worlds such as the Warhammer 40,000 (40k) franchise exemplify a resistance to this refusal to represent. Its shared universe constructs a middle ground between the draconic and the posthuman and with the language and visual art of embodied horror, a working example that attempts to represent such difficult terrain. 40k demonstrates a marked courage in the drawing of such unimaginable subjects. Horror representation, here, finds its footing, as it does with the early fiction of China Miéville, and becomes common practice in most TRPGs. Like that of the D&D case study, its primary analysis works through several mechanisms in the creation of its lore, a core aspect of how imaginary realized worlds are constructed with literariness in mind. It worked through a few major narrative elements, such as the mystery of the Emperor's death in the Horus Heresy, a complex storyline written by numerous authors and spread across a wide variety of gametexts. In contrast, the Beast Arises narrative is a compact, cohesive narrative that cements a particular portion of the overall lore of the 40k universe. It and the most recent addition of lore in the Gathering Storm demonstrate how, like the Horus Heresy, the wide 40k universe is a complex realized world comprised of 'written' gametexts. Yes, the intention by Games Workshop is to sell miniatures so that wargames can be played at tables. But the creation of lore as support for wargaming proves that 40k is exemplary as a realized world because of how it continues to expand its discursive meta-narrative.

The final case study of Numenera concludes with this TRPG that defies genre conventions as it subsumes within it any and all tropes from the modern fantastic. Miéville's attempt at echoing Lovecraft as a categorizer of material monstrosity can be seen in his early novels of Bas Lag. Miéville sees this type of representation in the service of a Weird writing that forces a 'numinous swillage' into a text. *Dread Trident* reads this as one more attempt by the literary to struggle with representation in a way that TRPGs embrace with ease. Miéville is a writer who exemplifies such an attempt, often with success, especially in his game-like use of monsters as objects of horror and narrative. His deft use of fantastic language finds a precursor in Jorge Borges, a supreme fantasist *Dread Trident* reads attempting to capture the ultimate mystery of the universe in both language and metaphysics. It sees the story, "Tlön, Uqbar, Orbis Tertius," as an example of how Borges's fiction prefigures the rise of realized worlds with its focus on how analog tools construct imaginary worlds. This acts as a literary example of the wider process of posthumanization at work, with traditional analog elements like gametexts and tools now bolstered by the digital, a combination that allows for the construction of the realized.

Numenera also finds a primary influence in the genre-resisting work of Gene Wolfe, especially in his Solar Cycle opus, a SF masterpiece that channels fantasy in such a way as to obscure genre boundaries. In fact, Wolfe's use of the mythic demonstrates how the modern fantastic rethinks magnification. These novels refuse a simple rational explanation, opting for the complexities involved in interpreting written language as a metaphor for understanding the imaginary world of the series. Such valorization of the magical demonstrates how a literary fantasy should admit its inherent fantasism. *Dread Trident* ends with a brief examination of the horror writer Thomas Ligotti as continuing Lovecraft's tradition of cosmic horror. Ligotti is helpful because he does take his horror seriously, even when he steps close to full representation yet ultimately refuses to collapse the cosmic into the material. By reworking Lovecraft with his own version of a nihilistic type of cosmic horror, Ligotti extends the game of Lovecraft's Mythos. Likewise, this demonstrates the continued expansion of such a complex realized world, even into the loose adaptation of Ligotti's thinking with the reuse of pulp material in HBO's first season of *True Detective*. The use of such Weird elements speaks to the season's inherent fantasy, a consistent theme that worked its way with full vigor before backing away in the end. *Dread Trident* sees in this a refusal not only to draw the ultimate horror, but even to posit its existence as a thing in *True Detective*'s imaginary world.

Dread Trident has attempted to capture the complexity within the realized imaginary worlds of key TRPGs. It has done so to foreground the embodied use of gameplay as an important factor in the experience of the fantastic as a way to resist a mundane, modern world. It has also done this to present SF and fantasy as two parts of the modern fantastic, both informing the other, both inseparably bound.

References

Aarseth, Espen. 2001. "Computer Game Studies, Year One." *Game Studies*. http://gamestudies.org/0101/editorial.html.

———. 2004. "Genre Trouble: Narrativism and the Art of Simulation." In *First Person: New Media as Story, Performance, and Game*. Cambridge, MA: MIT Press.

Abnett, Dan. 2005. *Eisenhorn*. Edited by Marc Gascoigne. Nottingham (UK): Games Workshop.

———. 2009. *Ravenor: The Omnibus*. Nottingham (UK): Games Workshop.

———. 2012. *Know No Fear*. Nottingham (UK): Games Workshop.

———. 2014a. *Horus Rising*. Nottingham (UK): Games Workshop.

———. 2014b. *Prospero Burns*. Nottingham (UK): Games Workshop.

———. 2016. *I Am Slaughter*. The Beast Arises 1. Nottingham (UK): Games Workshop.

———. 2017. *The Founding: A Gaunt's Ghosts Omnibus*. Nottingham (UK): Games Workshop.

———. 2018. *The Saint: A Gaunt's Ghosts Omnibus*. Nottingham (UK): Games Workshop.

Adams, Henry. 1918. *The Education of Henry Adams*. 1st edition. Boston, MA: Houghton Mifflin Co.

Aldiss, Brian W., and David Wingrove. 1986. *Trillion Year Spree: The History of Science Fiction*. New York: Atheneum.

Alexander, Jeffrey C., and Philip Smith, eds. 2005. *The Cambridge Companion to Durkheim*. Cambridge: Cambridge University Press.

Allston, Aaron. 1992. *Wrath of the Immortals*. Game Accessory edition. Lake Geneva, WI: Wizards of the Coast.

Altman, Rick. 1999. *Film/Genre*. London: BFI Publishing.

Anderson, Benedict R. O'G. 1991. *Imagined Communities: Reflections on the Origin and Spread of Nationalism*. London: Verso.

Aniolowski, Scott David. 1999. *The Creature Companion: A Core Game Book for Keepers*. Oakland, CA: Chaosium.

———. 2006. *Malleus Monstrorum: Creatures, Gods, & Forbidden Knowledge*. Hayward, CA: Chaosium.

Aniolowski, Scott David, Fred Behrendt, and John Carnahan. 1994. *Ye Booke of Monstres: New Nightmares for the Call of Cthulhu*. Vol. 1. The Aniolowski Collection. Oakland, CA: Chaosium Inc.

Annandale, David. 2016a. *The Last Wall*. The Beast Arises 4. Nottingham (UK): Games Workshop.

——. 2016b. *The Hunt for Vulkan*. The Beast Arises 7. Nottingham (UK): Games Workshop.

——. 2016c. *Watchers in Death*. The Beast Arises 9. Nottingham (UK): Games Workshop.

Ansell, Bryan, Mike Brunton, and Simon Forrest. 1988. *Realm of Chaos: Slaves to Darkness*. Nottingham (UK): Games Workshop.

Appelcline, Shannon. 2015. *Designers & Dragons: The 70s*. 2nd edition. Silver Spring, MD: Evil Hat Productions.

Arneson, Dave. 1975. *Dungeons & Dragons Supplement II: Blackmoor*. Lake Geneva, WI: TSR.

Ashley, Mike. 2007. *Gateways to Forever: The Story of the Science-Fiction Magazines from 1970 to 1980*. The History of the Science-Fiction Magazine, Mike Ashley. Vol. 3. Liverpool: Liverpool University Press.

Attebery, Brian. 1992. *Strategies of Fantasy*. Bloomington: Indiana University Press.

Awlinson, Richard. 1989a. *Shadowdale*. Avatar Series 1. Renton, WA: Wizards of the Coast.

——. 1989b. *Tantras*. Avatar Series 2. Renton, WA: Wizards of the Coast.

——. 1989c. *Waterdeep*. Avatar Series 3. Renton, WA: Wizards of the Coast.

Bachelard, Gaston. 1994. *The Poetics of Space*. Boston, MA: Beacon Press.

Badmington, Neil. 2010. "Man Saved by Wolfe | Electronic Book Review." *Electronic Book Review*. October 25. www.electronicbookreview.com/thread/criticalecologies/savedbywolfe.

Bakey, Craig. 1979. "Of the Gods." In *The Dragon* 29.

Barad, Karen. 2007. *Meeting the Universe Halfway: Quantum Physics and the Entanglement of Matter and Meaning*. Durham, NC: Duke University Press.

Barlow, Tani, Yukiko Hanawa, Thomas LaMarre, and Donald Lowe. 2005. "Editors' Introduction." *Positions* 13(1): 1–8.

Barrowcliffe, Mark. 2009. *The Elfish Gene: Dungeons, Dragons and Growing Up Strange*. New York: Soho Press.

Baudrillard, Jean. 1995. *Simulacra and Simulation*. Ann Arbor: University of Michigan Press.

Baur, Wolfgang. 2007. "People of Bas-Lag." In *Dragon Magazine* 352.

Benjamin, Walter. 2006. *The Writer of Modern Life: Essays on Charles Baudelaire*. Cambridge, MA: Belknap Press.

Bennett, Jane. 2001. *The Enchantment of Modern Life: Attachments, Crossings, and Ethics*. Princeton, NJ: Princeton University Press.

Berman, Marshall. 1988. *All That Is Solid Melts Into Air: The Experience of Modernity*. New York: Penguin Books.

Bienia, Rafael. 2016. "Role Playing Materials." Ph.D. dissertation. Braunschweig: Zauberfeder Verlag.

Bjork, Staffan, and Jussi Holopainen. 2004. *Patterns in Game Design*. 1st edition. Hingham, MA: Charles River Media.

Bligh, Alan. 2012. *The Horus Heresy Book I: Betrayal*. Nottingham (UK): Forge World.

Bloom, Harold. 1999. *Shakespeare: The Invention of the Human*. New York: Riverhead Books.

Bogost, Ian. 2012. *Alien Phenomenology, or, What It's Like to Be a Thing*. Minneapolis: University of Minnesota Press.

Booker, M. Keith, and Anne-Marie Thomas. 2009. *The Science Fiction Handbook*. London: John Wiley & Sons.

Borges, Jorge Luis. 1964. *Labyrinths: Selected Stories & Other Writings*. Edited by Donald A. Yates and James E. Irby. New York: New Directions Publishing.

——. 2000. *Selected Non-Fictions*. Edited by Eliot Weinberger. Translated by Esther Allen and Suzanne Jill Levine. New York: Penguin.

Bostrom, Nick. 2009. "The Future of Humanity." *Geopolitics, History, and International Relations* 2: 41–78.

Botting, Fred. 1996. *Gothic*. 1st edition. London: Routledge.

——. 2010. *Limits of Horror: Technology, Bodies, Gothic*. Reprint edition. Manchester: Manchester University Press.

Bowman, Sarah Lynne. 2010. *The Functions of Role-Playing Games: How Participants Create Community, Solve Problems and Explore Identity*. Jefferson, NC: McFarland.

Boyd, Eric L. 2007. "The World Serpent Inn." In *Dragon Magazine*. 351.

Boyle, Rob. 2016. "[Game Feedback] Academic Research Article on Eclipse Phase." April 5. Email message to author.

Boyle, Rob, and Brian Cross. 2009. *Eclipse Phase*. Posthuman Studios.

——. 2012. *Eclipse Phase Rimward*. Posthuman Studios.

Braidotti, Rosi. 2013a. *The Posthuman*. 1st edition. Cambridge: Polity.

——. 2013b. *Metamorphoses: Towards a Materialist Theory of Becoming*. London: John Wiley & Sons.

Broderick, Damien. 2000. *Transrealist Fiction Writing in the Slipstream of Science*. Westport, CT: Greenwood Press.

Bryant, Levi R. 2011. *The Democracy of Objects*. Ann Arbor, MI: Open Humanities Press.

Bryant, Levi R., Nick Srnicek, and Graham Harman. 2011. *The Speculative Turn: Continental Materialism and Realism*. Melbourne: re.press.

Buchanan, Ian. 1999. *A Deleuzian Century?* Durham, NC: Duke University Press.

Buck-Morss, Susan. 1991. *The Dialectics of Seeing: Walter Benjamin and the Arcades Project*. Cambridge, MA: MIT Press.

Campbell, Ramsey. 1997. *The Cthulhu Mythos*. New York: Barnes & Noble Books.

——. 2017. *The Inhabitant of The Lake & Other Unwelcome Tenants*. Hornsea (UK): Drugstore Indian Press.

Cannon, Peter. 1989. *H.P. Lovecraft*. Boston, MA: Twayne Publishers.

Cardin, Matt. 2003. "Thomas Ligotti's Career of Nightmares." In *The Thomas Ligotti Reader: Essays and Explorations*. Edited by Darrell Schweitzer. Holicong, PA: Wildside Press.

Carroll, Noël. 1990. *The Philosophy of Horror: Or, Paradoxes of the Heart*. New York: Routledge.

Carter, Lin. 1976. *Lovecraft: A Look Behind the Cthulhu Mythos*. New York: Ballantine Books.

Cartwright, John H., and Brian Baker. 2005. *Literature and Science: Social Impact and Interaction*. Santa Barbara, CA: ABC-Clio.

Chambers, Andy. 2002. "Foreword." In *Index Astartes*. Paperback edition. Vol. 1. Nottingham (UK): Games Workshop.

Clark, Andy. 2003. *Natural-Born Cyborgs Minds, Technologies, and the Future of Human Intelligence*. Oxford: Oxford University Press.

———. 2010. *Supersizing the Mind: Embodiment, Action, and Cognitive Extension*. Oxford: Oxford University Press.

Clarke, Bruce. 2008. *Posthuman Metamorphosis: Narrative and Systems*. New York: Fordham University Press.

Cline, Ernest. 2012. *Ready Player One*. 1st edition. New York: Broadway Books.

Clute, John. 1983. "The Urth And All Its Glory." *Washington Post*, January 30. https://www.washingtonpost.com/archive/entertainment/books/1983/01/30/the-urth-and-all-its-glory/5c9884ed-fd8d-468a-a9df-b236f4ac92d7/?utm_term=.aec81a258783.

———. 2003. "Science Fiction from 1980 to the Present." In *The Cambridge Companion to Science Fiction*. Edited by Edward James and Farah Mendlesohn. Cambridge: Cambridge University Press.

Clute, John, and John Grant, eds. 1997. *The Encyclopedia of Fantasy*. New York: Palgrave Macmillan.

Clynes, Manfred E., and Nathan S. Kline. 1960. "Cyborgs and Space." *Astronautics*. September. http://cyberneticzoo.com/wp-content/uploads/2012/01/cyborgs-Astronautics-sep1960.pdf.

Colebrook, Claire. 2014a. *The Death of the PostHuman: Essays on Extinction*. Vol. 1. London: Open Humanities Press. https://quod.lib.umich.edu/o/ohp?type=simple&rgn=full+text&q1=Sex+After+Life.

———. 2014b. *Sex After Life: Essays on Extinction*. Vol. 2. London: Open Humanities Press. http://hdl.handle.net/2027/spo.12329363.0001.001.

Collins, Sean T. 2014. "'True Detective' Ends With a Bang." *Rolling Stone*. March 9. https://www.rollingstone.com/tv/news/true-detective-recap-a-light-at-the-end-of-the-tunnel-20140309.

Cook, David "Zeb." 1994a. *Planescape Campaign Setting: A DM's Guide to the Planes*. Lake Geneva, WI: Wizards of the Coast.

———. 1994b. *Planescape Campaign Setting: A Player's Guide to the Planes*. Lake Geneva, WI: Wizards of the Coast.

———. 1994c. *Planescape Campaign Setting: Sigil and Beyond*. Lake Geneva, WI: Wizards of the Coast.

Cook, Monte. 2004. *Injecting the Weird*. S.l.: Monte Cook Games.

———. 2013a. *In Strange Aeons: Lovecraftian Numenera*. S.l.: Monte Cook Games.

———. 2013b. *Numenera*. 1st edition. S.l.: Monte Cook Games.

Cook, Monte, and John Tynes. 2002. *Call of Cthulhu: Roleplaying Game*. Renton, WA: Wizards of the Coast.

Coole, Diana, and Samantha Frost, eds. 2010. *New Materialisms: Ontology, Agency, and Politics*. Durham NC: Duke University Press Books.

Counter, Ben. 2014. *Galaxy in Flames*. Nottingham (UK): Games Workshop.

Cover, Jennifer Grouling. 2010. *The Creation of Narrative in Tabletop Role-Playing Games*. Jefferson, NC: McFarland.

Crow, Charles L., ed. 2014. *A Companion to American Gothic*. Oxford: Wiley Blackwell.

Csicsery-Ronay, Istvan. 2008. *The Seven Beauties of Science Fiction*. Middletown, CT: Wesleyan University Press.

Darwin, Charles. 1859. *On the Origin of Species*. London: John Murray.

Davies, Tony. 1997. *Humanism*. London: Routledge.

DeCamp, L. Sprague. 1975. *Lovecraft: A Biography*. New York: Doubleday.

DeCerteau, Michel. 2011. *The Practice of Everyday Life*. Translated by Stephen Rendall. Berkeley: University of California Press.

DeLanda, Manuel. 2002. *Intensive Science and Virtual Philosophy*. London: Continuum.

——. 2015. "The New Materiality." *Architectural Design* 85 (September).

Deleuze, Gilles, and Félix Guattari. 1987. *A Thousand Plateaus*. Minneapolis: University of Minnesota Press.

Dembski-Bowden, Aaron. 2010. *The First Heretic*. Nottingham (UK): Games Workshop.

——. 2017. *The Master of Mankind*. Games Workshop.

Denning, Troy. 1998. *Crucible: The Trial of Cyric the Mad*. Reissue edition. Avatar Series 5. Renton, WA: Wizards of the Coast.

Derleth, August. 1958. *The Mask of Cthulhu*. Sauk City, WI: Arkham House Publishers.

Derrida, Jacques, and Alan Bass. 2001. *Writing and Difference*. London: Routledge Classics.

Disch, Thomas M. 2005. *On SF*. Ann Arbor: University of Michigan Press.

Dolphijn, Rick, and Iris van der Tuin. 2012. *New Materialism Interviews & Cartographies*. Ann Arbor, MI: Open Humanities Press.

Dovey, Jon. 2006. *Game Cultures: Computer Games as New Media*. London: Open University Press.

Dragon Magazine. 1977. 8.

——. 1984. 91.

Eagleton, Terry. 2003. *After Theory*. London: Allen Lane.

Eco, Umberto. 1990. *Travels in Hyperreality*. Reprint edition. San Diego, CA: Mariner Books.

Eden, Amnon H. 2012. *Singularity Hypotheses: A Scientific and Philosophical Assessment*. Heidelberg: Springer.

Eil, Philip. 2015. "The Unlikely Reanimation of H.P. Lovecraft." *The Atlantic*. August 20. https://www.theatlantic.com/entertainment/archive/2015/08/hp-lovecraft-125/401471/.

Eliade, Mircea. 1987. *The Sacred and The Profane: The Nature of Religion*. Translated by Willard R. Trask. San Diego, CA: Harcourt Brace Jovanovich.

Ewalt, David M. 2014. *Of Dice and Men: The Story of Dungeons & Dragons and The People Who Play It*. New York: Scribner.

Fine, Gary Alan. 2002. *Shared Fantasy: Role Playing Games as Social Worlds*. Chicago: University of Chicago Press.

Foucault, Michel. 1980. *Power/Knowledge: Selected Interviews and Other Writings, 1972–1977*. Edited by Colin Gordon. New York: Pantheon Books.

———. 1998. *Aesthetics, Method, and Epistemology: Essential Works of Foucault, 1954–1984*. Vol. 2. Edited by James D. Faubion. New York: The New Press.

Foucault, Michel, and Paul Rabinow. 1984. *The Foucault Reader*. New York: Pantheon Books.

Freedman, Carl Howard. 2000. *Critical Theory and Science Fiction*. Hanover, NE: Wesleyan University Press/University Press of New England.

Fricker, Paul, and Mike Mason. 2016. *Call of Cthulhu: Horror Roleplaying in the Worlds of H.P. Lovecraft*. 7th edition. Hayward, CA: Chaosium.

Gilsdorf, Ethan. 2010. *Fantasy Freaks and Gaming Geeks: An Epic Quest for Reality among Role Players, Online Gamers, and Other Dwellers of Imaginary Realms*. Guilford, CT: Lyons Press.

Gold, Matthew K., ed. 2012. *Debates in the Digital Humanities*. Minneapolis: University of Minnesota Press.

Graham, Elaine L. 2002. *Representations of the Post/Human: Monsters, Aliens and Others in Popular Culture*. Manchester: Manchester University Press.

Gray, Jonathan. 2010. *Show Sold Separately: Promos, Spoilers, and Other Media Paratexts*. New York: NYU Press.

Grebowicz, Margret, Helen Merrick, and Donna Haraway. 2013. *Beyond the Cyborg: Adventures with Donna Haraway*. New York: Columbia University Press.

Greenwood, Ed. 1981. "Down-to-Earth Divinity: One DM's Design for a Mixed and Matched Mythos." In *Dragon Magazine*. 54.

———. 1987. *Cyclopedia of the Realms: A Complete Cyclopedia of the Fabulous Forgotten Realms from Abeir-Toril to Zhentil Keep*. Lake Geneva, WI: TSR.

Greenwood, Ed, and Jeff Grubb. 1987. *Forgotten Realms: DM's Sourcebook of the Realms*. Lake Geneva, WI: Wizards of the Coast.

Grubb, Jeff. 1987. *Manual of the Planes, 1e*. Advanced Dungeons and Dragons. Lake Geneva, WI: TSR.

———. 1989. *SpellJammer: AD&D Adventures in Space—Concordance of Arcane Space*. Lake Geneva, WI: TSR.

———. 2018. "Brave New Planes. Variant Planes in Your Campaigns: A Manual of the Planes Web Enhancement." Wizards of the Coast. February 7. https://www.wizards.com/dnd/files/World_Serpent.pdf.

Guymer, David. 2016a. *Echoes of the Long War*. The Beast Arises 6. Nottingham (UK): Games Workshop.

———. 2016b. *The Last Son of Dorn*. The Beast Arises 10. Nottingham (UK): Games Workshop.

Gygax, Gary. 1979a. "Sorcerer's Scroll: Playing on the Other Planes of Existence." In *Dragon Magazine*. Vol. IV/6. 32.

———. 1979b. *Advanced Dungeons & Dragons: Dungeon Master's Guide*. 1st edition. Lake Geneva, WI: TSR.

——. 1980. *The World of Greyhawk: Fantasy World Setting*. Lake Geneva, WI: TSR.

——. 1984. *A Guide to the World of Greyhawk Fantasy Setting*. Lake Geneva, WI: TSR.

Habermas, Jürgen. 1985a. *The Theory of Communicative Action*. Vol. 1. *Reason and the Rationalization of Society*. Translated by Thomas McCarthy. Boston, MA: Beacon Press.

——. 1985b. *The Theory of Communicative Action*. Vol. 2. *Lifeworld and System: A Critique of Functionalist Reason*. Translated by Thomas McCarthy. Boston, MA: Beacon Press.

Haley, Guy. 2016a. *Throneworld*. The Beast Arises 5. Nottingham (UK): Games Workshop.

——. 2016b. *The Beheading*. Nottingham (UK): Games Workshop.

——. 2018. *Dark Imperium*. Nottingham (UK): Games Workshop.

Hallab, Mary Y. 2009. *Vampire God: The Allure of the Undead in Western Culture*. New York: SUNY Press.

Hansen, Mark B.N. 2000. *Embodying Technesis: Technology beyond Writing*. Ann Arbor: University of Michigan Press.

Haraway, Donna Jeanne. 1991. *Simians, Cyborgs, and Women: The Reinvention of Nature*. New York: Routledge.

——. 2008. *When Species Meet*. Minneapolis: University of Minnesota Press.

Hardt, Michael, and Antonio Negri. 2000. *Empire*. Cambridge, MA: Harvard University Press.

Harman, Graham. 2002. *Tool-Being: Heidegger and the Metaphysics of Objects*. 1st edition. Chicago: Open Court.

——. 2012. *Weird Realism: Lovecraft and Philosophy*. Winchester (UK): John Hunt Publishing.

——. 2018. *Object-Oriented Ontology: A New Theory of Everything*. S.l.: Penguin UK.

Harrigan, Pat, and Noah Wardrip-Fruin. 2004. *First Person: New Media as Story, Performance, and Game*. Cambridge, MA: MIT Press.

——, eds. 2010. *Second Person: Role-Playing and Story in Games and Playable Media*. Cambridge, MA: The MIT Press.

Hayles, N. Katherine. 1999. *How We Became Posthuman: Virtual Bodies in Cybernetics, Literature, and Informatics*. Chicago: University of Chicago Press.

——. 2002. *Writing Machines*. Cambridge, MA: MIT Press.

——. 2012. *How We Think: Digital Media and Contemporary Technogenesis*. Chicago; University of Chicago Press.

Herbrechter, Stefan. 2013. *Posthumanism: A Critical Analysis*. London: Bloomsbury.

Herbrechter, Stefan, and Ivan Callus. 2009. *Cy-Borges: Memories of the Posthuman in the Work of Jorge Luis Borges*. Lewisburg, PA: Bucknell University Press.

Hogle, Jerrold E. 2002. "Introduction: The Gothic in Western Culture." In *The Cambridge Companion to Gothic Fiction*. Cambridge: Cambridge University Press.

Hollinger, Veronica. 2009. "Posthumanism and Cyborg Theory." In *The Routledge Companion to Science Fiction*. Edited by Andrew M Butler, Adam Roberts, Sherryl Vint, and Mark Bould. London: Routledge.

Horkheimer, Max, and Theodor W. Adorno. 1972. *Dialectic of Enlightenment*. New York: Continuum.

Houellebecq, Michel. 2005. *H.P. Lovecraft: Against the World, Against Life*. Translated by Dorna Khazeni. San Francisco, CA: Believer Books.

Huizinga, Johan. 1949. *Homo Ludens: Study of the Play Element in Culture*. London: Routledge.

Hume, Kathryn. 1985. *Fantasy and Mimesis: Responses to Reality in Western Literature*. New York: Routledge.

Hurley, Kelly. 2002. "British Gothic Fiction, 1885–1930." In *The Cambridge Companion to Gothic Fiction*. Cambridge: Cambridge University Press.

Huyssen, Andreas. 1987. *After the Great Divide: Modernism, Mass Culture, Postmodernism*. Bloomington: Indiana University Press.

Ihde, Don. 1990. *Technology and the Lifeworld: From Garden to Earth*. Bloomington: Indiana University Press.

James, Brian R., and Ed Greenwood. 2007. *Grand History of the Realms*. First print edition. Renton, WA: Wizards of the Coast.

James, Edward, and Farah Mendlesohn, eds. 2012. *The Cambridge Companion to Fantasy Literature*. 1st edition. Cambridge: Cambridge University Press.

Jameson, Fredric. 1991. *Postmodernism, or, The Cultural Logic of Late Capitalism*. Durham, NC: Duke University Press.

———. 1998. *The Cultural Turn : Selected Writings on the Postmodern, 1983–1998*. London: Verso.

———. 2005. *Archaeologies of the Future: The Desire Called Utopia and Other Science Fictions*. London: Verso.

Johnson, Jervis. 1988. "The Imperium." In *Adeptus Titanicus: Epic Battles Between Gigantic Robots*. Nottingham (UK): Games Workshop.

Joshi, S.T. 1980. *H.P. Lovecraft: Four Decades of Criticism*. 1st edition. Athens: Ohio University Press.

———. 1996. *A Subtler Magick: The Writings and Philosophy of H.P. Lovecraft*. 3rd edition. Berkeley Heights, NJ: Borgo Press.

———. 2001. *A Dreamer and a Visionary: H.P. Lovecraft in His Time*. Liverpool: Liverpool University Press.

———. 2008. *The Rise and Fall of the Cthulhu Mythos*. 1st edition. Poplar Bluff, MO: Mythos Books.

———, ed. 2011. *Dissecting Cthulhu: Essays on the Cthulhu Mythos*. Lakeland, FL: Miskatonic River Press.

———, ed. 2013. *The Complete Cthulhu Mythos Tales*. New York: Fall River Press.

———. 2015. *The Rise, Fall, and Rise of the Cthulhu Mythos*. New York: Hippocampus Press.

Joshi, S.T., and David E. Schultz, eds. 2000. *Lord of a Visible World: An Autobiography in Letters*. 1st edition. Athens: Ohio University Press.

King, Bill. 1993. "Battle for Earth." In *Horus Heresy*. Nottingham (UK): Games Workshop.

King, Brad, and John Borland. 2014. *Dungeons & Dreamers: A Story of How Computer Games Created a Global Community*. 2nd edition. Pittsburgh, PA: ETC Press.

Konzack, Lars. 2015. "Mark Rein•Hagen's Foundational Influence on 21st Century Vampiric Media." *Akademisk Kvarter* 11 (Summer): 115–28.

Kucukalic, Lejla. 2009. *Philip K. Dick: Canonical Writer of the Digital Age*. New York: Routledge.

Kyme, Nick. 2014. *Vulkan Lives*. Nottingham (UK): Games Workshop.

——. 2016. *Deathfire*. Nottingham (UK): Games Workshop.

Lacan, Jacques. 2006. *Ecrits: The First Complete Edition in English*. Translated by Bruce Fink. New York: W.W. Norton & Co.

Lakoff, George, and Mark Johnson. 1999. *Philosophy in the Flesh: The Embodied Mind and Its Challenge to Western Thought*. Basic Books.

Latour, Bruno. 1993. *We Have Never Been Modern*. Cambridge, MA: Harvard University Press.

——. 1996. *Aramis, or the Love of Technology*. Cambridge, MA: Harvard University Press.

Lefebvre, Henri. 1992. *The Production of Space*. 1st edition. Oxford: Wiley-Blackwell.

——. 2000. *Everyday Life in the Modern World*. Translated by Sacha Rabinovitch. New York: Harper & Row.

Leiber, Fritz. 1980. "A Literary Copernicus." In *H.P. Lovecraft: Four Decades of Criticism*. Edited by S.T. Joshi. Athens: Ohio University Press.

Ligotti, Thomas. 1990. *Songs of a Dead Dreamer*. New York: Carroll & Graf Publishers.

——. 1994. *Noctuary*. New York: Carroll & Graf Publishers.

——. 2008. *Teatro Grottesco*. London: Virgin Books.

Loomba, Ania. 1998. *Colonialism–Postcolonialism*. London: Routledge.

Lovecraft, H.P. 1965. *Selected Letters I: 1911–1924*. Edited by August Derleth and Donald Wandrei. Sauk City, WI: Arkham House Publishers.

——. 1968. *Selected Letters II: 1925–1929*. Edited by August Derleth and Donald Wandrei. Sauk City, WI: Arkham House Publishers.

——. 1971. *Selected Letters III: 1929–1931*. Edited by August Derleth and Donald Wandrei. Sauk City, WI: Arkham House Publishers.

——. 1976a. *Selected Letters IV: 1932–1934*. Edited by August Derleth and James Turner. Sauk City, WI: Arkham House Publishers.

——. 1976b. *Selected Letters V: 1934–1937*. Edited by August Derleth and James Turner. Sauk City, WI: Arkham House Publishers.

——. 1995. *Miscellaneous Writings*. Edited by S.T. Joshi. Sauk City, WI: Arkham House Publishers.

——. 2008. *H.P. Lovecraft: The Complete Fiction*. New York: Barnes & Noble.

Lowder, James. 2003. *Prince of Lies*. Avatar Series 4. Renton, WA: Wizards of the Coast.

Luckhurst, Roger. 2005. *Science Fiction*. Cambridge: Polity.

——, ed. 2013. *The Classic Horror Stories*. 1st edition. Oxford: Oxford University Press.

Lyotard, Jean François. 1984. *The Postmodern Condition: A Report on Knowledge*. Vol. 10. Minneapolis: University of Minnesota Press.

McCaffery, Larry. 1990. *Across the Wounded Galaxies: Interviews with Contemporary American Science Fiction Writers*. Urbana: University of Illinois Press.

Mackay, Daniel. 2001. *The Fantasy Role-Playing Game: A New Performing Art*. Jefferson, NC: McFarland.

McNeil, Graham. 2011. *The Outcast Dead*. 1st edition. Nottingham (UK): Games Workshop.

——. 2014a. *A Thousand Sons*. Reprint edition. Games Workshop.

——. 2014b. *Fulgrim*. Reprint edition. Games Workshop.

——. 2014c. *False Gods*. Reissue edition. Games Workshop.

Maddox, Tom. 1991. "The Wars of the Coin's Two Halves: Bruce Sterling's Mechanist/Shaper Narratives." In *Storming the Reality Studio: A Casebook of Cyberpunk and Postmodern Science Fiction*. Edited by Larry McCaffery. Durham, NC: Duke University Press.

Mazlish, Bruce. 1995. *The Fourth Discontinuity: The Co-Evolution of Humans and Machines*. New Haven, CT: Yale University Press.

Meillassoux, Quentin. 2010. *After Finitude: An Essay on the Necessity of Contingency*. London: Bloomsbury Publishing.

Mellins, Maria. 2013. *Vampire Culture: Dress, Body, Culture*. London: Bloomsbury.

Mendlesohn, Farah, and Edward James. 2009. *A Short History of Fantasy*. London: Middlesex University Press.

Merleau-Ponty, Maurice, and Colin Smith. 2002. *Phenomenology of Perception*. London: Routledge.

Merrett, Alan. 2007. *The Horus Heresy: Collected Visions*. Nottingham (UK): Games Workshop.

——. 2014. *The Horus Heresy: Visions of Heresy*. [Place of publication not identified]: Games Workshop.

Miah, Andy. 2009. "A Critical History of Posthumanism." In *Medical Enhancement and Posthumanity*. Dordrecht: Springer: 71–94.

Miéville, China. 2000. *Perdido Street Station*. London: Pan Books.

——. 2009. "Weird Fiction." In *The Routledge Companion to Science Fiction*. Edited by Mark Bould, Andrew M Butler, Adam Roberts, and Sherryl Vint. London: Routledge.

Miller, Laura. 2015. "We're All Genre Readers Now: Can We Finally Stop the Tired 'Pixies and Dragons' vs. Literary Fiction Wars?" March 11. https://www.salon.com/2015/03/11/were_all_genre_readers_now_can_we_finally_stop_the_tired_pixies_and_dragons_vs_literary_fiction_wars/.

Mona, Erik, ed. 2007. *Dragon Magazine*. 352.

Moorcock, Michael. 1987. *Wizardry and Wild Romance*. 1st edition. London: Gollancz.

Nesmith, Bruce, and Andria Hayday. 1990. *Ravenloft: Realm of Terror*. Advanced Dungeons and Dragons. Lake Geneva, WI: TSR.

Newfield, Christopher. 2004. *Ivy and Industry: Business and the Making of the American University, 1880–1980*. Durham, NC: Duke University Press Books.

——. 2011. *Unmaking the Public University: The Forty-Year Assault on the Middle Class*. Reprint edition. Cambridge, MA: Harvard University Press.

Nieborg, David B., and Joke Hermes. 2008. "What Is Game Studies Anyway?" *European Journal of Cultural Studies* 11(2): 131–47.

Noys, Benjamin, and Timothy S. Murphy. 2016. "Introduction: Old and New Weird." *Genre* 49(2): 117–34.

Nussbaum, Emily. 2014a. "Cool Story, Bro." *New Yorker*. February 24. https://www.newyorker.com/magazine/2014/03/03/cool-story-bro.

——. 2014b. "The Disappointing Finale of 'True Detective.'" *New Yorker*. March 10. https://www.newyorker.com/culture/culture-desk/the-disappointing-finale-of-true-detective.

Oates, Joyce Carol. 1996. "The King of Weird." *New York Review of Books*. October 31. https://www.nybooks.com/articles/1996/10/31/the-king-of-weird/.

Panshin, Alexei, and Cory Panshin. 1989. *The World beyond the Hill: Science Fiction and the Quest for Transcendence*. Los Angeles, CA: J.P. Tarcher.

Parrinder, Patrick. 2000. "Introduction: Learning from Other Worlds." In *Learning from Other Worlds: Estrangement, Cognition, and the Politics of Science Fiction and Utopia*. Edited by Patrick Parrinder. Liverpool: Liverpool University Press.

Partridge, Christopher, ed. 2014. *The Occult World*. New York: Routledge.

Petersen, Sandy. 1988. *Petersen's Field Guide to Cthulhu Monsters: A Field Observer's Handbook of Preternatural Entities*. Edited by Lynn Willis. Albany, CA: Chaosium.

Petersen, Sandy, and Lynn Willis. 2005. *Call of Cthulhu: Horror Roleplaying in the Worlds of H.P. Lovecraft*. 6th edition. Hayward, CA: Chaosium.

Peterson, Jon. 2012. *Playing at the World*. 2nd edition. San Diego, CA: Unreason Press.

——. 2014. "The Ambush at Sheridan Springs." *Jon Peterson* (blog). July 28. https://medium.com/@increment/the-ambush-at-sheridan-springs-3a29d07f6836.

Priestley, Rick. 1987. *Warhammer 40,000 Rogue Trader*. Nottingham (UK): Games Workshop.

Priestley, Rick, and Bryan Ansell. 1990. *Realm of Chaos: The Lost and the Damned*. Nottingham (UK): Games Workshop.

Priestley, Rick, and Andy Chambers. 1993. *Warhammer 40,000: Codex Imperialis*. Nottingham (UK): Games Workshop.

Prigogine, Ilya, and Isabelle Stengers. 1984. *Order out of Chaos: Man's New Dialogue with Nature*. London: Heinemann.

Quinn, Zoe. 2017. *Crash Override: How Gamergate (Nearly) Destroyed My Life, and How We Can Win the Fight Against Online Hate*. 1st edition. New York: PublicAffairs.

Ralphs, Matt, and Marc Gascoigne, eds. 2006. *The Art of Warhammer 40,000*. Nottingham (UK): Games Workshop.

Ranisch, Robert, and Stefan Lorenz Sorgner, eds. 2014. *Post- and Transhumanism: An Introduction*. Beyond Humanism: Trans- and Posthumanism. 1st new edition. Frankfurt-am-Main: Peter Lang.

Raulerson, Joshua Thomas. 2013. *Singularities: Technoculture, Transhumanism, and Science Fiction in the 21st Century*. 1st edition. Liverpool: Liverpool University Press.

Readings, Bill. 1996. *The University in Ruins*. Cambridge, MA: Harvard University Press.

Rieder, John. 2008. *Colonialism and the Emergence of Science Fiction*. Middletown, CT: Wesleyan University Press.

Roberts, Adam. 2000. *Fredric Jameson*. New York: Routledge.

———. 2006. *The History of Science Fiction*. Basingstoke: Palgrave Macmillan.

Roden, David. 2014. *Posthuman Life: Philosophy at the Edge of the Human*. 1st edition. London: Routledge.

Said, Edward W. 1979. *Orientalism*. New York: Vintage.

———. 1994. *Culture and Imperialism*. 25447th edition. New York: Vintage.

Saler, Michael. 2012. *As If: Modern Enchantment and the Literary PreHistory of Virtual Reality*. 1st edition. Oxford: Oxford University Press.

Sanders, Rob. 2016a. *Predator, Prey*. The Beast Arises 2. Nottingham (UK): Games Workshop.

———. 2016b. *Shadow of Ullanor*. The Beast Arises 11. Nottingham (UK): Games Workshop.

Schwab, Klaus. 2017. *The Fourth Industrial Revolution*. New York: Crown Business.

Scott, Curtis M. 1992. *Spelljammer—The Complete Spacefarer's Handbook*. Edited by Barbara G. Young. 2nd edition. Lake Geneva, WI: TSR.

Sederholm, Carl H., and Jeffrey Andrew Weinstock, eds. 2016. *The Age of Lovecraft*. Minneapolis: University of Minnesota Press.

Segerstråle, Ullica. 2001. *Defenders of the Truth: The Sociobiology Debate*. Oxford: Oxford University Press.

Sharon, Tamar. 2012. "A Cartography of the Posthuman: Humanist, Non-Humanist and Mediated Perspectives on Emerging Biotechnologies." *Krisis: Journal for Contemporary Thought* 2: 4–19.

Shaviro, Steven. 2014. *The Universe of Things: On Speculative Realism*. Minneapolis: University of Minnesota Press.

Singh, Anandraj. 2016. "Eclipse Phase Questions," March 28. Email message to author.

Snipe and Wib. 2017. "10 Weird and Wonderful Things from Rogue Trader—Snipe and Wib." *Youtube*. June 30. https://www.youtube.com/watch?v=OCapveFed9U.

Spengler, Oswald. 1926. *The Decline of the West: Form and Actuality*. Translated by Charles Francis Atkinson. Vol. 1. New York: Alfred A. Knopf.

Spinrad, Norman. 1990. *Science Fiction in the Real World*. Carbondale: Southern Illinois University Press.

Stabb, Martin S. 1970. *Jorge Luis Borges*. Twayne's World Authors Series Argentina 108. New York: Twayne Publishing.

Stableford, Brian M. 2006. *Science Fact and Science Fiction: An Encyclopedia*. New York: Taylor & Francis.

Steele, Justin. 2014. "Interview: Nic Pizzolatto, Creator/Writer of HBO's True Detective." *Arkham Digest*. January 21. www.arkhamdigest.com/2014/01/interview-nic-pizzolatto-creatorwriter.html.

Stenros, Jaakko, and Markus Montola, eds. 2010. *Nordic Larp*. 1st printing. Stockholm: Fea Livia.

Sterling, Bruce. 1996. *Schismatrix Plus*. New York: Ace.

Sutton-Smith, Brian. 2001. *The Ambiguity of Play*. Revised edition. Cambridge, MA: Harvard University Press.

Suvin, Darko. 1979. *Metamorphoses of Science Fiction: On the Poetics and History of a Literary Genre*. New Haven, CT: Yale University Press.

Swallow, James. 2012. *Fear to Tread*. Nottingham (UK): Games Workshop.

Team, Fantasy Flight Games. 2009. *Rogue Trader: Core Rulebook*. Roseville, MN: Fantasy Flight Games.

——. 2010. *Deathwatch: Core Rulebook*. Roseville, MN: Fantasy Flight Games.

——. 2012. *Black Crusade: Core Rulebook*. Roseville, MN: Fantasy Flight Games.

——. 2013. *Only War: Core Rulebook*. Roseville, MN: Fantasy Flight Games.

——. 2014. *Dark Heresy: Core Rulebook*. 2nd edition. Roseville, MN: Fantasy Flight Games.

Team, Games Workshop. 1987. "White Dwarf." *White Dwarf Magazine*. September.

——. 1988. *Warhammer Chapter 40,000/40K Approved Book of the Astronomican*. A Games Workshop Publication.

——. 2002. *Index Astartes*. Vol. 1. Nottingham (UK): Games Workshop.

——. 2017a. *Gathering Storm: Fall of Cadia*. 1. Nottingham (UK): Games Workshop.

——. 2017b. *Gathering Storm: Fracture of Biel-Tan*. 2. Nottingham (UK): Games Workshop.

——. 2017c. *Gathering Storm: Rise of the Primarch*. 3. Nottingham (UK): Games Workshop.

Team, Monte Cook Games. 2015. *Cypher System Rulebook*. Monte Cook Games.

Team, White Wolf. 2004. *The World of Darkness: Storytelling System Rulebook*. White Wolf Publishing.

——. 2011. *Vampire: The Masquerade—20th Anniversary Edition*. 20th Anniversary edition. White Wolf.

——. 2012. *Werewolf: The Apocalypse—20th Anniversary Edition*. 20th Anniversary edition. White Wolf.

——. 2015. *Chronicles of Darkness: Storytelling System Rulebook*. White Wolf Publishing.

——. 2018. "Vampire the Masquerade: Storytellers Vault Style Guide." *DriveThruRPG.com*. January 22. www.drivethrurpg.com/product/218269/Vampire-the-Masquerade-Storytellers-Vault-Style-Guide.

Team, Wizards RPG. 2008a. *Dungeon Master's Guide*. 4th edition. Renton, WA: Wizards of the Coast.

——. 2008b. *Forgotten Realms Campaign Guide*. 4th edition. Renton, WA: Wizards of the Coast.

——. 2014a. *Player's Handbook*. 5th edition. Renton, WA: Wizards of the Coast.

——. 2014b. *Dungeon Master's Guide*. 5th edition. Renton, WA: Wizards of the Coast.

——. 2017. *Tales From the Yawning Portal*. Renton, WA: Wizards of the Coast.

Thacker, Eugene. 2011. *In the Dust of This Planet: Horror of Philosophy*. Vol. 1. Winchester (UK): Zero Books.

——. 2015a. *Starry Speculative Corpse: Horror of Philosophy*. Vol. 2. Winchester (UK): Zero Books.

——. 2015b. *Tentacles Longer Than Night: Horror of Philosophy*. Vol. 3. Winchester (UK): Zero Books.

Thorpe, Gav. 2016a. *The Emperor Expects*. The Beast Arises 3. Nottingham (UK): Games Workshop.

——. 2016b. *The Beast Must Die*. The Beast Arises 8. Nottingham (UK): Games Workshop.

Todorov, Tzvetan. 1975. *The Fantastic: A Structural Approach to a Literary Genre*. Translated by Richard Howard. 1st edition. Ithaca, NY: Cornell University Press.

Tolkien, J.R.R. 1965. *Tree and Leaf*. Boston, MA: Houghton Mifflin.

Torner, Evan, and William J. White. 2012. *Immersive Gameplay: Essays on Participatory Media and Role-Playing*. Jefferson, NC: McFarland.

Toulmin, Stephen. 1992. *Cosmopolis: The Hidden Agenda of Modernity*. 1st edition. Chicago: University of Chicago Press.

Tresca, Michael J. 2010. *The Evolution of Fantasy Role-Playing Games*. Jefferson, NC: McFarland.

Turner, Frederick. 1988. *Genesis : An Epic Poem*. Dallas, TX and New York: Saybrook; Distributed by W.W. Norton.

Vance, Jack. 2000. *Tales of the Dying Earth*. Fantasy Masterworks. London: Gollancz.

VanderMeer, Jeff. 2008. "The New Weird: 'It's Alive?'" In *The New Weird*. San Francisco, CA: Tachyon Publications.

Varela, Francisco J., Evan T. Thompson, and Eleanor Rosch. 1992. *The Embodied Mind: Cognitive Science and Human Experience*. New edition. Cambridge, MA: The MIT Press.

Vint, Sherryl. 2007. *Bodies of Tomorrow Technology, Subjectivity, Science Fiction*. Toronto: University of Toronto Press.

——. 2009. "Introduction: Special Issue on China Miéville." *Extrapolation* 50(2): 197–9.

Weber, Max. 2001. *The Protestant Ethic and the Spirit of Capitalism*. London: Routledge.

Weinstock, Jeffrey Andrew. 2016. "Afterward: Interview with China Miéville." In *The Age of Lovecraft*. Edited by Carl H. Sederholm and Jeffrey Andrew Weinstock. Minneapolis: University of Minnesota Press.

Wellek, Rene, and Austin Warren. 1949. *Theory of Literature*. 3rd edition. London: Jonathan Cape.

Wells, H.G. 2009. *The Time Machine*. Edited by Stephen Arata. 1st edition. New York: W.W. Norton & Company.

Williams, J. Patrick, Sean Q. Hendricks, and W. Keith Winkler. 2006. *Gaming as Culture: Essays on Reality, Identity and Experience in Fantasy Games*. Jefferson, NC: McFarland.

Wilson, Edmund. 1980. "Tales of the Marvelous and Ridiculous." In *H.P. Lovecraft: Four Decades of Criticism*. Edited by S.T. Joshi. Athens: Ohio University Press.

Wittgenstein, Ludwig. 1968. *Philosophical Investigations*. Oxford: Basil Blackwell.

Wolfe, Cary. 2010. *What Is Posthumanism?* Minneapolis: University of Minnesota Press.

Wolfe, Gary K. 2011. *Evaporating Genres Essays on Fantastic Literature*. Middletown, CT: Wesleyan University Press.

Wright, Peter. 2003. *Attending Daedalus: Gene Wolfe, Artifice, and the Reader*. Liverpool Science Fiction Texts and Studies. Liverpool: Liverpool University Press.

Index